HOKKAIDO

A HISTORY OF JAPAN'S NORTHERN ISLE AND ITS PEOPLE

IBRAHIM JALAL

EARNSHAW BOOKS

Hokkaido

By Ibrahim Jalal

ISBN-13: 978-988-8552-90-0

HISTORY / Asia / Japan

EB144

Published by Earnshaw Books Ltd. (Hong Kong)

Contents

HOKKAIDO

Introduction

HONSHU IS the main island of Japan and stretches along the Pacific Ocean for over 800 miles. Many of its cities, Osaka, Kyoto, and Tokyo, are world renowned and serve as cultural symbols of Japan. Tokyo and Osaka are the vibrant, modern metropolises of bustling streets bathed in neon beneath towering glass skyscrapers. Kyoto, the ancient heart of the country, made of wood and stone, a city of shrines, rickshaws and geisha. These major cities share a relative proximity as most of Japan's population cling to the 'Pacific Belt' strung from Tokyo in the east to Fukuoka on Kyushu to the west. So well-lit is the Pacific Belt that satellite images taken at night show it as a bright, unbroken orange strand - the lights of over half the country's population. Yet in terms of landmass, half of Japan is north beyond Tokyo, into the more rural Tohoku region of Honshu and then across the narrow sea to Hokkaido. Honshu, with the islands of Kyushu, Shikoku and Hokkaido form the core of the Japanese nation. But of these, one is a relatively new member to the 'home islands': Hokkaido.

This book is the story of Hokkaido. It is the most northern of Japan's main islands and the largest administration region in Japan's 47 prefectural system.

Readers will likely recognize Hokkaido, as Japan's outline is indistinguishable without it. The shape of Hokkaido somewhat resembles a manta ray with a long tail, the Oshima Peninsula that splits into two smaller peninsulas, to the west the Matsumae peninsula, to the east the Kameda Peninsula. Together these two almost parallel peninsulas make up the most southern tips of Hokkaido, stretch out towards the main island, Honshu. On the eastern side is Hakodate, one of the most-visited locations in Hokkaido, famous for its historical architecture, night views from Mt. Hakodate, and the star-shaped fortress, the Goryōkaku. On the western side is Matsumae, the location of the only traditional Japanese castle in Hokkaido and the most northern of all such castles in Japan. At the northern base of the tail, close to the Sea of Japan, is Sapporo, Hokkaido's largest city.

Past Sapporo, into the interior, Hokkaido's geography branches into two main regions, a small wing in the south on the Pacific side which is backed by the Hidaka Mountains, a range of steep folded mountains stretching over 150 kilometers. This region is also famous as the homeland of an Ainu leader who led an assault against the Japanese in the 17th Century, and also as a haven for wildlife such as the hazel grouse, arctic warbler and grizzily bears. The much bigger northern wing faces the Sea of Okhotsk and features the port city of Wakkanai, the most northern city in Japan. Further north from Wakkanai is the island of Sakhalin, now part of Russia, which is visible from Wakkanai on a clear day.[1] The east of Hokkaido is the head of this manta ray, where two points of land jut out from the mass of the island. One is the UNESCO World Heritage Shiretoko National Park, a vast expanse of nature situated on the Shiretoko Peninsula. The meaning of the Ainu name for Shiretoko, '*Sir etok*' means the 'place where the land protrudes'. On a small peninsula opposite Shiretoko is the port city of Nemuro, and in between these two peninsulas are the islands of Kunashir and Iturup, the most southern islands in the Kuril Island chain. East of Nemuro and Kunashir are the Habomai islands and Shikotan Island, leading north up to the Kamchatka Peninsula in Russia. These islands share a recent history in the ongoing Northern Territory dispute between Russia and Japan, in which Japan claim they are part of Nemuro, and Russia claims they were forfeited after Japan's surrender in 1945.[2] East of Shiretoko is Abashiri, famous for Japan's largest and most isolated prison, now a museum famous nationwide. Abashiri, like all of Hokkaido's north, faces the Sea of Okhotsk. In the late winter, tourists from the rest of Japan and all over the world come to see the sea ice that originates from the Amur river in Russia and drifts through the sea of Okhotsk until it reaches the north of Hokkaido, forming a surface of thick white amongst the deep blue of the northern pacific.

While ice is one feature of Hokkaido, fire is another. As with most of the Japanese archipelago, volcanos are prominent in Hokkaido and their geothermal energy creates hot springs such as the Noboribetsu Onsen's 'Valley of Hell' southwest of Sapporo. Northwest of Muroran is Lake Tōya, a caldera lake, ten kilometers in diameter and nine kilometers across. In the middle of this body of water is Nakajima island, the ninth-biggest lake in Japan. Like much of Japan, Hokkaido is a place of great diversity.

Unlike the islands of Honshu, Kyushu and Shikoku, through most of recorded history, Hokkaido was not inhabited by mainland Japanese (Wajin) at all. The indigenous people who were adept at surviving on this sub-arctic island called their land *Ainu Mosir*, which means 'the land of men', they themselves were the Ainu, placed under *Kamuy Mosir*, 'the land of gods'. The living space of the Ainu people was not limited to Hokkaido. Further north, the Kuril Islands (known as the Chishima Islands in Japanese) and Sakhalin in the Sea of Okhotsk also served as their home and in the south, they settled as far as the Tohoku region of Honshu.[3] By the early modern era, the Ainu living in Honshu had either integrated with the Japanese expanding north or had fled to Hokkaido. Even though the Ainu faded away in northern Honshu, their legacy remains in places names throughout Aomori and Iwate prefectures and even in the Aomori dialect which, for instance, uses the Ainu word *'chape'* for cat instead of the standard Japanese word *'neko'*.

From the late 15th Century, Japanese settlers expanded north, finally crossing the Tsugaru Strait at Honshu and arriving on the southern tip of Hokkaido's Oshima Peninsula. Here, they began to trade and fight with the Ainu. This settler population was a minority in Hokkaido, but they nonetheless gradually began to assert power over the majority Ainu. By 1604, the Shogun of Japan granted the samurai of the Matsumae clan the sole right to conduct trade with the Ainu and become the Wajin lords of Hokkaido. In time, the Matsumae increasingly exploited this monopoly, forcing the Ainu into indentured servitude and exploiting the land. The resentment this created amongst the Ainu erupted in numerous rebellions which continued until the late 18th Century.

During the 18th Century, Russians begun to colonize the Far East of Eurasia, expanding the borders of their nation and eventually entering Sakhalin and the northern Kuril Islands. The Ainu were now wedged between great states competing for what they both saw as unclaimed territory. With little concern for the indigenous people, the Shogunate (the samurai government, based in Tokyo) saw the Russian expansion south as a threat to its own sphere of influence and began to strengthen its own claim to the islands in the Sea of Okhotsk.

Today, Sakhalin and the Kuril Islands are Russian territories with Hokkaido remaining part of Japan. The boundaries drawn by the two nation states did not coincide with the actually living space of the Ainu and this led to a dramatic decline in their population, particularly in Sakhalin and the Kuril Islands. The distance between what is now Japan and Russia is small. There is a mere 43 kilometers between the southern point of Sakhalin,

Cape Crillion and the northern point of Hokkaido, Cape Sōya, and the southern Kuril island of Kunashir is only 13 kilometers away from Hokkaido. Geographically, Sakhalin and the Kuril Islands are intimately connected and on a clear day, both Sakhalin and Kunashir can be seen from Hokkaido with the naked eye. It was precisely this proximity that motivated the Shogunate to send numerous expedition forces north to stake their claim to the region, and as the fear of Russian occupation increased, the Shogunate decided to take direct control of Hokkaido, southern Sakhalin and the Kuril Islands on two separate occasions in the 19th Century.

But the Shogunate could not stop foreign ships from approaching Japan and in 1852, Commodore Matthew Calbraith Perry of the United States Navy forced the Shogunate to open relations with the United States. Among Perry's demands was the opening of the port of Hakodate in Hokkaido to foreign trade. The forced opening of Japan created a crisis within the samurai ruling class, who debated the legitimacy of the Shogunate and the question of whether the emperor should be restored as the head of state and the 'barbarians' expelled from Japan. The anti-shogunate faction won out and in 1868 the Shogunate was overthrown, the new Meiji government with the Emperor as its figurehead took its place and promptly began a campaign to modernize, reform and recreate Japan in the image of a contemporary western state, in a process of modernization, westernization and even colonization.

In Hokkaido, the new government saw a vast territory full of potential, akin to the American west. Through mass migration to colonize Hokkaido, the Ainu were largely displaced via a frenzy of land grabs, the introduction of European-style farming and industrial technology. After numerous negotiations and a war with Russia (1904-1905), the nation of Japan at last drew its northern boundaries at the northern Kuril Island of Paramushir and at the 50th parallel on the island of Sakhalin.

This incarnation of the nation of Japan was not to last. In the final days of the World War II, the Soviet Army poured into Sakhalin and the Kuril Islands, prompting those who were able to evacuate to Hokkaido. Others who survived were left behind in the land, that may have been the birthplace to some of them but was now a foreign country. Japan lost southern Sakhalin, and the northern territories dispute concerning the larger Kuril Islands of Kunashir and Iturup, and the smaller islands of Habomai and Shikotan continues to this day. The descendants of the Japanese, Ainu and Koreans who did not, or could not, flee to Hokkaido after the Russian occupation continue to live in Sakhalin.

The name 'Hokkaido' can be traced back to 1869 when the Japanese explorer Matsuura Takeshirō (1818-1888) coined it, claiming it to be an amalgamation of Japanese and the Ainu language. 'Hoku' (北) comes from the Japanese character for north, 'Kai' (海) for ocean, and 'Dō' (道) meaning route or way. A direct meaning can be read into these characters, the 'Northern Sea Way', similar to how Norway in Europe means the 'Northern Way'. However, Takeshirō himself provided a different explanation saying the choice of characters came from a conversation he had with the Ainu chief Aieto of the Teshiogawa river basin, who taught him that the word 'Kai' meant something born from this land.[4] While scholars of the Ainu language have failed to find a word that aligns with Matsuura's 'Kai', this book is written in the same spirit and aims to tell the story of Hokkaido not just from the perspective of the Japanese who colonized the island, or the Westerners who visited and lived there, but also from the perspective of the indigenous people.

A Japanese bookshop typically contains at least two types of Japanese history: the conventional history of Japan mainly consisting of the islands of Honshu, Kyushu and Shikoku and a separate history of both Hokkaido and also the islands of Okinawa Prefecture to the southwest. These latter regions only became formally part of Japan in the 19th Century, although they had a history of interacting with Japan long before this. In both regions, the indigenous people had separate languages, customs and political systems to those of the mainland Japanese. That is why even today, scholars working on these regions are specialists who are often apart from standard Japanese history.

Within Japan, the recognition of the Ainu as an indigenous people has been gradually increasing; the first Ainu politician in the Japanese Diet, Kayano Shigeru, served from 1994 to 1998. In 2001, 80% of place names in Hokkaido that have origins in the Ainu language were declared intangible cultural assets and in July 2020 the Shiraoi Ainu Museum reopened as *Upopoy*, the National Ainu Museum and Park.[5] Still, most English language works on Japan tend focus on mainland Japanese history, largely or wholly neglecting the history of Hokkaido and of those who lived in Sakhalin and the Kuril Islands. This book is aimed at addressing this imbalance, and hopefully giving the reader an entire new perspective of what constitutes the nation of Japan.

NOTES

THE ISLAND OF HOKKAIDO has had numerous names throughout history, including *Ainu Mosir, Ezo, Ezogashima* and *Ezochi*. For the sake of simplicity, this book uses present-day names for the islands throughout, for consistency and clarity. An exception is the term *Karafuto*, which is used to refer to the southern half of the island of Sakhalin under the Japanese government.

Japanese names are written in their traditional form of surname first and given name second. Ainu names are written in the romanization of the Ainu language where this information is available. Many of the records about the Ainu are written by Japanese contemporaries which has led to the Japanese transliteration of Ainu words.

In Japanese history books concerning Hokkaido, the term "Wajin" is now generally used to describe the people of mainland Japan. This contrasts with the Ainu and Ryukyu people who were historically viewed as different ethnicities to the mainland Japanese.

PART I

From Hokkaido's Pre-history
to the Early Modern era

HOKKAIDO

1

THE AINU AND THE MATSUMAE

To UNDERSTAND the origins of the Ainu and their common lineage with the Japanese (Wajin), it is necessary to go back thousands of years to the origins of humanity on these most eastern islands of Asia. Humans arrived in the Japanese archipelago via seven known routes: two from the sub-arctic, four from continental Asia, and one via the Pacific Ocean. On the sub-arctic front, the first people came down from what is now the Russian island of Sakhalin into Hokkaido. From the continent, there was a route across the sea from Manchuria to Honshu, from the Korean Peninsula to Kyushu and crossing the sea from East China into Kyushu. Finally, there was the possibility of island-hopping from Taiwan through the Ryukyu island chain and into Kyushu. Those who arrived in Japan through the Pacific Ocean may have come from Luzon, in today's Philippines. Following on from Japan's Paleolithic Age, when people first began moving to these islands, the Japanese archipelago had entered its first cultural period, known as the Jōmon Period (14,000BCE to circa 300 ~ 1000CE).

Whether these various migrants from such diverse backgrounds viewed each other as friend or foe is difficult to know and it is impossible to know what languages they each spoke at this time. The first migrants to Japan are collectively known as the Jōmon people. The Jōmon were predominately hunter-gathers and are characterized by archaeologists through a shared culture of pressing rope onto unfired pottery to create patterns.[6] Small stone figurines, from about ten to 30 centimeters in height, are commonly found from this period. These figurines, called Dogū, were produced mostly in eastern Honshu and Hokkaido, but their precise purpose has been lost to history. The Dogū often have bulbous faces and small hands. It is possible that they were effigies taking on people's illness or as totems of goddesses and gods.

After 300BCE there was a divergence, forming the Ainu in Hokkaido and northern Honshu and the Japanese (Wajin or Yamato people) in the three islands of Kyushu, Shikoku, and Honshu. South of Hokkaido migrants from continental China and Korea began to enter the Japanese archipelago through Kyushu, gradually expanding into Honshu in the coming centuries. In contrast to the hunter-gathering lifestyle of the Jōmon people, the Yayoi people brought with them a culture of rice farming, social hierarchy and organized methods of warfare. It was at this point that there was a clear divergence between Hokkaido and Honshu, with Jōmon culture continuing in Hokkaido until 700CE. While the Jōmon's descendants continued their way of life in Hokkaido, the influx of Yayoi migrants led to a mixing of Jōmon and Yayoi in the three main southern islands. By around the year circa 250 ~ 300CE, this new hybrid of people had formed clans and begun to build large keyhole-shaped tombs for their chiefs. These tombs, called Kofun, often contain terracotta figures whose role was to accompany their chiefs into the next world.

There was little Yayoi migration as far north as Hokkaido, but the influx of new migrants still had an impact on the culture of the Jōmon in Hokkaido. Through trade, they left the stone age behind and acquired metalware, bringing the Jōmon Period in Hokkaido to an end and giving birth to the Satsumon Period

(7th Century to the 13th Century). Before that, in the 5th Century, another non-Jōmon group of people began to arrive in the north of Hokkaido. In numbers far fewer than the Yayoi migrants, this group of people descended from the Sea of Okhotsk where they made their livelihood from the ocean by fishing and hunting whales. Very little is known about the people who brought the Okhotsk culture to Hokkaido, other than that their creation of bear figurines and other animal worship items came to play an essential role in the religion of the Ainu. There is a strong possibility that the indigenous Uilita and Nivkh peoples of Sakhalin are the direct descendants of this Okhotsk culture.[7] The Okhotsk people mixed with those already in Hokkaido and by the 12th Century some groups in Hokkaido began to move north to Sakhalin and the Kuril Islands where they became the Sakhalin and Kuril Ainu. While connected to the Ainu of Hokkaido, these two Ainu groups developed their own distinct cultures. The Sakhalin Ainu developed an instrument called the *Tonkori*, and the Kuril Ainu made their living primarily from hunting seals, sea otters, and whales; as opposed to the land-focused hunting of the Hokkaido Ainu. In a sense, the Kuril Ainu continued the legacy of the Okhotsk people.

In the islands south of Hokkaido during the Asuka Period (538-710CE), the battling Yamato chiefs consolidated power under the banner of an Emperor. Though there were challenges to the Emperor's authority, he held hegemonic power. It is also during this era that Buddhism arrived from China and the Chinese script was adopted, grafted on top of the Japanese language and changing it in all sorts of ways. During the Nara Period (710-794), a capital city was founded in present-day Nara Prefecture, modeled after the capital of the Tang Empire, Chang'an (today's Xi'an, home of the terracotta warriors), with refined Buddhist sculptures, temples and a planned network of roads connecting the surrounding provinces to the capital. In 794 the Japanese imperial capital was moved to Kyoto, remaining the seat of the Emperor until the 19th Century.

It was during the Nara Period, in the 8th Century, that the Yamato wrote some of the first documents concerning their history and mythology. In the second of these chronicles, the *Nihon Shoki*, there are hints of some of the earliest interactions between the Yamato and the ancestors of the present-day Ainu. The *Nihon Shoki* records numerous battles between the Yamato and those recorded as the 'Emishi'. These Emishi are likely the Jōmon or Yamato groups that did not prostate themselves before the Emperor in Nara. As the Yamato armies mounted campaigns in the Kanto and then Tohoku regions of Honshu, many of these groups appear to have been integrated with the Yamato, with the northern extremities of Honshu holding out the longest (present-day Aomori and Iwate Prefectures). While these people may not be considered Ainu in their cultural practices, there is evidence that they spoke the Ainu language, such as the numerous place names in Japan's northern Tohoku region with origins in the Ainu language.[8]

By the 13th or 14th centuries, a distinct Ainu culture had formed in Hokkaido. Just as modern Ainu culture was forming, a small number of Yamato people arrived in Hokkaido and began to create small settlements on the island's southern edge. By the 15th Century, they had consolidated their power on the Oshima Peninsula at the island's southern edge, and by the 18th Century had established indirect control of nearly all of Hokkaido's Ainu. The Yamato-inhabited region of Hokkaido in that era was confined to the south and Hokkaido remained largely the land of the Ainu until the 19th Century. Despite the issuing of numerous texts declaring the Emperor's triumph over the barbarian races, the grip of the Emperors was not to last, being reduced to a mostly

Depiction of Ainu in 1918 by Murase Gitoku (1877-1938)

symbolic role as a feudal class of samurai came to dominate. The Yamato people in Hokkaido, however, were here to stay.

In the early 12th Century, samurai lords known as Daimyō snatched de facto power away from the imperial court, relegating the Emperor to the role of figurehead. The first Shogun, the strongest of all the Daimyō, Minamoto Yoritomo (1147-1199), moved his headquarters from Kyoto to the town of Kamakura. The first shogunate, known as the Kamakura Shogunate (1185-1333), was eventually replaced by the Ashikaga Shogunate (1336-1563) which ended in the mid-15th Century, with Japan falling into a period of warring states with Daimyō fighting each other for supremacy (1467-1600). Stability returned to Japan with the rise of the Tokugawa clan and the shift of central power to Edo, present day Tokyo, at the beginning of the 17th Century. The Tokugawa Shogunate remained in power until the Meiji Restoration in 1868, and this period of history is referred to as the Edo Period.

When the dynasty's founder, Tokugawa Ieyasu (1543-1616) arrived in what later became the capital, Edo was a sleepy fishing town, although a castle had been built there in 1457, which had fallen into ruin during more than a century of warfare. To Edo,

Ieyasu brought with him a large number of retainers, and they set about constructing a new Edo Castle, larger than its predecessor, and also a waterway to bring building supplies from Edo Bay directly to the castle.

Ieyasu became the Shogun of Japan in 1603 and with this, Edo became Japan's economic, political and cultural center. To prevent Japan from being divided, Ieyasu created a system known as 'alternate attendance', under which all the Daimyō were required to build residential mansions in Edo. Their wives and first-born sons had to stay in Edo at all times, with the Daimyō having to alternate one year in their domain and one year in Edo. Under the Tokugawa Shogunate, Edo grew to become one of the most populous cities in the world. Though much of Edo Castle was destroyed by fire in 1873, the current residence of the Emperor, the Imperial Palace, is on the same site and is surrounded by the walls, gates and moat of Edo Castle.

As the need to travel to Edo grew, a network of roads was laid throughout the country, including the Tōkaidō road, linking Kyoto and Edo. This road and many of its scenes were captured in the woodblock prints of Utagawa Hiroshige in his 'Fifty-three Stations of the Tōkaidō' series. These stations, or rest-houses, provided lodging, food, and entertainment ready for the processions of samurai and retainers heading to and from Edo. However, the fringes of modern-day Japan, including Hokkaido to the north and the Ryukyu Kingdom to the south, remained borderland regions, populated by peoples with customs unrelated to and unfamiliar to most of the contemporary Japanese.

As the Tokugawa Shogunate was establishing Edo as the heart of Japan, in Hokkaido, the Yamato on the Oshima Peninsula were beginning to consolidate and extend their own power, though to a lesser extent. As Japan had been divided into warlord-controlled factions for so long, there was little consciousness of it being a unified country in the early 17th Century. Furthermore, the peoples on the fringes of the samurai, the Ryukyu Kingdom (1429-1879) in the South and the 'Ezo' north of Honshu, spoke different languages and neither recognized the Emperor or Shogun as the supreme power in their land. It is therefore no surprise that when the first missionary in Hokkaido, Jerome De Angelis (1567-1623) entered the Matsumae domain in southern Hokkaido in 1618, he was told that he was not in Japan any more.

The first missionary in Hokkaido is closely tied to the origins of missionary work in Japan, which began in 1534 when seven students met and pledged to save the souls of the world through Catholicism at the church of Saint Pierre de Montmartre. They founded the Jesuit Order and vowed to venture across the world to spread the word of Christ. The first missionary the order dispatched was a Portuguese man in his thirties named Francis Xavier (1505-1552). Leaving Lisbon on April 7, 1541, he first traveled to India and then made his way further east to the Malayan Peninsula and what is today Indonesia. After spreading the message of Christ in Southeast Asia, he returned to India in 1549 and prepared to make his most ambitious voyage yet. In 1549, he set sail for Japan, arriving at Kagoshima in the southern Japanese island of Kyushu. Xavier was brimming with hope. He had heard tales of the country from Portuguese merchants and felt confident at the prospect of its people embracing the word of God.

"If I go there, I shall do great service for God our Lord, more than with the pagans of India," Xavier wrote.[9] But he found the environment more hostile than he had anticipated. This first Jesuit missionary toiled to convert the Japanese masses and within three years, Xavier succeeded in meeting with the Daimyō of the Satsuma realm in southern Kyushu. But despite Xavier's zeal he failed to convert the Daimyō to Catholicism. Undismayed, Xavier travelled on to Kyoto, in the hopes of meeting the Emperor, but he was rebuffed.

That is not to say that the first Jesuit mission in Japan was a complete failure. When Xavier met Buddhist monks of the Shingon sect, he began to use the Japanese name for the Vairocana Buddha, 'Dainichi,' in reference to the Christian God and was delighted to find that the monks were receptive. In time, Xavier realized how different the Vairocana Buddha was from the Christian god and discarded the term, and in so doing, he lost favor with the monks whose trust he had painstakingly worked to gain. At the end of three years having had only mediocre success, Xavier made plans to return to India. His luck ran out while he was waiting for a boat at Shangchuan island off the coast of China, where he fell ill and passed away. Despite his lackluster success, his accounts of the islands in the Far East inspired others to venture to the end of Asia, and through their toil, the number of Christian converts in Japan gradually climbed.

The Christian concept of an omnipotent God sitting above all men was rejected and viewed as a threat by successive generations of Shoguns, who vowed to prevent this alien religion from taking root in Japan. Regardless, the persecution of Christianity did not prevent Jesuit missionaries from venturing into East Asia. Almost 70 years after Francis Xavier's expedition, The Sicilian Jesuit, De Angelis, journeyed to an island that was not yet under the full subjugation of the Japanese. Surrounded by the Sea of Okhotsk to the north and the Sea of Japan to the west, the island was many times bigger than De Angelinas' home of Sicily. He had arrived in Hokkaido, where he spent the years 1618 to 1621.

Starting in the Heian Period (794-1185CE) nobles in the imperial capital of Kyoto had called the island Ezo or Ezogashima (the island of the Ezo). It is not clear if 'Ezo' referred to Hokkaido alone or also to Sakhalin and the Kuril Islands beyond, since these were also islands of the Ezo: the Ainu people. De Angelis arrived in Japan in 1602 and first began his missionary work in Kyoto. It was not long before resistance from the Shogunate forced him to move north to what is now Shizuoka Prefecture. Under the shadow of Mt. Fuji, De Angeles continued his missionary work, gradually moving further north still to the more temperate region of Sendai. Sensing that even this far north was not safe, he moved further away from the central authority of the Shogunate and arrived in Hokkaido in 1618. Crossing the Tsugaru Strait, from Honshu to Hokkaido, the Sicilian happened to meet the nephew of Matsumae Kinhiro (1598-1641), the Daimyō of the outposts in southern Hokkaido under the rule of the Matsumae clan. De Angelis learnt that the Matsumae were a very different breed of samurai to those he had encountered in Honshu. Far from the supervision of the Shogunate, the Matsumae were free to act with a degree of autonomy. Yet the Matsumae did not occupy a great deal of land in Hokkaido and the land they did control was marginal, confined to the southern coast, reassuringly close to Honshu. They existed on the fringes of the Shogunate to the south with the indigenous Ainu population to the north.

In 1587, The Shogun and predecessor to Ieyasu, Toyotomi Hideyoshi (1537-1598), ordered that all missionaries were to be expelled from Japan. Yet the wilds of the north were hardly thought of as 'Japan' to that generation of the Matsumae. Thus, the Sicilian could pass into Hokkaido without question.

During his time in Hokkaido, De Angelis gave the world the first written description of the Ainu. De Angelis's description in 1618 reflected the world he had the most experience of, that of southern Europe. From the viewpoint of the Sicilian, the clothing of the Ainu resembled the garments of Muslims in nearby North Africa, noting the common use of geometrical patterns on the cloth. The geometric designs of the long-sleeved Ainu gowns likely reminded him of the geometrical Islamic architecture in Sicily, Spain and North Africa. De Angelis also noted the hooped earrings adorned with colorful stones, an ornamentation called *Ninkari* by the Ainu. He also saw similarities between the Ainu and the Japanese, such as how both ate with chopsticks. To the Ainu, these instruments are known as *Ipe-pasuy*.

South across the island of Honshu, through the late 16th Century, peasants were converting to Christianity, and in some cases starting rebellions. The Shogunate's punishments, aimed at suppressing Christianity, became increasingly harsh. In 1597 an infamous event for Christianity in Japan occurred when missionaries along with over 20 of their converts were rounded up in Kyoto and Osaka. These Christians were forced on an 800-kilometer march to Nagasaki where they were crucified. This was just one of many events in which Christians were publicly executed for refusing to renounce their faith, and it was in this climate that De Angelis met his end when he decided to give himself up believing mercy might be shown by the Shogunate to him and his Japanese converts. He was wrong. There was to be no leniency for those who had converted. In 1623, De Angelis was burned at the stake alongside 50 Japanese Christians in the Shogun's capital of Edo, becoming one of many European and Japanese martyrs of the era.

In the same century as De Angelis' encounter with the Ainu, Japanese venturing into Hokkaido began to depict the Ainu through their eyes. The Japanese artists focused on the things they found outlandish in this northern land — Ainu fishing for salmon with a harpoon-like contraption, the ritual scarification of bears and the tattoos on the Ainu women. As for the Ainu themselves, depictions vary. Sometimes the Ainu are pale, other pictures depict shirtless men revealing bodies of thick hair on dark brown skin. Little did the artists of the time know that they and the Ainu shared common ancestors.

The history of the Wajin in Hokkaido goes back about 200 years before the establishment of the Tokugawa Shogunate that ultimately put De Angelis to death. This history is centered around the Matsumae clan, whose tale begins far away from Hokkaido, in the year 1431 when a child was born in Aoi castle, the seat of Wakasa province. He was the son of the governor representing the Shogun in the realm and this young boy was set to inherit his father's title and all the power that this commanded. Wakasa, in present-day Fukui prefecture, located on Japan's southwest coast, not far from Kyoto, is part of Honshu's snow country, a region in which the yearly fall of heavy snow can put a stop to traffic even today. Although Wakasa is about one thousand kilometers from Hokkaido, events that took place in Wakasa came to shape the future of both the Japanese and Ainu in the lands north of Honshu. From a young age, Takeda Nobuhiro (1431-1494) believed that he was destined to become the governor of Wakasa, but fate intervened sending him on a very different path.

When Takeda was around 20 years old, rumors began circulating in the castle that Takeda was not the rightful heir, that he was only an adopted child. To make matters worse, the governor chose Takeda's younger brother as heir, confirming his worst fears. At 21 Takeda, accompanied by five loyal retainers, left the castle that had been his home and slipped into the night. He never again saw Honshu's southwestern coast, but he found fortune in a very different snow country north of the Tsugaru Strait. Takeda went on to become the founder of the Matsumae clan, the dynasty that over the course of the next three centuries gradually extended Wajin power over the indigenous Ainu of Hokkaido.

Under the Kamakura shogunate (1185-1333), Hokkaido was a

land of exile to which the disgraced were consigned. One means of staying alive for the banished in the wilderness was to travel to the hinterlands and join the indigenous Ainu who knew how to survive in what was to the exiles an alien land. But for the most part, Japanese settlers stayed on the Oshima Peninsula, the long tail of Hokkaido, keeping them in close contact with the Japanese in Honshu. On the peninsula, the Japanese were concentrated in 12 outposts, which were known as '*Tate*' in Japanese. The most prestigious of these outposts was the Matsumae outpost, located at the southern point of the peninsula a short boat ride away from Honshu across the Tsugaru Strait. The Matsumae outpost held its prestige precisely because the Shogun's main representative in Hokkaido was stationed there.

This representative, based in what was a frontier outpost far away from the cities of Kyoto and Kamakura, had little tangible power. If the Ainu of just the southern coast were to revolt, with their knowledge of the land and the effective use of poisoned arrows, the Japanese settlers would have proven to be no match for them. Yet the Ainu did not necessarily view these Japanese settlers as enemies. For the most part, the Ainu were satisfied with trading goods such as pelts, in return for Japanese products including lacquerware and alcohol. Unfortunately, there are no written records from this period. The Japanese did not leave any documents about their interaction with the Ainu and the Ainu did not possess a writing-based culture of any kind. But it is clear that resentment began to build between the Ainu of southern Hokkaido and the Japanese settlers. It erupted in 1456 in the most significant event in Hokkaido's history thus far; furious Ainu attempting to destroy the Japanese outposts. What had caused the Ainu to rise up against the Japanese?

The incident that sparked the uprising took place in the Japanese outpost of Shinori (now part of Hakodate) located on the eastern tip of the Oshima Peninsula in 1456. An Ainu boy by the name of Okkai was haggling with a local blacksmith who he had asked to make a blade for his *Makiri*, the versatile hunting blade of the Ainu. *Makiri* are particularly advantageous in rivers and out on the open ocean as the light wooden handle ensures the blade will rise to the surface if dropped into the water. *Makiri* are also characterized by their elaborate scabbards which feature skilled engravings by Ainu craftsman. There are sheaths with three-dimensional carvings of bears and whales as well as sheaths with the geometrical, almost Celtic-like patterns perfected by the Ainu. Each carving reflected the individuality of the craftsman. While their craftsmanship was exquisite, the Ainu of this era relied on Japanese blacksmiths to forge the blades of the *Makiri*.

On this occasion, Okkai was not impressed with the workmanship of the Shinori blacksmith. He refused to pay and the blacksmith was enraged: how dare this young Ainu challenge him? What do his people know about forging? Voices

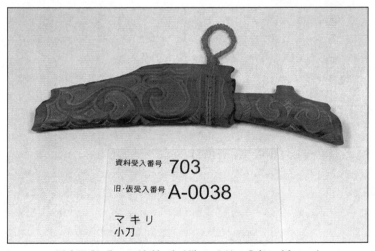

資料受入番号 703
旧・仮受入番号 A-0038
マ キ リ
小刀

Makiri *(kindly provided by the Nibutani Ainu Culture Museum)*

were raised and a crowd gathered. In a fit of rage, the blacksmith grasped the Makiri and thrust it into the young Ainu boy's chest. The color drained from Okkai's face and he fell to the floor, his blood spilling onto the cold ground.

News of Okkai's murder soon reached the Ainu throughout the Oshima Peninsula. Grievances amongst the Ainu appear to have been gradually building and for many this seems to have been the final straw. The Ainu rallied around a chief by the name of Koshamain, a figure about whom nothing is known except his name. The Ainu under Koshamain began by laying siege to the Shinori outpost. Eventually in May of 1457, Shinori was occupied and Okkai was avenged, then the Ainu continued along the coast destroying other Wajin outposts on their way. The pent-up resentment of these Ainu was evidently about more than just the murder of Okkai. Even the Matsumae outpost was no match for the furious Ainu. By 1457, only two of the 12 outposts remained standing, Mobetsu in the east and Hanazawa in the west of the Oshima Peninsula. It was in 1458 in the western outpost of Hanazawa, under Lord Kakizaki, that a now 26-year-old Takeda had settled. Hanazawa was the furthest outpost from where the Shinori blacksmith had lived and the Japanese there wondered if they too would fall before the wrath of Koshamain.

However, against all odds the Hanazawa outpost did not fall. Takeda set out with Lord Kakizaki and soldiers from Hanazawa outpost. Takeda managed to shoot and kill Koshamain, putting an end to the Ainu uprising. Lord Kakizaki was so delighted with Takeda that he offered him the hand of his daughter in marriage, making Takeda his heir. Takeda renounced his surname and took on the surname of Kakizaki. Five years after he had fled from the province of Wakasa, his role in defeating Koshamain had allowed Takeda to become the founding father of a new domain, Matsumae.

Takeda's son, Kakizaki Mitsuhiro (1479-1545) took the first step in raising the status of his clan by relocating to the derelict Matsumae outpost in 1514, of which another Ainu raid in 1513 had again laid waste to in the south of the Oshima Peninsula. Among the Japanese of southern Hokkaido there were rumors that Mitsuhiro himself had employed Ainu to sack the base, paving the way for his move there. No one, however, dared question the son of the man who had quashed the Ainu revolt of 1457. Since the Matsumae outpost was separated from Honshu by only 19 kilometers, it was the most important of all the outposts. By taking over Matsumae, Mitsuhiro ensured that trade links between the mainland and Hokkaido were under his family's control. It was also this move that lead to Mitsuhiro being accepted as the Shogun's main representative in the far north.

During this period of power consolidation, there was still the ongoing unrest and small-scale Ainu uprisings continued to occur after 1457. It was the great-grandson of Takeda, Kakizaki Suehiro (1507-1595) who finally reached conciliation with the Ainu of southern Hokkaido. It is not known what the Ainu demanded or what Suehiro offered, but this brief peace between the Ainu and Japanese brought an end to over 90 years of strife. Because of Suehiro's success in achieving peace with the Ainu, his son Kakizaki Yoshiro (1548-1616) could flaunt the power of his clan when a Japanese uprising began in the Mutsu Province in Honshu, a region that consisted of most of the present-day Tohoku region, comprising what is now Fukushima, Miyagi, Iwate and Aomori prefectures, which make up the northern part of Honshu. Yoshiro led an army of mostly Ainu soldiers to put down the revolt. Suehiro's command of an Ainu army established him as the most powerful man in Hokkaido, and when the Shogun Toyotomi Hideyoshi (1537-1598) planned a failed invasion of

Korea and China in 1592, Suehiro sent sea otter fur gathered by Ainu from the Kuril Islands to provide warm clothing during Korea's harsh winters. Sea otter fur is exceptionally resistant to the cold due to the thickness of the coat; it is the densest in the animal kingdom. The sea otter's habitat is confined mainly to the Kuril Islands, the Kamchatka Peninsula and the southern coast of Alaska. The Wajin strongly associate the Ainu with the sea otter, so much so that the Japanese word for the animal, '*rakko*', has its origins in the Ainu language. Suehiro's gift of these rare pelts further emphasized his position as the leader of the Japanese in southern Hokkaido. With this confidence, in 1599 Suehiro left behind his old surname of Kakizaki and rebranded his clan as Matsumae, a far more prestigious name.

Although battles between the Ainu and Japanese characterized the early years of Ainu and Wajin encounters in southern Hokkaido, there were also places they lived side by side, with archeological excavations of the Katsuyama outpost on the Oshima Peninsula's northwestern side suggest that some lived together. Whale and deer bone likely brought by Ainu hunters have been unearthed in Katsuyama outpost, which was built in the latter half of the 15th Century. While these items could be the products of trade, further evidence of cohabitation between Ainu and the early Wajin settlers has come from the unearthing of four *Ikupasuy* - a holy object used by the Ainu to communicate with the gods.

To understand the significance of the *Ikupasuy*, it is necessary for a digression into Ainu religious beliefs. The importance of Ainu spiritual tools is best explained by a contemporary Ainu, Kitahara Jirota (born 1976), an associate professor at the Center for Ainu and Indigenous Studies at Hokkaido University and a descendant of the Sakhalin Ainu. Kitahara talks about how the animist religion of the Ainu holds that spiritual beings inhabit a variety of both living and non-living things and that "everything other than air and soil is alive." For example, "when collecting water from a river late at night [...] Ainu chant, "Water *Kamuy* (diety), wake up, please. I am collecting water." It is considered rude to suddenly dip a bucket into the water as the Kamuy is in the river and sleeps at night." The *Ikupasuy* are one such tool for communication with the gods. The *Ikupasuy* are placed in alcohol, which, it is believed, is sent to the gods and to the ancestors in *Kamuy Mosir* (the realm of the gods). The *Ikupasuy* were used by a single family of Ainu and were passed down from generation to generation, and such a precious item is unlikely to have been traded to the Japanese. The presence of *Ikupasuy* at Katsuyama therefore suggests that Ainu were living together with the Japanese. There have also been excavations of 38 graves at the base of Iōzan Mountain which also suggest communal living of at least some Ainu and Japanese. While it cannot be known what sort of life these Ainu and Japanese had together, the graves near Iōzan suggest that there was no discrimination between the burial of Japanese and Ainu, at least in this particular case.[10] But despite instances of cohabitation and cooperation, confrontation between the Ainu and Japanese became the norm as the Matsumae consolidated their grip on Hokkaido.

2

REBELLION AND CONSOLIDATION

THE BALANCE of power began to increasingly tip in favor of the Matsumae during the early 17th Century with support from the Shogunate allowing for increased exploitation of the Ainu. Until 1604, Ainu had the freedom to trade with Japanese anywhere within southern Hokkaido or northern Honshu. The Ainu were allowed to negotiate, and if the offer of one domain was unattractive, they could seek a better deal elsewhere. This era came to an end in 1604 when the Shogun Tokugawa Ieyasu bestowed the Matsumae with a document known as the Black Seal, which stated that all trade with the Ainu was to be carried out under the sole supervision of the Matsumae.[11] This was a boon to the Matsumae samurai who now had a monopoly over trade with the Ainu, but it was a loss for the samurai of northern Honshu and devastating for the Ainu. The Black Seal also included clauses that allowed the Matsumae to impose taxes on any Japanese within their lands. This paid particularly large dividends during a gold rush that began in the 1630s.

Among Japan's samurai, the Matsumae were unique in being the only clan not to pay their retainers in stipends of rice, since contemporary farming techniques made it impossible to grow rice in the hemiboreal climate of Hokkaido. The Matsumae clan produced no rice themselves and survived from trade with the

Ainu. The historian Takakura Ichirō writing in 1942, went so far as to argue that the Matsumae were hardly samurai at all, given their dependency on the Ainu.

The Black Seal further integrated the Matsumae into the Shogunate that ruled all the domains of Japan to the south, and in 1606 the Matsumae were ordered to build a castle to oversee their domain while protecting Japanese interest in Hokkaido. The Matsumae or Fukuyama castle, as it is also known, is the most northern Japanese castle and the only one of its kind in the entirety of Hokkaido.

The Matsumae monopoly of Ainu trade began as a sort of tributary relationship with Ainu bringing goods to Matsumae castle in exchange for Japanese products. While tributary relationships usually involve one side recognizing the other as a superior power, prior to the Black Seal, Ainu *Ekashi* (chiefs) were treated as close to equals and during visits were seated alongside the Daimyō. This was an implicit recognition that the Matsumae depended on trade with the Ainu and had to offer a degree of respect in exchange. But as the Matsumae began to monopolize trade, the *Ekashi* were made to sit on a mat in front of the Daimyō in an obviously subservient position.

In 1618, the Sicilian missionary De Angelis was a witness to the influx of Japanese samurai from northern Honshu into the Matsumae domains that took place during the early decades under the Black Seal. De Angelis observed about 300 large ships make their way to Matsumae. All were stocked with rice and alcohol as these two items were indispensable when going to Matsumae, as they were among the most coveted items for trade with the Ainu.

During the first two decades under the Black Seal, while the Ainu's freedom to trade with the samurai of northern Honshu was restricted, they did at least have freedom within their own lands. Even this began to change during the latter half of the 17th Century when the Matsumae started to distribute parcels of Ainu land to the clan's highest-ranking retainers. These grants were not the right to own the land itself, but rather the right to trade with the Ainu within a designated area. This trading monopoly given to the Matsumae samurai led to further exploitation of the Ainu as the samurai began to enter lands that had previously been the sole territory of the indigenous people. It was also a system susceptible to corruption as samurai started selling contracts to merchants to operate within their territories, usually for a period of three to five years. In return, the merchants paid a tax called the *unjyōkin* to the Matsumae samurai. In many cases, the merchants operated large-scale fishing projects and paid the local Ainu as laborers.

This contract system did not cover Hokkaido in its entirety, nor did it cover all areas of trade. Ainu were informed by the merchants of goods they were seeking such as fish or pelts and were dispatched to get them. For the Ainu, this system was vastly inferior to the free trade they had been able to carry out in decades past. But for the Japanese, the contract merchant system extended the Matsumae clan's monopoly to vast areas of Hokkaido.

As the 17th Century progressed, the control of the Matsumae samurai extended further into lands which had previously been the exclusive living space of the indigenous Ainu. The Matsumae continued to expand these fiefs, and by 1751 trading posts had been established as far as the southern Kuril Island of Kunashir off Hokkaido's northeast coast. By 1772, the Matsumae had established fishing grounds as far as Cape Sōya on Hokkaido's northwestern edge, and even across the strait to Sakhalin.

The monopoly arrangement provided no incentives for reform, and this system led to gross mistreatment of the Ainu, which continued into later centuries. The 19th Century explorer Matsuura Takeshirō, the very same who christened the island as Hokkaido, witnessed Ainu men being sent to fishing grounds far away from their home villages and said that during their absence, their wives were forced by Matsumae guards to serve as concubines. The contract system and the corruption associated with the merchants continued until the abolition of the samurai and the feudal system with the Meiji Restoration of 1868.

Further tensions between the Ainu and Matsumae emerged with a gold rush which began in 1631. At the conception of the Black Seal, rumors of gold deposits in Hokkaido were reported to the Shogun who decided that the matter should be left to the Matsumae Daimyō, who paid little attention until later that year when gold was discovered at Shimamaki on the western side of the Oshima Peninsula. Further deposits of gold were found in southeast Hokkaido in Saru the following year, in 1633 near Shizunai and in 1635 at Tokachi. This led to a flood of Japanese miners, particularly to the region west of the Hidaka Mountains on Hokkaido's east coast. The Matsumae were only too happy to oblige them and demanded tax payments from the miners. Although some Ainu tribes profited from gold discovered on their lands, for the majority the gold rush simply created further tension as Japanese pushed them off their lands and disrupted their way of life. De Angelis estimated that as many as 50,000 miners crossed over to Hokkaido in one year alone.

Ainu discontent led to uprisings, such as in 1644, when Chief Henauke of Seta-nay (present day Setana) rose up in rebellion. However, it was only in 1669 that there was a rebellion that united numerous Ainu tribes and threatened Matsumae hegemony. After the 1669 rebellion, Maki Tadeamon of the Tsugaru Clan was sent to Hokkaido to investigate. His account is recorded in the *Tsugaru Itōshi* a collection of documents recording the history of the Tsugaru clan published in 1731.[12] Maki's recordings show that resentment had been building long before the events of 1669 itself.

One damning report received by Maki was from the Ainu chief of Shiranuka, who said that,

> "merchants come to catch salmon and cast huge nets that take all the fish from the river. When we complain, saying that no fish will be left for us, they tell us that the Ainu are too greedy and that this is a Matsumae fief. Sometimes they even beat us, and we have no choice but to sell the salmon we catch to them at meager prices."[13]

While Maki did not provide a precise date, he related how one Ainu chief attempted to bring their concerns directly to the Matsumae Daimyō. Maki wrote about Chief Kekushike, the leader of one Ainu community in Yoichi, who was already over seventy years of age when he went to appeal in Matsumae. Kekushike could remember when his people were free to take their boats across to Honshu to trade, when the resources of the land were divided only amongst the Ainu tribes and when the *Sisam* (Japanese) kept out of Ainu lands. Those days were now gone. His people had gone from equal partners in trade to being little more than slaves of the Matsumae. It is quite possible that Kekushike was fearful for the future of a younger generation of Ainu after seeing the power the Ainu held decline in his own lifetime, and this provided at least part of the motivation for him to travel south to Matsumae to seek a meeting with the Matsumae Daimyō. If he could just gain a meeting, he could explain the hardships brought on his people, and perhaps the Matsumae would understand.

When Kekushike arrived at the castle, the guards laughed at him. Who did this old man think he was? Not just anyone was granted a meeting with the Lord of Matsumae. Kekushike refused to leave until he was granted an audience, and for his indolence, the guards beat him. Furious, Kekushike returned to Yoichi, and attempted to rally support for a war against the Matsumae. If these *Sisam* were not expelled, he argued, conditions would only get worse for the Ainu. Kekushike's friends and family convinced him that it was sure to fail. The Matsumae had superior weapons, and uniting the Ainu tribes was going to be difficult. He abandoned the planned uprising, Maki records.

Chief Kekushike had not been simply naïve in seeking talks with the Matsumae; the Ainu had not always been exploited in such a way by the Japanese. A decree by Shogun Toyotomi Hideyoshi in the 16th Century reads: "Any merchants who travel to Matsumae to trade with the Ezo (Ainu) must treat the natives as if they are your own countryman. Let no harm fall onto them and refrain from doing them any injustice."[14] This was in stark contrast to the treatment the Ainu experienced later in the time of Chief Kekushike in the 17th Century, but Hideyoshi's proclamation reveals more about the weakness of the Japanese position in Hokkaido at the time rather than any moral awareness of the need to treat the Ainu with respect. In the 16th Century, the Matsumae had established little more than a trading colony on the Oshima Peninsula, and their prosperity depended upon good relations with the Ainu. Regulations were therefore enforced in that era which prevented Japanese from freely entering Hokkaido in order to maintain a degree of harmony.

The man who led the 1669 rebellion against the Matsumae was an Ainu man by the name of Shakushain, born far to the east of Yoichi who had far more success than Kekushike.[15] Shakushain united the Ainu of southern Hokkaido in 1669 and led an army against the Matsumae. Shakushain has become a figure of legend shrouded in mystery with the Japanese records of the time offering various and sometimes conflicting accounts. Out of all the confrontations between the Ainu and Japanese in Hokkaido, the uprising led by Shakushain came the closest to toppling Matsumae's hegemony and it was the first unified offensive composed of multiple Ainu tribes. It is precisely this that accounts for the almost superhuman descriptions of Shakushain by contemporary Japanese chroniclers, such as the 1710 record *Ezo Danhiki* which describes Shakushain as possessing an immense body, three times the size of an ordinary man.[16] Shakushain's god-like physique is coupled with his venerable age of 80, and his legendary age does not prevent him leading an army against the Matsumae. The *Ezo Danhiki* creates a ferocious image, yet its author had likely never met Shakushain. Other records such as the *Tsugaru Itōshi* estimated Shakushain's age during the revolt at around 60. From these records, it is likely that Shakushain was born at the beginning of the 17th Century.

Since Shakushain was born around the implementation of the Black Seal, it is likely that in his youth he had visited Matsumae castle to pay tribute. From the elders in the community, Shakushain had knowledge of the days when the Ainu were free to trade with the Japanese living as far south as Honshu. Despite the lofty goal of the uprising to rid Hokkaido of the Japanese and free the Ainu from oppression, the revolt had much humbler origins in a local feud between the Menaskur (also written as menas-un-kur) and Haekur (also written as hay-kur or sar-un-kur) Ainu clans in the vicinity of the Shizunai river, a roughly 700-meter-long watercourse that begins in the Hidaka Mountains and makes its way to the Pacific Ocean on Hokkaido's south side.

According to the *Tsugaru Itōshi* in 1665, Chief Shakushain of the Menaskur tribe caught two bear cubs. In the Ainu religion, bears are seen as *Kamuy* (gods) that have come to the human realm of *Ainu Mosir* from the realm of *Kamuy Mosir*. Cubs were raised to maturity and then during the festival of *Iomante*, they are sent via sacrifice back to the realm of the gods, leaving the people with the spirit's worldly garments — its fur — and its meat. Being in possession of bears was thus a sign of a prosperous tribe, and of being in favor with the *Kamuy*. While Shakushain had caught two bear cubs, the neighboring chief of the Heakur, Onibishi had had no such luck, and he beseeched Shakushain to gift him one of the two. Shakushain, however, resented Onibishi for killing Chief Sentain of the Menaskur tribe in 1648. Shakushain ignored Onibishi's request, and the feud between the two sides grew. There are at least three accounts of what happened next. According to the *Tsugaru Itōshi*, the feud escalated when the Menaskur killed the nephew of Onibishi. The Nanbu clan's record, *Ezo Ikki Kakigaki,* also cites this as being the trigger of an all-out war between the Menaskur and Haekur.[17] The latter describes the killing as an accident and the former as a deliberate act. In another account, the Matsumae record *Ezo Hōki* describes Shakushain's son, Kanririka as being murdered at the hands of the Haekur.[18]

Regardless of how it happened, tension between the two chiefs culminated in 1668 with chief Onibishi being killed in a Japanese mining camp by the Menaskur. According to the Shogunate's record, *Ezo Danhiki,* Onibishi was felled by a spear as he attempted to retreat. The death of Onibishi did not end the Menaskur-Haekur feud. Onibishi's brother-in-law, Utafu went to Matsumae to seek aid in the form of weapons and supplies to fight the Menaskur, but his pleas fell on deaf ears. On his way back, Utafu fell ill and died at Yakumo in the middle part of the

Oshima Peninsula. Rumors began to circulate that Utafu had been poisoned by the Matsumae, and that the devious samurai were aiming at nothing less than wiping the Ainu off the face of Hokkaido. In reality, Utafu likely died of smallpox, not poison, and since the Matsumae clans' survival depended on the ability to trade with the Ainu they had nothing to gain from attempting genocide. But the resentment within Ainu society was stoked by this death which acted as a rallying point to challenge Wajin power.

The Menaskur and Haekur subsequently made peace and united to overthrow the Matsumae. Shakushain spread his message to the neighboring Ainu tribes. According to the *Tsugaru Itōshi*, he proclaimed:

> "The Matsumae have poisoned the food they have traded with the Ainu. We can have no doubts that they seek nothing less than the obliteration of the Ainu. We know the Matsumae poisoned Utafu! Let us take our bows and rain arrows on their vessels and then let us press on to Matsumae!"[19]

Ainu across Hokkaido joined the struggle, and while not every Ainu chief consented, the overwhelming majority of southeastern and southwestern Hokkaido rallied behind Shakushain.

On July 22, 1669 unexpected news reached Matsumae castle. Four Japanese falconers had been murdered at Shikotsu (present-day Chitose, the main airport entry point into Hokkaido). Soon, other messages began to pour in. Wajin in the dozens were being killed along Hokkaido's east coast. Something was amiss. There had been small-scale Ainu uprisings as far back as anyone could remember and the Matsumae had always been able to appease the Ainu, whether through trade or sheer might. What the Matsumae failed to realize was that now Ainu across southeastern and southwestern Hokkaido were uniting to overthrow their oppressors. Not fully comprehending the gravity of the situation, the Matsumae waited three days before dispatching a messenger to Edo.

The Matsumae messenger crossed the Tsugaru Strait from Hokkaido to Honshu and arrived at the Matsumae Daimyō's Edo residence two weeks later, on July 11. The Matsumae messenger told the clan's representative in Edo about the Ainu army. The representative was unable to believe what he was hearing. He went back and forth in his mind about how to best inform the Shogunate. The Black Seal was bestowed on the Matsumae precisely because they were entrusted to look after the interests of the Japanese in Hokkaido. If rumors of an Ainu army were to be believed, this was an embarrassment. After two days of deliberation, the representative at last plucked up the courage and informed the Shogunate about events that were developing in Hokkaido. The Shogunate, unlike the Matsumae, was quick to respond and ordered the Tsugaru, Nanbu and Akita clans of Tohoku to prepare weapons and send troops to support the Matsumae. Meanwhile, the Ainu were making their way towards Matsumae, targeting Japanese falconers, fisherman and gold prospectors on the way. About 153 Japanese were killed in eastern Hokkaido and 120 in the west. Among them, 98 of the Japanese were from Honshu attempting to make a profit on the northern frontier.

The Ainu targeting of the Japanese in Hokkaido was a strategic means of attacking the Matsumae's lifeline, the ability to trade. Shakushain aimed to unite the Ainu of Hokkaido, and possibly even as far as Sakhalin and the Kuril Islands, against the Matsumae preventing them from access to trade in the process. By the end of August, the samurai and Ainu armies met at Kunnui at the northern point of the Oshima Peninsula. The number of Ainu who took part in the battle varies according to each record, the *Ezo Danhiki* states 2,000 while the *Tsugaru Itōshi* and *Ezo Hōki* state between 300 to 350. The samurai undoubtedly had better weapons in the form of arquebus guns and katanas, but the Ainu proved a worthy foe and they struggled to gain an upperhand over the Ainu, with the battle dragging on for over a month. The Ainu with their knowledge of the land used guerrilla tactics, retreating into the mountains when they were disadvantaged and bringing down volleys of poison arrows when they had an opening. The Ainu frequently attacked in what were unfavorable conditions for the samurai, during the dead of night or when rain caused the samurai's arquebus to jam. After weeks of grueling fighting, the samurai eventually overwhelmed the Ainu, forcing Shakushain to retreat to his territory in Shizunai. By September 20th, the Matsumae had succeeded in forcing the complicit chiefs to surrender and to pledge their allegiance to the Matsumae. The challenge to Matsumae hegemony had for now been placated.

For the Matsumae, there was still the problem of Shakushain and his potential to lead another rebellion as a figurehead. Thus, the Matsumae offered Shakushain a peace treaty with the ulterior motive of assassinating him. According to the *Ezo Danhiki*, the Matsumae General Sato Gonzaemon offered a peace with Shakushain at Pipok (present-day Niikappu, at the base of the Hidaka Mountains), and Shakushain agreed. At the very least he had shown that the Ainu were not slaves to the Matsumae. To celebrate, a banquet was held during which a scheming Gonzaemon decided to turn the rumors that started the war into a grim reality as he poisoned the drinks of the Ainu. Shakushain believed the Matsumae were genuine in their peace overtures and only when he realized he had been poisoned did his eyes lock with those of his murderer.

"Gonzaemon, you conniving fiend!" he is said to have shouted. Shakushain knew it was too late, and his curses were the last air to leave his lungs before he collapsed. This is not the only account of Shakushain's demise and other records offer slightly different versions of events. The prevailing story is that the Matsumae came to Pipok and Gonzaemon pledged that no more Ainu would be harmed if they agreed to peace. After agreeing and celebrating with a banquet, Gonzaemon broke his promise, murdering not only Shakushain but many of the accompanying Ainu. After Shakushain was murdered, Gonzaemon proceeded to Shizunai and burnt down the Menaskur *Chashi* (Ainu fortress).[20] It was not only the rebelling Ainu who faced repercussions; the Shogunate also scolded the Matsumae for allowing events to get so out of hand. The Matsumae murder of Shakushain was their revenge for making them look like fools.

Over one hundred years after Shakushain's murder, there was one final attempt by the Ainu of Hokkaido to overthrow the Matsumae, in the battle of Kunashir-Menashi (1789). It was at Kunashir Island, today a disputed territory between Japan and Russia, just off Hokkaido's north-east coast that the Ainu rose against the slavery of the Japanese merchants in an attempt to restore some autonomy to the Ainu of north-eastern Hokkaido and the southern Kuril Islands. When the Japanese first came to Kunashir, they had conducted trade in tobacco, alcohol and rice for pelts collected by the Ainu. But just as in the mainland of Hokkaido, this mutual trade gave way to contracting by 1754. For the Hidaya Merchants, from present-day Gifu Prefecture north of Tokyo, the Ainu of Kunashir worked nonstop to catch herrings in the spring and salmon in the autumn. Even this did not satisfy the appetite of the merchants who scolded the Ainu for taking breaks. To those who disobeyed, they doled out beatings. Nothing had been learned from Shakushain. Instead with the backing of the Matsumae and the Shogunate, contractors saw fit to mistreat the Ainu with the knowledge that if push came to shove, they ultimately had the upper hand. As with Shakushain the inhuman treatment of the Ainu boiled up in resentment. Once again, rumors began circulating that the Wajin had poisoned the meager rations of food. This poison became a personification of the fear that the Wajin sought to wipe out the Ainu race and 41 Ainu rose up to fight. This zeal spread to the Menashi Ainu on the Hokkaido coast opposite Kunashir Island. In total, 71 Wajin were killed. Fears of another Shakushain rebellion led the Matsumae to send troops and the Shogunate once again ordered the Tsugaru and Nanbu clans of Tohoku to hasten to Kunashir. In the two-month period before the Matsumae arrived, the Ainu chief Shonko, understanding the consequences of attempting to overthrow the Matsumae, called for the younger Ainu to end their vendetta. The Matsumae arrived, led by General Niida Magosaburō (died 1807). Niida acknowledged the corrupt acts of the merchants, but he scolded the Ainu for taking matters into their own hands instead of seeking assistance and decided punishment was in order. It is of course doubtful if the Matsumae would have done anything to better the plight of the Kunashir Ainu if they had sought aid. The Ainu who were deemed to be perpetrators were placed in cages and were in turn executed. As the Ainu watched their compatriots escorted out one by one to meet their end, they begin chanting *Peutanke* - a chant to the gods to drive away evil spirits. This infuriated the Wajin even more.

In total 71 Japanese and 37 Ainu died during the battle, and its immediate aftermath and Magosaburō took a further 39 Ainu to Matsumae as hostages. The Ainu of Hokkaido never again rose up in battle to challenge the Matsumae. However, while the Japanese had been increasing their hegemony over the Ainu, a new threat to the Shogunate had been expanding into East Asia and eventually onto the Shogunate's northern frontier. This was the Russians, who were known to the Japanese who first encountered them as the 'Red Ezo'. Though the Shogunate feared losing territory, it was the Ainu who became trapped between the Japanese expansion north and Russian expansion south.

Shakushain's legacy continues to this day. Beginning in 1961, the Shizunai Board of Tourism arranged a Shakushain festival. But protests from the Shinhidaka Ainu Association led to the management of the festival being transferred to the local Ainu. This yearly festival continues to this day in Shinhidaka's Mauta Park, not far from where Shakushain reigned during his time. The park also includes a memorial museum to Shakushain and an archive concerning the Ainu. Until 2018 the centerpiece of the park was a statue of a furious Shakushain with a hand raised calling for battle. However, many years of heavy snow had caused the statue to crack, and in 2015 the Shinhidaka Ainu Association decided it was time for a new reincarnation of Shakushain to grace Mauta Park. Speaking to a reporter of the *Hokkaido Shimbun* newspaper, the spokesman of the association said, "we have entered a period where the Ainu and Wajin live side by side," and because of this, the new Shakushain statue today reflects a more somber Shakushain with his hands raised in prayer.[21]

3

CROSSROADS IN THE SEA OF OKHOTSK

THE KAMCHATKA PENINSULA lies at the furthest edges of the Eurasian continent. This vast peninsula is larger than either the island of Great Britain or the Korean Peninsula. Kamchatka is linked geologically to the American continent and the Japanese archipelago through two volcanic island chains. To the east, is the Aleutian Islands which links Kamchatka to Alaska, and the southern cape of Kamchatka which leads down into the Kuril Islands and Hokkaido. By the end of the 18th Century, a new colonizing people not native to this region began to appear in Kamchatka, Sakhalin and the northern Kuril Islands, eventually making expeditions to the fringes of Hokkaido. These interlopers into the Far East were the Russians and their presence in the north deeply disturbed the Shogunate. Coming from as far as eastern Europe, and for even the hardiest Russian explorers, these expeditions into northeast Asia were by no means an easy feat, and many died in the biting cold. During their treks of conquest east, the Russian settlers faced resistance from the indigenous people, the harsh Siberian weather and the dilemma of carrying enough food supplies across the continent while travelling light enough to cover a vast distance. Regardless of these difficulties the Russians gradually made their way east and by 1639 had reached the Sea of Okhotsk in which sits the

Kamchatka Peninsula, Sakhalin, the Kuril Islands and northern Hokkaido.

Over the next few decades, Russians pushed further south and by 1778 had made it to the most southern islands of the Kurils. Like many place names in Sakhalin, the Kuril Islands and Hokkaido, the Russians (like their Japanese counterparts) transliterated the original Ainu place names to fit their language. The Russians took the name 'Iturup' from the original Ainu name for the island 'Etuworop', Japanese interpreted the same name as 'Etorofu'.

The first recorded Russian encounter with the Ainu was in 1697 by an exploration party led by the Siberian Cossack Vladimir Atlasov (1661/1664-1711) in the Kamchatka Peninsula. Here, the Russians met the indigenous Itelmen, as well as Ainu who had come from the Northern Kuril Islands. Regardless of their different languages and culture, the Russians christened all the native peoples as 'Kamchadals': from the point of view of the Russians they were all natives of Kamchatka.

As with the indigenous people of northern Eurasia, when the Russians took over native land, they demanded a fur tax from the Kuril Ainu. As indigenous people had likewise responded further west, the Ainu protested and built a fort to resist the Russian invaders. The Ainu's resistance proved to be futile, with the Russians overwhelming the Ainu and killing 50. Having overcome the small resistance presented by these Ainu; Russians descended further south into the Kuril Islands until they arrived in Hokkaido. In the Kuril Islands, the Russians designated the native Ainu as 'Kurils' after the Ainu word for man. The Kuril Ainu, meanwhile, began to call the Russians the '*hūre-sisam/ hūre-shamu*' - the scarlet people. This moniker was either from the red coats that characterized the Russian settlers or their pale faces which became bright red as blood rushed to their cheeks in the frigid climate.

As was the case in Kamchatka, Russian expeditions into the Kuril Islands were met with indigenous resistance. In 1711, Russians again entered the most northern Kuril Islands of Paramushir and Shumshu just south of Kamchatka, and once again clashed with both the Itelmen of southern Kamchatka and the Ainu of the northern Kuril Islands. Just as the Shogunate did not tolerate Ainu rebellions in Hokkaido, the Russians did not tolerate their resistance in the Kurils. Two years later Russians returned to subjugate these Ainu and force them into paying the fur tax.

Ainu wishing to escape the Russians moved further south along the archipelago, although this proved to be only a brief respite with Russian influence extending deeper into the Kuril Islands. The Ainu who had not forsaken their homes had the Russian way of life forced upon them. Cows were bought from the mainland and the farming of potatoes, cabbage and daikon was encouraged over hunting, the traditional means of living. The Ainu in the northern Kuril Islands were forced to adopt Russian names and on Shumshu Island, a Russian language school was erected. Religion, such a central part of Russian life at the time, was also transmitted to these Ainu as they were made to adopt the Russian Orthodox faith, with later generations of northern Kuril Ainu becoming sincere adherents of this faith.

As the Russians descended to the southern Kuril Islands they met with further resistance. In 1770, Ainu from the southern island of Iturup regularly went to the neighboring island of Urup to hunt seal, otter and striped mullet, and it was on Urup that tensions erupted between the Ainu and a group of Russians who had entered the hunting grounds which had been under the control of generations of Ainu. In the skirmish, two chiefs from the Iturup were killed by the Russians. The following year, Ainu from Iturup again crossed over to Urup to fight the Russians before moving on to kill Russians on the less populated and smaller volcanic island of Broutona. Ainu resistance toward Russian influence also took place in neighboring Sakhalin. While Ainu armed resistance against the Japanese in Hokkaido came to an end with the battle of Kunashir-Menashi in 1789, in Sakhalin Ainu battles with the Russians continued to as late as 1891 when 16 Russian prisoners attacked Ainu around Lake Tunaycha who were partaking in *Iomante*. During this incident, eight Ainu women were killed by Russians during their most important religious ritual, further enraging the Ainu. The sacrilege of the interlopers prompted these Sakhalin Ainu to take up arms. The event at Lake Tunaycha is just one of many examples of Ainu armed resistance against the Russians in Sakhalin and the Kuril Islands.

The indigenous people lacked the technology of the Russians and Japanese, but in the Kuril Islands the Ainu resistance prevented the Kuril Islands from becoming a Russian colony in its entirety. Although their resistance slowed down the Russian expansion south, it did not prevent Russians from making expeditions to the southern Kuril Islands including Iturup. It is from Iturup that the Russians could see Hokkaido and it was not long before they crossed over to Nopamappu, present-day Nemuro, on Hokkaido's northeastern shore in 1778. The following year Russian merchants once again appeared off the coast of Hokkaido, this time at Akkeshi, where they petitioned the Matsumae officials to open trade with the Russian Empire. The Russians failed to understand the increasing paranoia of the Shogunate as they encroached on what was considered Japanese territory under the control of the Matsumae.

With the Russian expansion south and east from Siberia, the Japanese in Hokkaido began to have increased encounters with the Russians. It was a doctor of Sendai domain, Kudō Heisuke (1734-1801), who presented the first written report of the Russians to the Shogunate. Doctor Kudō had never seen such devilish people with such pale skin and outlandish hair. The Ainu, however, were a foreign people of the north he was well acquainted with. Just as the Wajin called the Ainu 'Ezo', Doctor Kudō titled his report 'Description of the Red Ezo.' Following Doctor Kudō's report, the Shogunate assembled a team of 37 surveyors to investigate the suspicious 'Red Ezo' appearing from the north. After their arrival in Hokkaido, the team of surveyors split into two groups: the western group crossing over into Sakhalin and the eastern group heading for the Kuril Islands. The eastern team encountered many Russians on the island of Iturup and were even more concerned by an Ainu who spoke Russian and had adopted a Russian name. Their fears were not only that the Red Ezo had encroached into Japanese territory but the Red Ezo held the potential to turn the precarious Ainu people into their allies and set them against the Japanese.

The most famous explorer from the survey expedition was Mogami Tokunai (1755-1826). Mogami was born in today's Yamagata Prefecture to an impoverished peasant family. At the age of 26, his father passed away, prompting him to move to the world's biggest city during the 18th Century, the Shogun's capital of Edo. In the bustling streets of Edo, Mogami became the pupil of the renowned mathematician Honda Toshiaki (1743-1821). Honda had opened his own school in Edo at the age of 24 and had advocated both Westernization and the colonization of Hokkaido in order to maintain Japan's hold over the island. Honda's ideas were eventually realized with the Meiji Restoration of 1868 which saw both a Westernization of Japan as well as the colonization of Hokkaido. The Shogunate chose Honda for the first mission to survey the islands north of Hokkaido. However, a sudden illness led to Honda sending his young disciple Mogami in his place. Due to his background, Mogami was an unusual fellow to undertake such an expedition. During the Edo Period (1603-1868) laws prohibiting an individual changing their class were established to prevent uprisings and to maintain the social hierarchy. This class order placed samurai at the top, followed by farmers, craftsman, merchants and outcasts. In reality, while merchants were ranked lower, many were able to become wealthier than their samurai counterparts, but the system held them in place and prevented them partaking in certain activities reserved for their supposed social betters. In a system aiming to maintain the feudal order of the Shogunate, farmers were forbidden from wielding swords, preventing them from revolting and challenging their samurai superiors. How Mogami managed to transcend such a rigid system demonstrates his skill and luck in an age of very limited social mobility.

Upon reaching the north of Hokkaido, Mogami and his party managed to cross over to the northern point of Kunashir Island with the help of an Ainu guide. The following year, Mogami once again set out from Matsumae and with another Ainu guide, successfully crossed over to Iturup. It is at Iturup that Mogami encountered Russians living on the island. Unlike the paranoia of the Matsumae officials, Mogami's experience of the Russians was more constructive. Using an Ainu who could speak Russian, Mogami was introduced to three Russians with whom he lodged for over three months. On the first day, the Russians performed for him a traditional song; Mogami was moved by the performance and offered them some rice as a token of his appreciation. It was during this period that Mogami heard from the Russians about their country and the numerous Japanese castaways who had become stranded on Russian shores. Having collected enough information, Mogami went with the three Russians to Kunashir

Island, embracing them before parting ways.

Mogami had come to form a friendship with the Russians on Iturup that transcended his mission to survey the islands. The Shogunate, however, had a very different reaction to Mogami's encounter with the Russians. By 1807 the Shogunate designated the entirety of Hokkaido as territory under its direct control. This had begun with eastern Hokkaido in 1779, and was followed by western Hokkaido, including Matsumae in 1807. The port of Hakodate was made the capital city with Shogunate officials dispatched to govern the island. This period lasted until 1821, after which the Shogunate returned power to the Matsumae clan as fears of Russian incursion waned, albeit temporarily. In what was good fortune for the Shogunate, Napoleon's invasion of Russia in 1812 put a stop to Russian interest in Asian expansion as resources became increasingly redirected toward its European frontier. Subsequently, Russian expansion east increased in the middle of the century following Napoleon's defeat. During this time, Hokkaido again came under the direct control of the Shogunate in 1855. Under the second phase of the Shogunate's rule, the central city of Hokkaido again shifted from Matsumae to Hakodate.

Mogami made numerous voyages throughout his life to Sakhalin and the Kuril Islands. He was a man well-versed in the Ainu language and without the guidance from the local Ainu, Mogami's surveys would have been greatly inhibited if not impossible. It was thanks to an elderly Mogami meeting a German doctor by the name of Philipp Franz von Siebold (1796-1866) that maps of the islands north of Hokkaido made their way to Europe. Seibold was born into a family of physicians and his reading of the travels in Latin America of the German explorer Alexander von Humboldt (1769-1859) awoke a wanderlust in him. Like von Humboldt, Seibold desired to travel to distant lands and at the age of 26, much like Mogami, he made a decision that shaped his life from then on. Seibold became a military physician for the Dutch, one of the most active colonial powers of the era with a particular relationship with the Japanese.

The hostility to Christianity that Francis Xavier encountered as the first missionary to Japan eventually culminated in the banning of all foreign ships from trading with Japan by 1639, with the important exception of the Dutch who pledged to the Shogun that their only purpose in Japan was to conduct trade and not to convert the masses of Japan to Christianity, destabilizing the Shogunate in the process. Thus, the Dutch were permitted to set up a base on the artificial island of Dejima in Nagasaki Bay. This gave them access to Japanese trade along with the Chinese merchants also stationed in Nagasaki. Today Dejima has become an integral part of the city through land reclamation projects.

In the summer of 1823, Seibold arrived at Dejima and the German doctor left quite a legacy behind him. Seibold introduced vaccination and pathological anatomy to Japan and began a medical school in Nagasaki. The founding of the medical school resulted in Dutch becoming the language of modern medicine in Japan, for example *katēteru* from the Dutch *khateter* meaning a catheter and *supoito* from *spuit* meaning syringe. He also fathered a daughter with Kusumoto Taki (1807-1865) who went on to become the first female physician in Japan, Kusumoto Ine (1827-1903). Seibold had an appreciation for Japan and sent gifts back to Holland such as the prints of the renowned woodblock artist Katsushika Hokusai (1760-1849) as well as Japanese fauna and wildlife, including the first Japanese giant salamander in Europe.

When Seibold journeyed to Edo in 1826 he met the elderly Mogami on several occasions. He was fascinated by Mogami's exploration to the northern islands and Seibold even learnt some of the Ainu language from the veteran explorer. Mogami likely saw something of himself in Seibold, who had traveled to distant lands far from home. Through their friendship Mogami allowed Seibold to borrow some maps of Hokkaido and Sakhalin.

However, the Shogunate was increasingly paranoid about Christian missionaries penetrating Japan and the situation was not improved by the Russians appearing in Hokkaido from the north. Accepting the maps from Mogami proved to be a mistake for Seibold. Mamiya Rinzō (1775-1844), another famous Japanese explorer of Sakhalin, is believed to have discovered that Seibold possessed the maps of the northern territories. It is thought his jealousy of the older explorer Mogami led to him informing the authorities, which resulted in Seibold's expulsion from Japan. Seibold did eventually return during his later life, however. During his second trip to Japan (from 1859-1862), Seibold gathered one of the oldest collections of Ainu objects, including types of Ainu garments: *Retarpe* (woven from nettles) and *Attus* (woven from bark), both now held in the Museum Five Continents in Munich.[22]

On his return to Europe, Seibold introduced the Strait of Tartary between Sakhalin and the Eurasian continent in his book *Nippon: Archiv zur Beschreibung von Japan* (1832–54) as the 'Mamiya Strait' after the Japanese discovery of the area (on Japanese and Korean maps of Sakhalin, the Strait of Tartary is still described as the Mamiya Strait). Seibold never knew that it was Mamiya who likely reported him to the Shogunate. As for Mamiya himself, he has been credited with proving that Sakhalin was not connected to the continent and is instead a long island north of Hokkaido.

Like Mogami, Mamiya was also aided by the Ainu in his exploration of the northern islands. Mamiya even had a child with an Ainu woman whose descendants continued to play an active role in the Ainu Community in the 21st Century.[23]

4

Sakoku and Hokkaido

The Shogun's hostility to foreigners entering Japan culminated in the execution of Christian missionaries and converts, gradually closing off the country from the outside world from end of the 1630s, and in Hokkaido and beyond, from organized surveys by Russians in the northern lands. Such acts were not entirely reactionary, as they aimed to maintain stability within Japan. In Japanese, this period is known as '*Sakoku*,' or 'chained country' if the Chinese characters of 鎖 (chain) and 国 (country) are read literally.

The Tokugawa Shogunate (1600-1868) was the first form of government to comprehensively tie regional Daimyōs vying for power under the Warring States Period (1467-1600) into a centralized state. It is with the formation of the Tokugawa Shogunate that a state resembling the nation of Japan began to emerge. The internal politics underlying *Sakoku* was the motivation to prevent regional Daimyō from acquiring power through trade or challenging the Shogun's hegemony through religions such as Christianity, which professed allegiance to a higher power. Once the founder of the dynasty, Tokugawa Ieyasu had successfully consolidated his control over most of what contemporaries recognize as Japan. He created a system called 'alternate attendance' to keep power concentrated in the hands of the Tokugawa clan. Under this system, the wives and children of each regional Daimyō were housed in the Shogun's capital of Edo. Every year each Daimyō and his samurai retainers were ordered to come to Edo – this long march and lavish processions to the capital city which drained the coffers of each regional Daimyō while at the same time allowing for a close watch to be kept on them, right under the Shogunate's nose. If any single Daimyō could empower his clan through trade and alliance with a foreign nation, this fragile system could come tumbling down, sending Japan back into a period of warring states. It was this underlying fear that shaped the Shogunates' reaction to the Russian contacts with Hokkaido.

Regardless of official policy, Japan was not completely shut off from the outside world during this period. The Dutch and Chinese could conduct trade, although it was limited to Nagasaki. There was also the Ryukyu Kingdom (present-day Okinawa Prefecture and parts of Kagoshima Prefecture), which was an independent kingdom that traded in the form of 'tribute' with China and states in Southeast Asia, although an invasion from the samurai of Satsuma domain in 1609 robbed the king of absolute rule. There was also the island of Tsushima, almost directly between Kyushu and the Korean Peninsula that served as a trading outpost. Finally, there were the trade links between the Ainu and the Matsumae domain.

From Hokkaido, Sakhalin, and the Kuril Islands the Ainu could trade with the Russians and Chinese as well as other indigenous groups. For the Russians who encountered Ainu on the island of Paramushir, the island closest to the Kamchatka Peninsula, they found Ainu in possession of porcelain, silk, and cotton as well as pans and knives from their trade with the Matsumae. The Ainu were quite willing to profit from trade with the Russians, so much so that the Ainu chief Ikotoi of Aketsu in eastern Hokkaido met with the Russians yearly to conduct trade in the Kuril Islands. Not just Japanese goods entered Russian hands through the Ainu. The Ainu chief Yaenkoroaino of Sakhalin successfully used the Amur River region of the island to conduct trade with Manchu officials from China. The Ainu thus acted as trade intermediaries even though Japan was officially closed to the outside world.

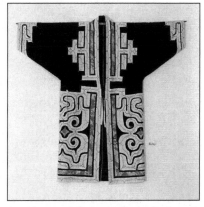

An Ainu garment in the Rūnpe *style made from cotton (kindly provided by the Nibutani Ainu Culture Museum) Cotton was an item the Ainu acquired through trade*[24]

This connection can be seen in some rarer Ainu garments which have embraced Chinese designs such as dragons, one example of which can be seen at the Hakodate City Museum of Northern Peoples.

The Ainu could trade the spoils from hunting with both the Russians, Matsumae and Chinese as well as Russian products to the Japanese and Japanese products to the Russians. This trade allowed the Matsumae clan to proposer thanks to the Ainu, nonetheless the rules of *Sakoku* were strict. Officially, no foreigners could enter Japan and any Japanese who left were forbidden from returning. Whether leaving Japan was of their own violation or circumstances outside of their control, the punishment was always exile, as was the case with Japanese castaways.

Between the years 1661 and 1862, more than 40 Japanese were cast away from their homeland by typhoons, storms, and shipwrecks, sending seafarers as far as the North American continent and Siberia. The majority of castaways ended up in

Hokkaido, but at least ten Japanese were stranded on the Kuril Islands, three on the Russian-controlled Kamchatka Peninsula and even as far as the Coast of Mexico in 1813, California in 1815 and Washington state in 1833.

It is through such castaways that the Russian Empire attempted to crack the Shogunate's *Sakoku* policy and open formal trade links with Japan. A potential chance came in 1695, when a ship leaving Osaka bay was set adrift, eventually landing on the frigid coast of the Kamchatka Peninsula. The sole survivor, Denbe, was washed up from the shipwreck, but he was powerless as curious natives ransacked the remains of the ship. The locals did not know what to make of the gold coins in the ship's cargo and gave them to their children as toys. The cargo was lost, but Denbe managed to stave off death by living with the natives. Denbe's luck further improved when a Cossack called Atlasov came across Denbe and escorted him to the Tsar's residence in Moscow. The Russians saw Denbe as a potential key to opening up Japan, and after his command of Russian had improved, he became the empire's first teacher of the Japanese language. The opportunity to further Russian knowledge about Japan increased when a ship from the Tohoku region washed ashore, leaving a Japanese man by the name of Sanima who became the assistant Japanese teacher to Denbe.

These were by no means the last Japanese to wash ashore in Russia. In 1729 a ship by the name of the *Wakashō-Maru* left Satsuma domain in southern Kyushu and became stranded on the Kamchatka Peninsula. Only two of those on board, Sōza and Gonza, survived. In 1736, they also became Japanese teachers, this time at a language school affiliated with the Academy of Science. These first Japanese castaways in Russia never returned to their homeland.

One particular castaway played a prominent role in Russia's

efforts to open Japan to trade and was the first castaway to successfully re-enter Japan from Russia. Daikokuya Kōdayū (1751-1828), was the captain of the *Shinsho-Maru*. Kōdayū spent over ten years in Russian territories before being able to return home.

The *Shinsho-Maru* was a large Benzaisen junk with the capacity to transport up to 150,000 kilograms of rice. In December of 1782, the ship set sail from Kishū domain's Shiroko port (present-day Mie Prefecture), in western Honshu's Kansai region bound for Edo. Led by Captain Kōdayū, there were 16 crewmembers and the ship's cat onboard, and after being caught in a storm, they spent eight months adrift in the Pacific Ocean, before arriving at the Amchitka Island on the Aleutian island chain which stretches from Alaska to the Kamchatka Peninsula. Those who survived Amchitka with the help of Russians on the island made it to the mainland, where they faced numerous hardships including famine and adverse weather, as they transversed the country seeking permission from the Russian authorities for passage back home. Through a meeting with one Erik Gustavovich Laxman (1737-1796) a member of the Saint Petersburg Academy of Science and founder of the museum in Irkutsk, the Japanese obtained a meeting with the Tsarina, Catherine the Great (1729-1796). Russia, seeing an opportunity to establish trade links with Japan, was more than happy to send the surviving castaways back, and with Erik's son Adam Laxman, the survivors left the port of Okhotsk for Hokkaido in 1792.

When the ship arrived in Hokkaido, the three Japanese, (soon to be two as one who had survived the ordeal in Russia passed away in Hokkaido), were treated with suspicion by the Matsumae officials stationed there. The surviving members who made it to Edo were Capitan Kōdayū and crew member Isokichi (1763-1838). Once the *Yekatrina*, the ship carrying the Japanese and the Russians made landfall, Isokichi and a member of the Russian crew were sent to survey the area. The two spotted a Matsumae guardhouse in Betsukai. As they approached, a group of Ainu suddenly appeared. Isokichi asked the Ainu if this was Hokkaido, which they confirmed and subsequently took him to the Matsumae officials. The Matsumae guards were suspicious of the two men in Russian clothes and doubted whether Isokichi was even Japanese. To buy more time they ordered the *Yekaterina* to move east to Nemuro while the Matsumae were informed of these Red Ezo. Guided by two Ainu elders aboard a small towboat, the *Yekaterina* was escorted to Nemuro where the crew were made to wait for months as the Matsumae consulted with the Shogunate about what was to be done.

The Russians, however, did not come just to return the castaways out of the goodness of their hearts. Adam demanded to be taken to Edo and begin trade negotiations with the Shogunate. Of course, his requests were repeatedly ignored. Not wanting to idle away their time as they waited in Nemuro, the Russians built a Russian-style steam bath, created a temporary base to observe Hokkaido's fauna, geography, and resources and also attempted to study Ainu-Japanese relations. These activities were soon stopped by the Matsumae officials. In their free time, the Russians skated on the frozen port of Nemuro, astonishing the Matsumae with this alien custom.

It was also during this time that the first Japanese-Russian dictionary was created. By early May, the Russians were at last granted a meeting with the Matsumae and were ordered to move along the eastern coast of Hokkaido towards Matsumae at the southern point of the Oshima Peninsula. A strong southerly wind prompted an unscheduled stop in Hakodate. Isokichi recalled in his memoirs how the local people rushed to the port to see this foreign ship docking in their small town. There was also a record of local people thoroughly scrubbing down the places the Russians touched after they left, suggesting an underlying fear among the Hakodate denizens of these strange people. At Matsumae, three rounds of discussions were held between Adam and Shogunate officials, and at last a deal was made with the Shogunate tolerating one Russian ship, if it called at Nagasaki, as did the Dutch and Chinese traders. Adam believed he had successfully achieved his mission and after bidding farewell to his Japanese companions the *Yekatrina* set sail for Russia.

Even though they may have made it back to Japan, the Shogunate viewed Kōdayū and Isokichi with suspicion and promptly escorted them to Edo for interrogation about their time in Russia. After they had professed that they had not converted to Christianity and were not Russian spies, Kōdayū and Isokichi boldly spoke the truth, stating that the Russians desired to open up trade relations with the Japanese. Their testimony became part of two records, invaluable documents for understanding Japanese-Russian relations under *Sakoku*.[25] After questioning, Kōdayū and Isokichi were given residences in what is today the Koshikawa Botanical Gardens of Tokyo University. Kōdayū lived to the age of 78, passing away in 1828, and Isokichi lived to 75, passing away ten years later. Both were laid to rest at Kōan-Ji temple where a record of Kōdayū and Isokichi has been recorded in the temple's death register (present-day Bunkyo Ward, Tokyo). Kōdayū and Isokichi experienced the Russians not through a combination of rumors and suspicion but as real living people. This makes them exceedingly rare individuals in a period where Japan was all but closed off from the outside world.

While Adam Laxman was satisfied that he had opened up trade relations with the first Russian-Japanese treaty of commerce, the reality was far more complicated. The Shogunate had agreed to a Russian ship gaining access to Nagasaki. But when this was put into practice in 1802, the officials at Nagasaki refused to let the Russian ship anchor, exclaiming that Japan was closed to foreign nations other than the Dutch and Chinese. Japanese-Russian relations further deteriorated when in 1811 the Golovnin Incident erupted as four sailors of the Russian ship the *Dianne* were captured on Kunashir Island and imprisoned in Hakodate. Any goodwill created by talks between the Shogunate and Adam Laxman was rendered null when Nikolai Rezanov (1764-1807) attempted to put into effect what had been previously agreed between the two parties. When Rezanov attempted to land in Nagasaki, he was told by the Nagasaki Magistrate that only China, Korea, Ryukyu and Holland had a right to trade in Nagasaki and that he had best be on his way. Leaving for Russian Alaska, an infuriated Rezanov convinced Lieutenant Chwostoff stationed there that there may be chances to profit from the Japanese situation on Sakhalin and the Kuril Islands. In 1806, Chwostoff attacked Japanese villages on Sakhalin and in 1807 chased off 300 Tsugaru samurai stationed on the island of Iturup. This in turn prompted the Shogunate to become increasingly harsh towards foreign ships and in 1806, an order was given to open fire on any ships that did not turn back.

It was in this climate that in 1812 Vasily Golovnin (1776-1831) had come to Kunashir Island to conduct a survey. With six of his crewmembers, Golovnin alighted from the *Diana* and was guided by an Ainu named Alexi (Oseki in Japanese records), when suddenly the eight of them were seized by samurai stationed on the island. They were imprisoned in Hokkaido for two years and three months. With the capture of the ship's captain the deputy captain, Petr Rikord (1778-1855) saw a chance to negotiate when he spotted a Japanese merchant ship sailing nearby. The crew of the *Diana* raided the ship, capturing the lead merchant, Takadaya Kahei (1769-1827), showing some mercy by allowing the rest of the crewmembers to alight on Kunashir Island. Takadaya who was a successful merchant from Awaji Island (present day Hyogo Prefecture) had set up his trading company in Hakodate. Rikord forcibly took Takadaya to Kamchatka as collateral in the hopes that he could be able to free his fellow sailors in the hands of the Shogunate.

During Takadaya's imprisonment, he and Rikord spent hours talking together, eventually building a relationship of trust. Takadaya was sympathetic to the capture of the crew of the *Diana* and proposed to Rikord that he stress that the Russian crew had no relationship to the ransacking of Lieutenant Chwostoff on Sakhalin. Rikord took up Takadaya's plan and released Takadaya on Iturup Island as a sign of good will. Takadaya, true to his word, submitted the Russian letter explaining the situation to the Shogunate and made a push for the release of the Russian prisoners. He was successful, and in 1813, the crew were released.

Upon his return to Russia, Golovnin went on to write an account of his experiences in '*Captivity in Japan During the Years 1811, 1812, 1813*'. This book became an instant classic that would go on to inspire future Russian diplomats and missionaries in Japan once the port of Hakodate opened. Takadaya, who had learned the Russian language during his imprisonment in Kamchatka, later played a role in mediating the border dispute in the Kuril Islands between the Japanese and Russians. For his mercantile work building up the port of Hakodate and his diplomatic role with the Russians, Takadaya was enshrined at the Kaitaku-Jinja shrine, or 'colonizers shrine' in Sapporo in 1938. The Golovnin Incident shows how the escalating tension between the Japanese and Russians led the two powers to the brink of war in the early 19th Century. But despite the tension between the Shogunate and the Russian Empire, it was not the Russians who broke *Sakoku*, but the Americans.

Despite multiple failed Russian attempts, the isolationist policy of *Sakoku* could not continue in a world of expanding imperial powers, and just 26 years after Kōdayū's death, Commodore Matthew Perry of the United States Navy forced Japan open with gunboat diplomacy. Perry required the Shogunate to sign the Convention of Kanagawa in 1854, a treaty that opened the ports of Shimoda and Hakodate to American ships. The following year, Vice-Admiral Putiatin (1803-1883) of the Imperial Russian navy saw an opportunity, thanks to Perry, and signed the Treaty of Shimoda, opening the ports of Nagasaki, Shimoda, and Hakodate to the Russian Empire. The Hakodate locals who were once so suspicious of the strange people on board the *Yekatrina* came to embrace their status as a melting pot in the 19th Century, one of the first places in Japan to which European culture was introduced.

Alongside active attempts to prevent the Russians interloping on the Shogunate's sphere of influence, there were also attempts to make the Ainu more Japanese. The Russian Orthodox Church never attempted a mission in Japan on the same level as the Portuguese Catholics, but some Ainu in the Kuril Islands had converted to the Russian Orthodox faith. If the Ainu could be made to follow the Buddhist practices of Japan instead, it could be claimed that They too, were in a sense Japanese, making their homeland of Hokkaido an unquestionably Japanese territory for the Shogunate. In 1804, the Shogunate ordered the creation of three temples to convert the Ainu to Buddhism with the immediate aim of turning them away from their animist religion in the process. These temples were known as the 'Three Ezo Temples'.[26] The temples, which continue their religious services to this day are Kokutai-Ji, Tojū-In and Usuzenkō-Ji, each representing a different school of thought within Japanese Buddhism. Kokutai-Ji is a Zen temple of the Rinzai School, emphasizing transcendental meditation, Tojū-In is a Tiantai temple that places importance on the Lotus Sutra (which teaches that all living things have the potential to reach enlightenment), and Ususenkō-Ji is of the pure land school where anyone who recites the Bodhisattvas Amitābha's vow has the potential to be saved from the sufferings of this world. Even though each school emphasis different tenets of Buddhism, the three Ezo temples were united in their purpose to propagate Buddhism amongst the Ainu.

Buddhism was the central religion of the Tokugawa Shogunate and a few years after the establishment of the regime in 1603, every Japanese was ordered to register their family at their local Buddhist temple. All funerals were conducted according to Buddhist teachings, and the founder Tokugawa Ieyasu's spirit was even shrined as a reincarnation of a Buddha in Tōshō-gū shrines across the country.[27] Throughout the three Ezo temples, there is ample evidence that attempts were underway to convert the Ainu to Buddhism.

An 1804 document at Kokutai-Ji lays out the temple's aims of educating the Ainu by bringing them into the Buddhist faith, and at the same time encouraging them to adopt Japanese customs. It is written that memorial services for the Ainu's dead were to be held at the temple, displaying no prejudice against Japanese or Ainu devotees, at least in the written word. There were also efforts to reach the Ainu through their language. At Usuzenkō-Ji wooden printing blocks of Buddhist prayers written in both Japanese and the Ainu language in katakana script. With these printing blocks, the priests at the temple could mass-produce prayers and circulate them amongst the Ainu everywhere. At Kokutai-Ji, prints of the five Buddhist precepts (abstain from killing, abstain from stealing, abstain from sexual misconduct, abstain from false speech and abstain from intoxicating substances) were circulated among the Ainu.

The Shogunate's attempt to make the Ainu culturally Japanese ultimately stemmed from a fear that the Ainu might become allies with the Russians on the fringes of Hokkaido. Since the Ainu made up a majority of the population, it was vital that the Shogunate found some way to emphasize an association of the Ainu with Japan. However, the relatively laissez-faire methods of the Shogunate paled in comparison to the reforms of the Meiji government which overthrew the Shogunate in 1868 and ushered in a wave of reforms for both the Ainu and Japanese alike.

5

HOKKAIDO'S FIRST INTERNATIONAL PORT

WITH HIS VICTORY over rival Daimyō at the Battle of Sekigahara in 1600, Shogun Tokugawa Ieyasu declared that there were to be no more wars in Japan. All were to be subservient to the Tokugawa dynasty, and peace to prevail. By the 19th Century, the samurai had been living in an unprecedented 200-year period of peace. Although it had been decades since any samurai had seen combat, they proudly held on to traditions of swordsmanship, archery, and loyalty to their Daimyō. It seemed to them as if this stability might go on for an eternity and that history itself had come to an end. The Tokugawa forever ruling, the samurai never fighting again and Japan remaining isolated from the troubles of the outside world. Yet, just as the Goths had put pressure on the Roman Empire or the Mongols on China's Song dynasty, the pressure of Western nations on the fringes of Japan eventually caused the Tokugawa Shogunate to collapse. By the 1850s, the Shogunate was struggling to maintain the *Sakoku* isolation policy as the American and Russians opened the port of Hakodate in Hokkaido to foreign trade. With commercial treaties signed between the Shogunate and numerous foreign nations, diplomats and merchants poured into these ports. The semi-opening of Japan introduced new technology, trading opportunities and ways of thinking, but many samurai resented what they saw as humiliating treaties signed under the threat of foreign attack. There were worries that these foreigners would desecrate Japan or reduce it to a colony, like the Philippines, India and many other Asian territories.

The opening of Japan sparked a movement to 'revere the Emperor and expel the barbarians' which developed into the Meiji government and nation-state of Japan in 1868.[28] While the Meiji government dropped extremist ideas concerning expulsion of 'the barbarians', the desire to create a modern nation-state with the Emperor as its figurehead culminated in 1869 in the Battle of Hakodate, the last battle of a civil war to determine the future direction of the country. In Hakodate, the remains of an army loyal to the Shogunate attempted to establish a separate republic in Hokkaido, to which the new Meiji government was willing to fight against to see a unified Japan. All the landmark events — the opening of Japan, the influx of foreigners and civil war — all involved the Hokkaido port city of Hakodate. Situated at the southern point of the Oshima Peninsula, at the beginning of the 19th Century, it was little more than a sleepy seaport, but by the end of the century, Hakodate was one of the most cosmopolitan cities in Asia. Such a dramatic transformation was only possible with the opening of Japan.

On July 14, 1853 Commodore Matthew Calbraith Perry (1794-1858) of the United States Navy arrived off the coast of Uraga in Edo Bay on a mission to end the Shogunate's isolation policy once and for all. The Shogunate had set up the Uraga Magistrate precisely to monitor these foreign ships on the doorstep of Edo. Under the orders of President Millard Fillmore (1800-1874), Perry had been instructed to open up Japan by brute force if necessary and this was precisely what he did. From his flagship, the USS *Mississippi*, Perry ordered the ships' cannons to fire blank shots at Uraga. With the might of the Americans firmly established,

Perry warned the Uraga Magistrate that they had until March of next year to prepare for talks. After only nine days off the coast of Uraga, the four ships: *Mississippi*, *Plymouth*, *Saratoga* and *Susquehanna*, set sail for Hong Kong leaving a shocked Shogunate in their wake. On January 12, Shogun Tokugawa Ieyoshi (1793-1853) died suddenly of heart failure at the age of 60, prompting Perry to return sooner than he had threatened. Upon his return, Perry demanded that five Japanese ports be opened to the Americans, including Matsumae in Hokkaido. Under the 30-year-old son of Ieyoshi, the Shogunate agreed to negotiate and in March of 1854, 500 American sailors landed in the tiny fishing village of Yokohama, just south of Edo. Within five days, the Convention of Kanagawa was concluded between the United States and Japan. Among its 12 clauses was a provision for the opening of not Matsumae, but Hakodate to American ships.

Perry's opening of Japan and his acquisition of U.S. access to Hokkaido was keenly watched by the Russians. Despite resistance from the Shogunate, Admiral Yevfimiy Putyatin (1803-1883) eventually succeeded in negotiating the Treaty of Shimoda on February 17, 1855.[29] Like the Convention of Kanagawa, the Treaty of Shimoda guaranteed the Russians the right to trade and included a clause that agreed to set the Russian-Japanese border at the Kuril Islands of Kunashir and Iturup. Under the treaty, the northern Kuril Islands became Russian territories while the southern Kuril Islands became Japanese; the status of Sakhalin was left open, allowing both countries to operate on the island for the time being.

With these two treaties, the port of Hakodate had been opened for both the Americans and Russians. Perry was first to make use of the new American privileges, and after concluding the Convention of Kanagawa in Yokohama, he set sail to survey the soon-to-be-open port of Hakodate.

But before Perry could get to Hakodate, a flustered Shogunate ordered the Matsumae to maintain order and the Matsumae elder, Kageyu, sent 47 retainers to oversee Hakodate. The Matsumae samurai had no idea what to expect from the American barbarians and, fearing the worst, began stripping the temples and shrines of precious objects they believed were liable to theft. With little real understanding of who the Americans were, the samurai wrote a proclamation on April 5 which reflected their anxiety. In it, the samurai concluded that since the Americans were likely to be ravenous and short-tempered, women and children should take refuge in the hills of Hakodate before their arrival. Furthermore, during the Americans visit, small boats were prohibited from entering the harbor and all houses facing the ocean were to have their *Shōji* paper doors boarded up to prevent curious residents looking out. Pilgrimages to the sacred Mt. Hakodate were prohibited and if funerals were necessary, they were to be carried out quietly in the dead of night. Ten days later, the *Macedonian*, *Susquehanna* and the *Bandolier* arrived in Hakodate harbor. Six days after, on April 21, Perry himself arrived aboard the *Powhatan*, accompanied by the *Mississippi* frigate.

Upon Perry's arrival, Hakodate was little more than a cluster of buildings confined to the base of the mountain, protected from southern winds by this natural barrier. After Hakodate opened to foreign trade, the few buildings on the island gradually expanded along the tombolo onto the mainland, creating a city. One of Perry's first actions was to climb Mt. Hakodate, and as he ascended the 334-meter mountain, members of his crew collected botanical samples along the way. Looking down, he could see the wooden frames of Japanese houses, the sands of the tombolo and the unending green forests stretching over the horizon. In his account of his expedition to Japan (*Narrative of the expedition of an American Squadron to the China Seas and Japan; with Francis*

L *Hawks; 1856*), members of Perry's crew remarked how the geography of Hakodate bore a striking resemblance to Gibraltar, another tide island dominated by a mountain. Perry was first to make this observation and the first of many Westerners to mispronounce Hakodate as 'Hakodadi'.

The topography of Hakodate is recorded in the narrative thus:

"The appearance of the place on entering the harbor is striking and picturesque. The town stretches for the space of three miles along the base of a lofty promontory, divided into three principal peaks, which reach a height of from six hundred to a thousand feet. Their lofty summits are bare, often covered with snow; their upper slopes are but scantily clothed with underwood and some scattered pines, while below, where the mountains begin to rise from the level land, there is a rich profusion of verdant growth, with groves of wide-spreading cypresses, tall forest maples, and fruit-bearing trees, the plum and peach. This abundant vegetation presents a pleasing contrast to the bolder and more barren aspect of the higher acclivities and summits of the surrounding hills. The town thus appears to be nestling in repose under the cover of the shade of the trees in the midst of a scene of rural beauty, while all around in the distance is the wild, bleak massiveness of nature."[30]

As the vast nature of Hokkaido was noted, so too was the constant battle with the cold:

"The poorer classes kept much within doors huddled around their meagre fires in their hovels, which, without chimneys, and with a scant light from the paper windows, were exceedingly cold, gloomy and comfortless. The richer people strove to make themselves more comfortable by enveloping their bodies in a succession of warm robes, but succeeded indifferently, as they were constantly complaining of the severity of the weather."[31]

There are a number of anecdotes about Perry's crew and while many may be tall tales, they expressed the contemporary Japanese mindset towards the Americans as well as the American interest in Japan. The people of Hakodate were anxious about the arrival of the Americans and the Matsumae samurai's proclamation on April 5 only served to heighten anxiety. But the image of the American barbarians that had been fanned by rumors soon evaporated when Perry's crew arrived. In one such anecdote, a sailor finds a discarded bedpan in the sand, thinking it a novel Japanese hat he places it on his head, much to the amusement of the on-looking Japanese. Perry's crew bought large quantities of souvenirs, including paper parasols and tobacco pipes. A painter of the Tsugaru clan records in 'Strange Tales of the Western Ezo' that the Americans bought so many Mokugyo (fish-shaped wooden gongs) that not a single one could be found in all Hakodate.[32] The Americans' interests were not limited to handicrafts and five stone statues of the Bodhisattva Kṣitigarbha (Jizō) were among the items loaded onto the American ships.

The Narrative also offers a description of Hakodate's architecture in the years before it began to rapidly develop:

"The buildings in [Hakodate] are mostly of one story, with attics of varying heights. The upper part occasionally forms a commodious apartment, but it is ordinarily merely a dark cockloft for the storage of goods and lumber, or the lodging of servants. The height of the roofs is seldom more than twenty-five feet from the ground. They slope down from the top, projecting with their eaves beyond the wall, are supported by joints and tie-beams, and are mostly covered with small wooden shingles of about the size of the hand. These shingles are fastened by means of pegs made of bamboo, or kept in their places by long slips of board, which have large rows of cobble stones put upon them to prevent their removal. The stones are, however, said to have the additional advantage of hastening the melting of the snow […] the gable ends, as in Dutch houses, face towards the street […] A few of the better houses and temples are neatly roofed with brown earthen tiles […] The poorer people are forced to content themselves with mere thatched hovels, the thatch of which is often overgrown with a fertile crop of vegetables and grass, the seeds of which have been deposited by vagrant crows […] the Japanese woodwork is never painted […] the buildings consequently have a mean and thriftless look. In the wintry, moist climate of [Hakodate], the effect of weather upon the unpainted pine boards was strikingly apparent, causing them to contract, mould and rot, so that the whole town had a more rusty, ruined appearance than its age should indicate."[33]

Despite Perry's historic arrival in Hakodate, his crew could not escape the harsh realities of contemporary naval travel. During their time in Hakodate, two of Perry's crew: the 52-year-old James G. Wolf and 29-year-old G.W. Remick passed away from scurvy. The denizens of Hakodate who were once so fearful of the Americans, treated the fallen with dignity and buried them in what is today the foreign cemetery of Hakodate, overlooking the ocean. After spending just over two weeks in Hakodate, Perry and his crew set sail for Shimoda on May 8. Commodore Perry never returned to Hakodate, but he went down in history as the man who forced the Shogunate to open Japan to the wider world, and commemorative monuments to him can be found as far south as Okinawa (Naha), on Honshu (Shimoda, Miura, and Yokohama) and of course in Hokkaido (Hakodate). By opening Japan, Commodore Perry became one of the most influential figures in Japanese history.

While the Shogunate had been forced to open Hakodate, it attempted damage control measures to limit the influence of the Americans as much as possible. The first approach was to seek to keep the Americans separate from the people of Hakodate by replicating the Dutch settlement on Dejima in Nagasaki.

1891 depiction of Hakodate, Mt. Hakodate can be seen in the background with the settlement spread out along the tombolo

An 1858 map shows plans for the creation of Tsukijima; made from digging canals to create an artificial island in the waters just off Hakodate. Tsukijma was to have a 300-meter wharf and three hectares set aside for living quarters and was intended to serve as a point of commerce and taxation for the Americans in Hakodate. The Shogunate was forced to cancel these plans on February 24, when the Diplomat Townsend Harris (1804-1878), who was negotiating The Treaty of Amity and Commerce (July 1858), balked at the idea of a segregated settlement. The Shogunate was forced to concede. The Americans made use of Hakodate proper.

The presence of foreigners led to changes in the political control of Hokkaido. As early as the 18th Century, the Russian presence throughout the Kuril Islands and Sakhalin had created an anxiety within the Shogunate about territorial claims over Hokkaido. The Shogunate's response was to take direct control of Hokkaido from 1802 to 1821. Once anxiety about the Russians died down, the Shogunate once again allowed the Matsumae clan free reign over the island. Following the Convention of Kanagawa, the Shogunate's claim over Hokkaido again appeared to be in jeopardy and the Shogunate took direct control of the island once more in 1854, declaring that southern Sakhalin, the Southern Kuril Islands and all of Hokkaido, with the exception of Matsumae, were the Shogun's lands. Regardless of which countries claimed sovereignty, the majority of the inhabitants of these lands were the Ainu.

Under both periods of Shogunate rule, Hokkaido's center of government was the Hakodate Magistrate, serving a similar role to the Uraga Magistrate during the period 1802 to 1821. The Hakodate Magistrate was built on the hills of Motomachi, in what is now Motomachi Park. High upon the hills the Magistrate could spy ships far out on the open sea. The Magistrate was built in the *Shointsukuri* architectural style, typical to samurai houses beginning in the Muromachi Period (late 15th Century). Prominent features of this style are gabled roofs, *tatami* mats and rooms separated by *fusuma* sliding doors. Some other famous examples of this architectural style are the Nishihongan-Ji temple and the Temple of the Silver Pavilion in Kyoto. The defining features of the Hakodate Magistrate were the red tile roof and drum tower rising from its center. From this tower, a drummer used a *Taiko* drum to announce the time. The tower stood five stories tall, making it the tallest building in Hakodate at the time and visible with the naked eye from almost anywhere in the city. In addition to the Magistrate's imposing height, the complex was also 3,000 square meters in area and divided into an officer's quarters occupying the front of the building and family quarters for the magistrate's family at the rear. Like numerous buildings from the Edo Period, the Magistrate was built from cypress, cedar, pine and zelkova wood and was furnished with the hollyhock black and gold crests of the Tokugawa Shogunate. To greet both Japanese officials and foreign dignitaries the entrance of the Magistrate was constructed to give the impression of entering a temple.[34]

With the arrival of the Americans and the commencement of the Magistrate's second term, two officials were assigned to the role and this was eventually increased to a three-man system. Though based in Hakodate, the Magistrate sought to govern, albeit loosely, the entirety of Hokkaido, an island of over 70,000 square kilometers. Under this system, one magistrate was to deal with affairs in Hakodate, mainly concerning foreigners, the second magistrate was to tour the entirety of Hokkaido, which served the purpose of emphasizing the Shogunate's claim on the territory, and the third magistrate was stationed in Edo. After the opening of Hakodate to foreign trade, the Magistrate became the point of contact between the consulates of various nations and the Shogunate. The Magistrate was also at the center from which policy towards the Ainu and Japanese was enacted in Hokkaido. The final magistrate, Sugiura Makoto (1826-1900), kept a detailed journal about his life during his two-year term and the writings he has left behind offer a glimpse into the daily activities of the Hakodate magistrate. In an entry written in August 1866, Sugiura recalled, "I was invited to attend a celebration for the King of Portugal's birthday by the Portuguese consular. Around twelve o'clock I arrived after a banquet, we took a commemorative photograph. At four o' clock I left and went to inspect some merchants before returning in the evening."[35] The exchange of knowledge between the Magistrate and Western nations changed the everyday lives of the people of Hakodate, bringing them new technology such as canning, stoves and streetlights. The Magistrate thus proved to be a melting pot of Westernization and modernization, which made the citizens of Hakodate some of the most cosmopolitan in Japan.

The Hakodate Magistrate was not an entirely new form of governance and was modeled on the Nagasaki Magistrate, constructed in the 18th Century to oversee Dutch and Chinese traders in Nagasaki. In Hakodate and Kanagawa, two new magistrates were erected due to the international treaties forced on the Shogunate. What made the Hakodate Magistrate unique was the sheer size of land under its jurisdiction. The Nagasaki Magistrate and Kanagawa Magistrate oversaw the control of port cities, the Hakodate Magistrate's jurisdiction extended over the world's 21st largest island as well as parts of southern Sakhalin and the Kuril Islands.

Due to this vast amount of territory, in 1860 the Magistrate ordered the six samurai clans of the Tohoku region to guard against any invasions in the northern territories.[36] The Matsumae

The Reconstructed Hakodate Magistrate (photograph by Eri Yasuda)

clan, who previously had supervised these areas up to this period, were permitted to maintain their control of the southern part of the Oshima Peninsula. The Magistrate also ordered the Aizu, Sendai, Akita and Shōnai clan to supervise the southern half of Sakhalin across the Sōya Strait from Hokkaido. Due to the expenses it took each clan to station samurai far away, each took turns stationing samurai in Sakhalin. In 1861 the responsibility was on the Sendai clan, in 1862 the Aizu clan, in 1863 the Shōnai clan and 1864 the Akita clan. The Shimoda treaty had left the status of Sakhalin vague, allowing both Russians and Japanese to inhabit the island during this period, with the Russians in the north and the Japanese in the south. The stationing of all clans in the northern territories was to emphasize that this land belonged to the Shogunate and was part of Japan.

While the Magistrate on the hills of Motomachi could oversee foreign ships coming into Hakodate; this gave the Magistrate the advantage of spying ships long before they could dock, this also had its drawbacks since it provided an opportunity to attack an exposed target on the hills for any hostile forces. While America and Russia had signed treaties with the Shogunate, these were at the threat of superior military power. It was still possible that Japan could come under attack, and the Shogunate decided that some form of defense was necessary for Hakodate should these new relationships deteriorate. The Magistrate turned to the Dutch studies scholar Takeda Ayasaburō (1827-1880) to construct such a defense. Takeda came from a century-old tradition of Dutch Studies (*Rangaku*), as until the Convention of Kanagawa the only Europeans prohibited to trade with the Japanese were the Dutch in Nagasaki. Through *Rangaku*, Japanese could study the sciences and arts from western countries through the Dutch on Dejima Island. With the Convention of Kanagawa, Rangaku scholars were in a particularly valuable position as foreign experts. Takeda's inspiration for the city's defenses came after an invitation to board the 30-gun French frigate *Constantine* in Hakodate harbor, where he was permitted to peruse documents. For Hakodate, Takeda choose not the multilayered wooden castles of Japan but opted instead for the Bastion style fort of early modern Europe. Construction on the fort began on June 14, 1857 and after eight years construction was completed in May 1865. The fort was named the Goryōkaku, the 'five-sided fort' due to its shape. Goryōkaku is a formidable fortress surrounded by a moat 30 meters wide and six deep and thick impregnable walls. While the architectural design of Goryōkaku is European in origin, it is not without Japanese elements, such as the construction of the walls built in the *Kirikomi-Hagi* style of Edo Period castles. This form of stone masonry involves shaping large rocks into squares before stacking them to leave no gaps creating a vertical wall in the process. Compared to the exposed hills of Motomachi, the Goryōkaku proved to be a much more fortified position and as such, the Magistrate was reassembled inside the Goryōkaku in July 1864, just before the completion of the fort in the following year. Despite building the Goryōkaku for a potential war with foreigners, the only time the fort's military capabilities were put to the test was in a civil war.[37]

While the Magistrate was preparing the defenses of Hakodate, western countries began to establish their position in the up-and-coming port city. By the late 19th Century America, Russia, Britain, France, Holland, Portugal, Switzerland, Germany, Denmark, Austria, Italy, The United Kingdoms of Sweden and Norway (Sweden and Norway formed a single Kingdom during this period) and China had all established consuls in Hakodate. In the year 1859 (only one year after signing of The Treaty of Amity and Commerce), there were 66 merchant ships from the United States and the United Kingdom, six from Russia, five from Holland and one from France docking at Hakodate. Military vessels were also prominent during the same period in which two were from Russia, 13 from the United States and the United Kingdom, one from France and two from Holland. The large number of Russian ships was due to a desire to find a winter port resistant to freezing over and effectively forcing a halt to shipping – this was the same motivation for Russian involvement in the Crimean War (1853-1856).

The influx of foreigners into Hakodate made the denizens of the city some of the most urbane in Japan. Western medicine came to Hakodate and smallpox was eliminated through vaccination programs. Opportunities to speak English, Russian, and Dutch in particular increased, leading to a rise in Japanese interpreters. Western technology such as streetlights made its way to the northern port. One innovation that would change the living conditions of the people of the city, helping them to resist the cold noted by Perry's crew, was the stove, which made the harsh winters of Hokkaido considerably more bearable. The people of Hokkaido have the architect of the Gōryokaku fort, Takeda Ayasaburō, to thank for the first Japanese stove. Takeda first came into contact with a western stove in 1856 when he was invited aboard a British ship. Takeda quickly realized that such a stove would be ideally suited to Hokkaido's environment. After seeking permission from the Hakodate Magistrate, Takeda created a mold and the first Japanese stove was produced shortly thereafter. The Magistrate was so impressed with Takeda's stove that it commissioned blacksmiths to make a further 22. As many of the Western government officials, soldiers, missionaries, doctors and engineers brought their families with them to Hakodate, they founded a foreign settlement in the hills of Motomachi. The same hills in which women and children had taken shelter before the arrival of Perry's fleet of black ships. The opening of Hakodate also brought samurai and merchants from across Japan's domains, seeking to profit from this new trade. The people of Hakodate acclimatized to living in their new, international city.

The first foreign representative to arrive in Hakodate came before such changes could take place, arriving at the dawn of Hakodate's opening not as a career diplomat but as a man of commerce. Three years after Commodore Perry had concluded the Convection of Kanagawa, in the spring of 1857 a 500 ton whaler arrived off the coast of Hakodate. From the open sea, the crew of the whaler could see Mt. Hakodate, which they christened 'Telegraph Hill' after the very same Telegraph Hill they saw leaving San Francisco to transverse the Pacific. On board the whaler stood a bearded man six feet tall. With one hand he grasped a map labelled 'Hakodai' from Perry's survey. His other hand was in his pocket as he confirmed the safety of a letter from President Franklin Pierce (1804-1869). This man was Elisha E. Rice and he had come to Hakodate to carry out clause 11 of the Convention of Kanagawa: "There shall be appointed by the government of the United States consuls or agents."

Rice came to Hakodate as a commercial agent to oversee the commercial and diplomatic affairs between America and Japan. As the whaler entered the harbor, the crew noticed the outline of a figure watching them from the Magistrate. The Magistrate had prepared sweets, alcohol, and tobacco as the officials anxiously awaited the arrival of the Americans. At the Magistrate, Rice handed over President Pierce's letter and was informed that the American's annex of Jogen-Ji temple, a short stroll from the Magistrate would become the American commercial office.[38] After the Americans settled into the temple, the captain of the whaler sent a wooden staff as a gift to the Magistrate to thank them for their hospitality. The Magistrate, in turn, sent a box of pears to Jōgen-Ji temple. This was the beginning of the exchange of gifts and customs between Rice and the Magistrate. On one occasion, Rice gave a can of sardines to the Magistrate; the new technology of canning having been discovered in Europe at the beginning of the 19th Century. This was the first time the officials at the Magistrate had seen canned food. Canning allowed food to be stored for long periods and the heat used to seal the containers ensured that bacteria were eliminated. When the can was opened one official turned to Rice and asked, "so is this the flavor of your country?"[39] Another contribution by Rice was milk, with Rice undertaking the first milking of a cow in Hokkaido. The dairy industry became part of Hokkaido's economic backbone with the establishment of the Development Commission in 1869 under the new Meiji government.

From an annex in Jōgen-Ji temple, Rice proudly hung the star-spangled banner and on May 1, sent a letter to the department of state; "I opened my office as a commercial agent that I have been well received all facilities granted that I could ask."[40] Although Rice arrived as a commercial agent, he became the American consular in Hakodate nine years after his arrival.

Rice's experience and knowledge led to his reappointment under presidents Buchanan (president from 1857-1861), Lincoln (1861-1865), Johnson (1865-1869) and Grant (1869-1877), since each new president was free to choose a new consular Rice's long-term as commercial agent and consular was a sign of their confidence in him. When Rice arrived in Hakodate, the city was roughly two kilometers in length. Communication was no easy task, upon his arrival Rice was forced to use an outdated Dutch and English dictionary to communicate with the Magistrate, and the officials in the Magistrate had a hard time attempting to decode the presidential letter.

Despite the small size of Hakodate and some communication difficulties, Rice was fond of the city, remarking that the port reminded him of Nantucket in his native New England. Rice's contemporary, the novelist Herman Melville (1819-1891), described Nantucket in the Great American Novel *Moby Dick* (1851) as; "two-thirds of this terraqueous globe are Nantucketer's. For the sea is his; he owns it, as Emperors own empires", and many Nantucket whalers made their way to Hakodate after the opening of the port. Over Rice's long career, Hakodate rapidly expanded as foreign dignitaries and merchants poured into the city. English became the lingua Franca replacing Dutch as the language of commerce and science. In a letter to the Secretary of State, Rice extolled Hakodate for its safety remarking that there were no cases of murder in Hakodate and that unlike Yokohama and Nagasaki it was not necessary for foreigners to carry pistols since the people of Hakodate were interested in commerce above all else. Furthermore, it was unnecessary to have personal bodyguards and even after the British consul arrived, Rice expected the pace of life to continue. Rice noted:

"[the British consul] appeared to be a quiet man and

judging by his looks, is more fond of beer and pleasure than business or fighting, and on the whole I am of the opinion that everything will go on as quietly here as it has for the last two years or more."[41]

Rice arrived in Hakodate as a commercial agent but played the role of a diplomat from the beginning. While the citizens of Hakodate might have been cordial, Rice found that the American sailors were quite the contrary. When whalers came ashore, rowdy sailors often stole alcohol, in one case when a merchant asked to be paid his rightful due, he was met with a knuckle to the face. Rice scolded the sailors, asking them to control themselves during their stay in Hakodate, was this how America wanted to present itself to the world? The sailors were not interested in international diplomacy and the rowdy behavior continued. To resolve the pandemonium, Rice consulted the Magistrate about the possibility of banning the sale of alcohol to foreigners. The ban ruined the revel of many a sailor, and the Magistrate was quick to agree and the selling of alcohol to foreigners was prohibited.

There was also the problem of ships running aground on reefs in the natural harbor. As Rice had done, ships coming into Hakodate made use of Perry's 'Harbor of Hakodadi' chart. This was an imperfect record as Perry's survey had lasted only five days, leaving many blind spots where ships could run aground on reefs. In the winter of 1857, the *Covington*, a whaling barque ran aground becoming the first of many that became stranded. To address the problem, Rice commissioned a lighthouse and donated it to the Magistrate, who installed it on a ship stationed in the harbor. Rice was the first foreign representative to arrive in Hakodate and his behavior and actions set a precedent for other nations seeking to establish a consular in Hakodate. Rice was also in a unique position to witness Hakodate transform from a small mainly Japanese settlement into an international port.

America may have been first to establish trading relations in Hakodate, but it was Russia which established the first foreign consulate, as agreed during the Treaty of Shimoda. With this, on January 6, 1858 the Russian diplomat Isoif Antonovich Goshkevich (1814-1875) arrived in Hakodate. As a missionary Goshkevich had spent ten years in China during which he encountered Vasily Golovnin's (1776-1831) autobiographical book, *Captivity in Japan During the Years 1811, 1812, 1813*. This book had become a sensation in Russia and inspired Goshkevich to seek a position further east. Like Rice, Goshkevich took temporary residence in a temple, Jitsugyō-Ji temple in Mōtomachi, until the Russian consulate had been constructed.

The Magistrate had particular motivation for assigning temples as residences for foreign dignitaries. Practically, the large size of temples made them suitable for housing the large staff of the delegate and the steep temples roofs that rose above the town below allowed the Magistrate to identify the location of foreigners with ease as well as to keep them isolated from the general populace.

While Rice had struggled to communicate upon his arrival, he generally had a cordial relationship with the Magistrate. Goshkevich however, soon came into conflict with the Magistrate over the location of the nascent Russian consulate. While the building of a consulate in Hakodate had been agreed in the Treaty of Shimoda, its location within Hakodate had not. Much to Goshkevich's displeasure, the Magistrate had chosen land three kilometers outside of the city. As Rice's commercial office was in the center of Hakodate, it is likely that the Magistrate was wary of Goshkevich, arriving as a Russian diplomat, Rice had come as only a commercial representative. An angry Goshkevich argued that such tactics might have worked with the Dutch in Nagasaki, the same was not true for the Russians here in Hakodate. The Magistrate eventually gave in to Goshkevich, and after residing in Jitsugyō-Ji temple for two years, the construction of the Russian consulate was finished in 1860. The Russian consulate was the first Western building in Hakodate and immediately became a local landmark. Although the Russian consulate had a European façade, the Japanese laymen had no experience with the interior of Russian buildings and the inside was built in line with a traditional Japanese style. Unfortunately, the Old Russian Consulate was lost to The Great Fire of Hakodate in 1907, and the consulate in Hakodate today was constructed in 1908.

Unprepared for the opening of Japan, the majority of foreign diplomats in Hakodate were only equipped with European languages. Goshkevich stood out from his contemporaries with his proficient Japanese. Goshkevich had a unique opportunity that allowed him to achieve proficiency in Japanese long before his contemporaries thanks to a runaway samurai by the name of Masuda Kōsai (1820-1885). Masuda was a samurai of the Kakegawa clan (Shizuoka Prefecture), who was jailed for his role as the kingpin of a gambling syndicate. During his time in prison, Masuda vowed to change his ways and began following Buddhism. Upon his release, Masuda found work as the secretary of the Ikegamihonmon-Ji temple in Edo before leaving his post to take up the life as a wandering monk. While Masuda was sojourning in the Izu Peninsula's coastal town of Heda (present-day Numazu city), he happened to see a Russian ship in the harbor. Masuda's curiosity got the better of him and before long he was talking with the ship's interpreter, none other than Goshkevich. Masuda was convinced to leave with Goshkevich to Russia. During his 18 years in Russia, Masuda worked as an interpreter, compiling a Japanese-Russian dictionary in the process. Thanks to Masuda, Goshkevich was able to gain a firm command of Japanese long before he arrived in Hakodate. As for Masuda, he eventually returned to Japan in 1873 after a diplomat of the new Meiji government, Tomomi Iwakura (1825-1883) informed him that the new administration did not intend to persecute him for the *Sakoku* policy of the former Shogunate. Masuda returned to Japan, with the Russian government providing him a pension and travelling expenses in recompense for almost two decades of service.[42]

Due to Masuda's language instruction, Goshkevich was able to establish a rapport with the officials of the Magistrate and many came to the Russian consulate to discuss matters with Goshkevich, even issues that did not concern Russia. The Russian consul was not just popular with the Magistrate, the local people of Hakodate also saw value in Goshkevich. Under his supervision, the consulate's doctor Mikhail P. Albrecht established a free clinic open to the public in the Motomachi district. Albrecht also inspected the living conditions of Hakodate's residents, concluding that while the houses were clean, the streets were certainly not, as Hakodate suffered a pervasive foul stench emitting from open drains. When Goshkevich brought Albrecht's concerns to the Magistrate, there was little understanding of the science behind hygiene and the officials ignored his advice.

The Russian consulate's most significant architectural legacy was the Hakodate Orthodox Church. The Orthodox Church that can be seen in Hakodate today has its origins in a church established within the Russian consular in 1859. By 1861 a separate church had been erected, although this was lost to the Great Fire in 1907. The church that can be seen today was built in 1916. Alongside Mt. Hakodate, the Orthodox Church has become a quintessential symbol of the city.[43] But what is more fascinating than the building itself is the story of the man behind Hakodate's most iconic building.

Since 1612, the practice of Christianity was forbidden in Japan, but after Perry, Japan was open to other, technologically advanced, European nations, and as was to be expected, much of the Western laity in Hakodate almost instantaneously began covert missions despite stipulations against this. On October 19, 1856 Russia agreed for orthodox priests coming to the embassy with the Shogunate, paving the way for the introduction of Orthodox Christianity in Japan. Goshkevich was quick to make use of this new religious freedom and arranged for a priest to be dispatched from Russia. On November 5, Vasily Makov arrived in Hakodate. The elderly Makov, who was 60 at the time of his arrival, promptly began supervision over the construction of a small church attached to the Russian consulate in addition to a Russian language school for the people of Hakodate in the consular's garden. Makov spent only four years in Hakodate before returning to Russia.

His successor came to be known as Saint Nikolai of Japan (1836-1912) and was the only figure in the Orthodox Church in the 20th Century to earn the title 'Equal-to-the-Apostles'. Before he was a Saint, or even adopted the name Nikolai, he was simply known as Ivan Kasatkin and was known as such until he graduated from the Petersburg Theological Academy in 1860.

Like Goshkevich, Nikolai came across the writings of Golovnin's confinement, which piqued his interest in the islands bordering Russia's far eastern frontier. Nikolai was fortunate also, as during this very same time the Russian consular in Hakodate was searching for a new priest. The Petersburg Theological Academy put four of its best students forward of whom Nikolai was selected. On June 22, 1860 Nikolai graduated from the Academy, formally changing his name from Ivan to Nikolai. Ready to begin his life for the Orthodox faith on foreign shores he bid farewell to his family in August the same year.[44] Like those before him, Nikolai traveled by horse-drawn sleigh across the Siberian tundra, arriving at Irkutsk in late August. Having arrived in the Asian part of Russia, Nikolai crossed the Amur River. During this passage harsh winds rocked the small boat, with Nikolai praying to God to make it to Hakodate safely on his trans-Siberian journey. Such a journey had proved fatal to many before him. As the Siberian winter grew increasingly intense, Nikolai arrived at the town of Nikolayevsk-on-Amur, opposite the northern tip of Sakhalin. If he could take a boat south, he could arrive in Hokkaido before New Year. However, in the dead of winter, ships were not able to navigate the frozen ocean of Okhotsk and Nikolai spent the season in Nikolayevsk-on-Amur.

Nikolai's wait was not in vain as he was fortunate enough to meet the veteran missionary Innocent of Alaska (1797-1879) who had spent years amid the Aleutian Islanders and had even translated parts of the Bible into the Aleutian language. Through this chance encounter, Nikolai learned how to preach Christianity to peoples such as the Aleutians and Japanese, as well as the necessity of proficiency in the native language. Taking Innocent of Alaska's advice to heart, Nikolai began studying Japanese and Chinese while he waited for the ice to thaw. The young Nikolai, having still not set foot in Japan, was confident that his missionary zeal combined with his study of Japanese would be enough to convert the masses of Japan.

Spring began and he was at last able to leave for Hakodate aboard the Russian battleship the *Amur* in April 1861, arriving in Hakodate on July 2. Having set foot on Japanese soil, an idealistic Nikolai found that the confidence he had before his arrival was shaken.

He recorded in his journal that when he arrived:

"I was young and overflowing with creative energy and I imagined that the word of God would ring out through Japan as the masses took up the faith. After I arrived, I was confronted with a reality that was nothing like what I had expected [...] The Japanese of the time looked on foreigners with a great deal of suspicion as if they were a kind of beast and the teachings of Christ were viewed as if they were some black magic."[45]

Nikolai happened to arrive in Japan during the period when the samurai were debating the competency of the Shogunate for allowing foreign powers to impose unequal treaties on Japan and her seaports. In a time where the Qing dynasty in China was being subjugated in the Opium Wars (the first between 1839 and 1842, and a second between 1856 and 1860) this fear was not in itself unfounded. However, as the Qing dynasty's resistance had shown, fighting with the foreigners could only result in harsher treaties. One image that captures the *Sonnō Jōi* spirit of the age is that of a sumo wrestler (*rikishi*) throwing a Westerner to the ground with the on-looking foreigners throwing their arms up in awe of his might. This *Sonnō Jōi* sentiment prompted defiant samurai to attack Westerners and officials of the Shogunate. Despite this, *Sonnō Jōi* played little role in the new Meiji government, it was a catalyst for challenging the authority of the Shogunate.

Nikolia's first Japanese convert was considerably different from the open-minded Japanese willing to embrace Christ that he had envisioned. Sawabe Takuma (1834-1913) was one of many samurai caught up in the fever of *Sonō Jōi*. Born on the island of Shikoku under the Tosa clan, Takuma had married the daughter of a Shinto priest in Hakodate, and after her father's death moved to take up the position as head priest of the Yama-no-Ue shrine in Motomachi. Takuma read numerous works of the time on the importance of expelling the barbarians and like many others, carried a fundamentalist rage, convinced that the only way to save Japan was to purge the foreigners by any means. For Takuma, nothing was more immoral than the preaching of the Christian missionaries and he began plotting to assassinate Nikolai. On numerous occasions, Takuma visited the Russian consulate, yet on every occasion he failed to find Nikolai. When Takuma did manage to track him down he confronted Nikolai asking why he was spreading this Christian heresy in Japan, but a collected Nikolai managed to calm Takuma down. A hesitant Takuma, surprised by Nikolai's resolve, listened to him talk about original sin, the Trinity and the undying soul, causing Takuma to question his role as a Shinto priest and the logic of *Sonō Jōi*. While the seeds of doubt were sown in Takuma's beliefs, he was not yet convinced of Nikolai's teachings and on numerous occasions returned with a barrage of questions hoping to find the flaws in Nikolai's arguments. At first, these questions were critical, as time passed they gradually transformed into questions of genuine curiosity. In April 1868, Takuma was secretly baptized with two other converts in Nikolai's house and Takuma took up the name Paul. For a brief spell, Takuma continued his role at Yama-no-ue shrine, replacing part of the Shinto chants with quotes from the Bible until he eventually retired from the position altogether. While it may have been legal for foreigners to practice Christianity in Japan, the Shogunate still prohibited the conversion of Japanese and when rumors begin to circulate that Takuma had converted, he was eventually seized and imprisoned. This failed to break Takuma's resolve and during his imprisonment, he converted many inmates. Upon his release, he became the first Japanese priest of the Orthodox Church. By 1872, 50 Japanese had converted to the Orthodox faith, and in the same year the Hakodate Orthodox Church was constructed in the Byzantine architectural style, once again the consular employed Japanese craftsmen to raise the building. The locals of Hakodate had never seen such a 'temple' and soon gave it the nickname of 'clanging temple' after the bells that rang out from Motomachi during church services.

Nikolai continued to work for the cause of Orthodox Christianity in Japan and in 1872, he and Takuma left Hakodate for Tokyo, bringing an end to Nikolai's life in Hokkaido, which had been the first point in a lifelong mission to Japan. By 1891, under Nikolai's supervision, the Holy Resurrection Cathedral was constructed near today's Ocha-no-Mizu station in Tokyo. Today the cathedral is open to the public, and its green domes and ringing bell tower make it distinct amongst the high-rise buildings of Tokyo's Bunkyō ward. In 1905, when war broke out between Russia and Japan, Nikolai refused to return, stating: "I cannot leave Japan, I cannot turn my back on the believers of the faith in this country."[46]

Nikolai continued his work for the Orthodox faith until his death in 1912 and was buried in the Yanaka cemetery in Tokyo. In 1923, the Great Kanto Earthquake shook the metropolises of Tokyo, Kawasaki and Yokohama killing over 100,000 people, destroying much of the cities and leaving around two million people homeless. Amongst this calamity, the bells of the Hakodate Orthodox Church were transported to the orthodox cathedral so that those of the orthodox faith could find comfort during trying times. Thus, for 45 years the 'clanging temple' of Hakodate was silenced. In 1968, a Greek ship-owner was working in Hakodate's shipyard when he was moved by the silence of his faith's church. To resurrect the 'clanging temple,' he donated two 575-kilogram bells to the church which continue to be rung to this day.

Like Russia and the United States, the British also established a consulate in Hakodate. But it was these first two nations that had the biggest impact being the first to arrive. The British consul was engulfed in controversy in 1865 when the constable and jailer assigned to the consulate, Henry Trone and George Kernish, alongside the British naturalist Henry Whitely, robbed an Ainu grave in Mori, north of Hakodate, and sent the artefacts found inside to Britain. In Europe, there was much curiosity regarding the origins of the Ainu, with many falsely believing they were from a lost Caucasian race. When the crime reached the ears of Koide Hozumi (1834-1869) at the Magistrate, he challenged the British consular Francis Howard Vyse about the whereabouts of the Ainu remains. Vyse at first claimed that Koide was mistaken, but after mounting pressure tried to give back different remains, failing to deceive anyone involved. It transpired that the bones had been sent to Vyse's brother, making the consul an accomplice in the crime, and he was subsequently forced to resign. Any good brought to Hakodate by the British then was not from the consular, but from the missionaries who attempted to lift the Ainu out of poverty, something which will be explored in later chapters.

6

THE BATTLE OF HAKODATE

THE INCREASE OF foreigners who had forced open Japan led
to resentment amongst some samurai, who took it upon
themselves to assassinate officials of the Shogunate and any
foreigner who dared set foot in the treaty ports. But terrorism
in itself could not shake the hegemony of the Shogunate.[47]
The pivotal man who united two of the Tozama, the Daimyō
who had been deemed to be less loyal to the Shogunate, and
challenged the Shogunate was Sakamoto Ryōma (1836-1867) of
Tosa domain (present-day Kochi Prefecture). Much like Takuma,
who had attempted to assassinate Nikolai, this young samurai
in his 20s believed that by targeting officials of the Shogunate,
Sonnō Joi could be realized. Sakamoto sought to assassinate
the high-ranking official, Katsu Kaishū (1823-1899) a believer
in the necessity of modernization. However, Sakamoto did not
succeed; Katsu persuaded Sakamoto that long-term reform was
necessary. Sakamoto left behind the mantra of *Sonnō Jōi* to begin
working as his assistant. As the Shogunate started to crack down
on opposition, Sakamoto fled to Kagoshima in 1864 where he
successfully acted as an intermediary to bring about the alliance
of the Chōshū clan (present-day Yamaguchi Prefecture) and the
Satsuma clan (present-day Kagoshima Prefecture) in 1866. The
Satsuma-Chōshū alliance began a campaign to restore power

to the Emperor and overthrow the Shogunate. It is from this alliance of Tozama clans that organized resistance became a stark challenge to the Shogunate in the form of an imperial alliance. In 1868, this alliance declared a new government under the Emperor and entered battle with the Shogunate at Kyoto in January. By May of 1868, Edo was surrounded. Ironically, the Satsuma clan received weapons from the British and the anti-foreign zeal, which had provided the basis for the restoration, had little role in the new Japan, instead shifting more to the west regarding politics, industry and imperial ambitions.

Although the Shogunate surrendered in June, resistance continued in Edo into July, until the imperial alliance triumphed at the battle of Ueno. However, the leader of the Shogunate's Navy, Enomoto Takeaki (1836-1908) refused to surrender. Though samurai clans as far north as the Matsumae had come to accept the new Meiji government, Enomoto and his troops stayed loyal to the Shogunate. Their allegiance did not waiver and with 2,000 members of the navy, Enomoto fled Shinagawa port with the dream of preserving the Shogunate. In a snowstorm in the early hours of November 12, the Enomoto army arrived at the south of Hokkaido and landed at Washinoki, north of Hakodate. Here they engaged the Matsumae army, which had already pledged its allegiance to the new Meiji government.

After repulsing the Matsumae, they proceeded towards Hakodate and on November 14, the Enomoto army defeated the magistrates' forces at the village of Nanae. The government officials in Hakodate, who had already become loyalists of the new Meiji government, were uncertain of their future in Hokkaido - perhaps this island no longer even formed a part of the Japanese nation-state. Taking action before it was too late, the governor inside the Goryōkaku fled aboard a Prussian steamship to Aomori on the 26, leaving behind supplies of munitions and grain in the Goryōkaku. When the Enomoto army eventually arrived in Hakodate, they were able to walk through the snow directly into Hakodate's great fortress unchallenged. In an outcome unseen by the Magistrate at the time of its creation, the fortress built to protect Hakodate from foreigners fell to Japanese soldiers. With the center of Hokkaido's government captured, Enomoto wrote a letter to the imperial court stating that all that he and his men wished for was to continue the legacy of the Tokugawa Shogunate in Hokkaido, there was no need for prolonged war. However, if the Meiji government did decide to attack, he and his men would retaliate.

Enomoto was serious about building an alternative Japanese state and even began minting currency, although the people of Hakodate called this new currency "desertion money", a sign of the disdain many held for the occupying army. During preparations for war, the foreigners in Hakodate were forced to recognize the Enomoto army as the *de facto* government. Many diplomats in Hakodate were also confused about what was going on and how their business might be affected. To clear confusion, the United States Consul, Elisah E. Rice decided to meet with Enomoto in the Goryōkaku on November 22. Rice was concerned about the safety of American citizens and their property in Hakodate and demanded to know what Enomoto was planning. Enomoto calmly explained that he was committed to upholding the commercial treaties undertaken by the Shogunate, but with a war looming overhead, each nation began to prepare to protect its people and property in spite of this reassurance. Rice found the American government almost flippant about the matter, causing him to write an angry, though reserved, letter to the Secretary of State:

"If only a small war steamer would be spared instead of being constantly stationed in Kobe where all is quiet, come to this port where American interests are in actual need of protection, and remove the obligation we may have to incur on Great Britain and France, who see the necessity of keeping a powerful war vessel here constantly."[48]

After Rice's letter was received, one American warship was eventually released to Hakodate, joining the one Russian, nine British and four French ships already harbored in Hakodate.

Despite Enomoto's success in securing the largest city in Hokkaido, the Matsumae clan in the south remained a thorn in his side. A decision was soon made to purge the Matsumae from Hokkaido. In December, Enomoto sent an army led by Hijikata Toshizō (1835-1869) and Hitomi Katsutarō (1843-1922), to launch an attack on Matsumae castle. Hijikata and Hitomi besieged the castle with cannon fire from their ships and troops from the land. The Matsumae were cornered and the Daimyō, Matsumae Tokuhiro (1844-1869) abandoned the castle. The Matsumae samurai, refusing to let their land fall into the hands of the enemy, resorted to setting the castle alight. By the time the fire faded out, two-thirds of the castle town had been destroyed by the flames. When Hijikata led his troops into what he believed to be the abandoned castle, he found only eight women of the Matsumae family, crying in despair as the Matsumae men had abandoned them. Feeling a pang of empathy, Hijikata opted to let them live and allowed them to board a ship to Hirosaki in Honshu.[49]

While Enomoto had hoped to acquire Hokkaido without any bloodshed, this was not to be. After the defeat of the Matsumae, there was a brief period of tranquility. This was brought to an end with the arrival of the Meiji army who began their march towards Matsumae in April of 1869.

Alongside this, the Meiji army used a fleet consisting of warships such as the *Kasuga* to bombard Katsutaro's armies forcing them to retreat to Hakodate. Shortly after, the Meiji army led by Kuroda Kiyotaka (1840-1900) finally arrived in Hakodate to begin the offensive. The Meiji forces had successfully established their government throughout Japan and were not going to relinquish Hokkaido; this was to be the final battle of the civil war. Sensing a bloody battle both the Japanese citizens of Hakodate and foreigners fled the city. The Japanese left on foot, and the foreign nations retreated to their nation's ships and sailed two miles off the coast of Hakodate on the eve of the battle. As for the Enomoto army, they held a loose grip on Hakodate at best. Katsutaro, knowing the odds were stacked against them, penned a death poem, Hijikata was shot from his horse and killed, a martyr to the cause. A week after Hijikata's death, Enomoto surrendered. Enomoto's dream of a new nation in Hokkaido, a 'Republic of Ezo', had not come to pass, with Enomoto's grip on Hakodate lasting a mere half year. Enomoto and Hitomi likely expected to be executed and named as traitors in the history of the nation, but the times had indeed changed and following a period of imprisonment, both became influential politicians in the new Japan. Hitomi became the governor of Ibaraki Prefecture and Enomoto went on to become the Naval Minister, signing the Treaty of Saint Petersburg in 1875, ceding Japanese claims to the island of Sakhalin in exchange for the Kuril Islands.

With the battle of Hakodate deciding the future of Hokkaido and even Japan, the Meiji government now controlled the area from Kyushu in the south to Hokkaido in the north. The people of Hakodate began to return to their city, only to encounter piles of dead from both the Meiji and Shogunate factions in the streets. Their town reduced to the burnt-out shells of buildings.

THE BATTLE OF HAKODATE

On Hakodate's Ōmori beach the Meiji government carried out a mass funeral for their fallen soldiers, then carved out a mass grave into the hillside of Mount Hakodate. In 1869, a shrine was established on the site which is now the Hakodate Gokoku-Jinja shrine. However, similar respect was not afforded to the rebel army and a resentful Meiji government decided to leave the fallen of the Enomoto army to rot in the streets. Despite the view of the people of Hakodate who wished to bury the dead, rebuild the city and continue their lives, the Meiji government prohibited any funerals for the enemy. The people of Hakodate held hands, gritted their teeth and bore the stench of the rotting corpses.

There was one individual however, who wished to put things right, Yanagawa Kumakichi (1825-1913). Born in Asakusa in Edo, Yanagawa first came to Hakodate in 1856 to run an employment agency, which assisted with the building of the Goryōkaku. Yanagawa was aghast at the orders of the Meiji government, believing that all souls deserved funeral rights. With a conviction that the fallen of the Enomoto army deserved better, Yanagawa began visiting temples throughout Hakodate. However, every time Yanagawa talked to a priest about the possibility of funeral rites they turned him away, saying that although they were sympathetic, they dared not go against the new government - these were unstable times. After hours of walking until his feet were sore, Yanagawa entered Jitsugyō-Ji, the very same temple that Goshkevich had stayed in upon his arrival in Hakodate. Like the priest at prior temples once again Yanagawa tried to convince the priest, Matsuo Nichiryū, about his desire to give funeral rites to the fallen of the Enomoto army. Unlike the other priests, Matsuo listened to Yanagawa sympathizing with his humanism and offering the grounds of the temple. Having found a willing temple, Yanagawa began sneaking out at night carrying the dead one by one to Jitsugyō-Ji Temple. Night after night Yanagawa continued this task until one citizen of Hakodate, moved by Yanagawa's bravery, began to help. Soon others followed until they had cleared the dead from the ruins. Yanagawa understood that he was going against the orders of the Meiji government and was prepared to pay with his life. When eventually Yanagawa was questioned by the authorities he was asked who his associates were - he alone could not have moved over 700 corpses. Yanagawa replied, "I did the job by myself and I have done nothing wrong, I will not grovel before you for my life."[50] With his lips sealed, Yanagawa was sentenced to execution and was imprisoned.

Fortunately, Yanagawa was spared as a naval officer with the new government, Tajima Keizō (1843-1899), who had brought Enomoto in after his surrender intervened. He put forth the case that Yanagawa could not be executed for such chivalrous behavior. Enomoto cried in prison when he heard the news. Thanks to Tajima's generosity, Yanagawa was freed. With this freedom, Yanagawa focused on finishing the job he had started and in 1871 purchased land at the base of Mt. Hakodate to lay the fallen to rest. Gradually the remains were moved from Jitsugyō-Ji temple to the new location and in 1874, the Meiji government allowed religious services to be held for the enemy army. In 1875 with the help of a now pardoned and free Enomoto, Yanagawa built a memorial for the dead called the Hekketsu-Hi. Yanagawa lived to the age of 88, and upon his passing in 1913, the priests of Jitsugyō-Ji temple built a monument dedicated to him alongside the Hekketsu-Hi.[51]

With the burial of the fallen Hakodate at last moved into a new era under the Meiji government and the end of the century saw dramatic changes throughout Hokkaido. A new government agency called the Development Commission oversaw a new wave of colonization for Hokkaido, bringing Wajin in their tens of thousands north. In this new era, Sapporo proved to be a more suitable location than Hakodate for the colonization and development of the island as it was located deeper in the interior of Hokkaido, in contrast to Hakodate at the island's southern edge.[52] The Development Commission also led to changes in Hakodate as well, such as in 1869 when the city's name was changed from 箱館 to 函館 (both read as Hakodate). This cosmetic change caused much confusion with the local people and bureaucrats as they continued to use both versions until the latter eventually became the norm, which it remains to this day. While Hokkaido's capital city was moved to Sapporo, Hakodate continues to hold the legacy of being the first city in Hokkaido open to foreign trade and the site of the final battle of a civil war that decided Japan's future.

HOKKAIDO

PART 2

The Modern Era and the
Meiji Restoration

HOKKAIDO

7

COLONIZATION AND MODERNIZATION

FOLLOWING THE defeat of Enomoto's army at Hakodate, the Meiji government had at last gained complete control over Japan. Seizing the helm of the state, the new government now had to modernize the country to compete with the Western powers rapidly dividing up the globe; great regions of Asia, Africa, and America had already been carved out as colonies. While Japan had developed economically throughout the era of the Tokugawa Shogunate (1603-1868) the country was still at heart a feudal society led by a warrior class of samurai. Like the Ming and Qing dynasties in neighboring China, the Tokugawa Shogunate had attempted to seal their country off from the outside world and its influence. This attempt to prevent association with the outside world had failed.

The Qing dynasty in China was forced to sign unfair treaties with foreign powers and attempts to resist British influence lead to the two Opium Wars. The new Meiji government in Japan took a different approach. The oligarchs of the new government chose to follow a path of industrialization, westernization and modernization eventually culminating in the colonization of overseas territories in Asia and the Pacific.[53] However, such changes demanded a new political and economic system and through a series of reforms throughout the 1870s the foundations of the nation state of Japan were laid. One such monumental reform dates from August 29, 1871 when the Meiji government announced the abolishment of feudal domains and the establishment of prefectures. The following year, the Daimyō throughout Japan were summoned before Emperor Meiji (1852-1912) and informed that all land was to be returned to the state. The Daimyō lost absolute control of land that had been in their families for generations. In return many were given the chance to become governors of the new prefectures and eventually members of the House of Peers following its formation in 1889. The former Daimyō, once the strongest samurai in Japan and descendants of ancestral warriors who had battled to defend and expand their domains, became servants of the government.

In this new era, what was to become of Hokkaido, or Ezo as it was known to contemporaries? Although the Matsumae clan had established a Wajin stronghold in the Oshima Peninsula, Hokkaido was never unified under a single Daimyō, even as late as the final era of the samurai under the Tokugawa Shogunate. It was precisely because of Hokkaido's status as an insecure territory that Russian expansion south proved to be such a point of contention for the Shogunate.

When the Meiji government took direct control over Hokkaido, most of the interior geography of the island was uncharted and the population stood at only 100,000. The Meiji government faced the challenge of cultivating this vast amount of land that had been left largely in a state of nature. Before any development could take place, it was necessary to assert that Hokkaido was an indisputable part of Japanese territory. In July of 1869 an edict announced the government's claim to the island, while simultaneously scolded officials stating that bribery was not to be accepted under the new government; unlike the era of the Shogunate. Maps from the early Meiji era also included the entire Kuril Island chain as part of Hokkaido and on July 17, the Japanese name for the island 'Ezo', was changed to Hokkaido. During the first few decades under the Meiji government, the administration of Hokkaido took many forms before finally settling on the 'Hokkaido Government' in 1886. The former Hokkaido Government Building (the Hokkaido government has since relocated) with its baroque revival architecture, red bricks, and stately garden remains a popular tourist spots in Sapporo today.

The first wave of significant reforms to Hokkaido came in 1869 with the creation of the Development Commission. This arm of the government was charged with the development of the island and of aligning this frontier of the empire to the same economic strength as the mainland. The Development Commission was first established in Tokyo, and was shifted to Hakodate in 1870, before being moved again to Sapporo in 1871, which has remained Hokkaido's political epicenter ever since. The Development Commission was a great plastered white hall, complete with green accents and a large dome from which the *Hinomaru*, the Japanese national flag, or the symbol of the Development Commission, a red star on a blue background could be hoisted for all to see.[54]

During these early years, the majority of Hokkaido's population was concentrated in the south of the island, in the former Matsumae domain and Hakodate. Sapporo was designated the capital city precisely because it was situated in the center of Hokkaido, far from the already developed areas to the south. To construct the new city, the chosen planner Shima Yoshitake (1822-1874), oversaw the development of a river running through the city, a grid-like street plan and separate government and civilian districts. However, Shima was unprepared for the difficulties of building in Hokkaido's long winters and soon ran over budget. This led to his dismissal from the project but Shima's development left a legacy on the city that is still felt today. One example is the north to south man-made Sōsei River, constructed in the 1860s, which joins the Ishikari (Japan's third largest river), and flows through Asahikawa to Sapporo and onto the Sea of Japan.

While Sapporo's urban design had Japanese roots in the ancient gridded cities of Nara and Kyoto, parallels could also be drawn to American cities of the era, and from 1881 the street names in Sapporo were likewise changed to ordinal numbers. Sapporo's planning also allowed for a safer city; from its inception in Shima's plans, Ōdori Street separated the city north to south and acts as a fire breaker. Ōdori Street later became the famous Ōdori Park of Sapporo, today the location of the Sapporo Snow Festival in Winter, Sapporo Beer Festival in Summer and a local produce festival in Autumn. Outside festival time, Ōdori is reminiscent of New York's Central Park: a breathing space in the center of a bustling metropolitan city. Despite Sapporo being the political center of Hokkaido, its isolation meant that it took time to attract colonizers to this remote outpost. It was not until 1922 that Sapporo's population overtook neighboring Otaru and only in 1936 did Sapporo overtake Hakodate to become the biggest city of Hokkaido.

Similar to many aspects of the Meiji era, Sapporo is an amalgamation of Western and Japanese styles. The Sapporo police station, Sapporo Agricultural College (later Hokkaido University) as well the Hōheikan Government Guest House are in distinctly Western architectural styles. The Hōheikan was built as a Western style hotel in 1880 to accommodate a visit from Emperor Meiji the following year. With white clapboards covering the façade and its wide circular porch the Hōheikan captured the modern feeling of the new city. But the building which is most symbolic of the city is the Sapporo Clock Tower, built in 1878 as the drill hall for the Agricultural College in the carpenter gothic style common in America at the time. Covered in wooden clapboards and coated in white paint, this like many other contemporary buildings in Sapporo at the time gave the city a quasi-American atmosphere and with this atmosphere came a feeling of optimism and potential. The Clock Tower continues to have a special place in the hearts of Sapporo's residents. The former mayor of the city, Itagaki Takeshi (1916-1993) described the clock tower thus:

> "The bells ring out as if they are to envelope the town. They are more than a mere signaling of time, they are a sign of the love and warmth to those who live and make their way to Sapporo."[55]

Sapporo Clock Tower – Photography by the author

While Sapporo's most iconic buildings are in frontier and gothic architectural styles, designs were not limited to Western architecture. Sapporo also embraced a more traditional Japanese atmosphere, with the houses and shops in the west and south of the city being characteristic of Meiji Period Japanese buildings being built of wood rather than brick.

Given the sheer size of Hokkaido it is understandable why the choice of a political center away from Hakodate was necessary. Today Hokkaido is Japan's largest administrative region with an area of 83,424 kilometers square. In comparison, the second largest administrative region by area is Iwate Prefecture which has an area of 15,275 kilometers; less than 20% of Hokkaido. Apart from size, Hokkaido is also the only one of Japan's four home islands that is not divided into multiple prefectures (Honshu is divided into 34, Kyushu into seven and Shikoku into three), although there are sub-prefectures within Hokkaido. From a contemporary standpoint, it is therefore easy to think of Hokkaido as having always been a unified entity. As the reforms of the island throughout the Meiji era show, it was quite possible that Hokkaido could have been split up between multiple prefectures, and there were even times when prefectures existed within Hokkaido in the early Meiji era.

With the 1871 establishment of prefectures and the abolition of feudal domains, the Matsumae domain in southern Hokkaido was formed into the short-lived Tate Prefecture. Two months later, it was integrated into Aomori (Hirosaki at the time) prefecture across the Tsugaru Straits in Honshu. There was particular significance in this decision. By joining the former Matsumae domain to Honshu, the Development Commission signaled a new colonial Hokkaido, with the feudal part of Hokkaido belonging to the Matsumae being cast off to Honshu. The difficulties of managing a prefecture straddling the straits led to Aomori (Hirosaki) Prefecture petitioning the Grand Council of the State for the return of Tate Prefecture to Hokkaido. This brought an end to the short-lived prefecture and returned Hokkaido to the state of one political unit. Hokkaido's first significant political entity, the Development Commission, lasted 13 years from 1869 to 1882. Then following criticism over insufficient development of the land, Hokkaido was again divided, this time into three prefectures, which lasted until 1886. The lands that had been the center of Wajin activity in southern Hokkaido were organized into Hakodate Prefecture, the areas surrounding the former Development Commission became Sapporo Prefecture, and the northeast of Hokkaido became Nemuro Prefecture. In 1883 Hokkaido's population was 216,251, of whom 65% lived in Hakodate Prefecture, 28.3% lived in Sapporo Prefecture, and only 6.7% in Nemuro Prefecture. Despite promises, the three-prefecture system failed to provide rapid development. Coupled with an austerity policy and the deflation economics of the Japanese government, the three-prefecture system actually led Hokkaido into a depression; precisely the opposite environment necessary for development and continued colonization. Unification into one administrative unit under the Hokkaido Government occurred in January 1886; and has remained so ever since. The northern frontier did not stop at Hokkaido, however, with the colonization of Karafuto, the Japanese territory below the 50th parallel On the island of Sakhalin, also proceeded apace.

The first colonizers of Hokkaido under the new government were disgraced samurai of Sendai Domain who had fought on the losing side of the civil war. The beginning of the Meiji era was in many ways a reverse of the Tokugawa Shogunate. As previously mentioned, during the Warring States Period (1467-1600) the Daimyō of Japan had vied with each other for power and territory. This period of warring states culminated with the Battle of Sekigahara after which the newly established Tokugawa Shogunate divided the Daimyō into two broad categories. Those who had fought on the side of the Tokugawa became *Fudai* Daimyō and having demonstrated their loyalty were given key political positions throughout the Shogunate's 200-year reign.

Those who had fought against the Shogunate were branded as *Tozama* Daimyō, viewed with suspicion and watched by the *Fudai*. This power dynamic began to weaken during the final years of the Shogunate as the regime was forced to agree to unfair treaties with the Western powers. Eventually this dynamic reversed as the Tozama domains of Satsuma and Chōshū launched a war that overthrew the Shogunate in 1868, concluding with the Battle of Hakodate in 1869. Domains that had opposed the Meiji Restoration such as Sendai, Yonezawa and Aizu had huge tracts of their land seized as punishment for their resistance. The Sendai domain had their 620,000 koku reduced to 280,000 koku of land (a koku was an amount of rice to feed one person for a year and was used as a means of measuring land size under the Shogunate). Much of the land taken from Sendai was given to Nanbu domain including the symbol of Sendai power: Shiroishi castle. With this loss of power and livelihood, the fate of the domains who had defied the reformation government was uncertain.

In Sendai domain, there was one man who found opportunity amongst this hardship, Date Kuneshige (1841-1904) who led his retainers to start a new life on Japan's northern frontier. Within Sendai, the land that Date oversaw was part of the land that was victim to such a severe reduction, it was now impossible to grow sufficient crops to support his retainers and their families, numbering 8,000. Date was distraught to see his loyal retainers in such a crisis. Furthermore, he suspected that the samurai class no longer had a place under the new modernization reforms. Date wrote an urgent plea to the heads of the new government requesting the opportunity to develop land in Hokkaido.[56] Date wrote; "no payment is necessary; my only wish is that we are able to become farmers."[57] Date's letter required a great deal of bravery: to renounce his status as a samurai, the highest of social classes, to become a worker of the land would have been unimaginable to his ancestors. But he was astute in seizing an opportunity to modernize before modernization was thrust upon the samurai. The new government, still faced the problem of Russian expansion south and having samurai stationed in Hokkaido would be a useful bulwark and agreed.

With the blessing of his former adversaries on March 29, 1870, Date with 220 men, women and children, left for Muroran and made landfall on April 6. When the colonists arrived, the local Ainu helped carry luggage off their boats to the shore. They then began to make their way to what is now Umemoto-chō in Date City, south of Lake Tōya, which at the time was wild country. Here Kuneshige took his hoe to clear the land and planted 13 plum trees, the genesis of Date City.

Despite the positive start for the former samurai, farming was no easy matter. Under the Tokugawa Shogunate samurai had depended upon stipends and even those who had experience of farming found it difficult to grow crops in the cold hard earth of Hokkaido. By the first harvest season, the settlers had only managed to produce a few daikons (radishes) and potatoes, hardly enough to sustain themselves. They were forced to eat *Fuki* (giant butterbur) a herb that provides very few calories. The local Ainu joked that while they had no objection to the Wajin arriving to cultivate the land they would protest if the Wajin started to reek of *Fuki*. Despite their jesting, when the settlers harvest took a turn for the worse, the Ainu taught them how to fish there. Since Date and his men volunteered to colonize Hokkaido as a form of atonement, they were given no support from the government. If their colonization mission failed, this was to be their punishment for choosing the wrong side in the civil war. but with the help of the Ainu and their determination, Date's followers managed to not only survive but also flourish, allowing other settlers of the Watari-Date to make their way in separate waves of immigration.

Ono Fukashi (1876-1952) who was the eldest son of a third wave colonizer captured the spirit of the endeavor through his artwork. In one piece titled 'Building a Cabin' settlers build a simple log cabin: cutting down a tree and gathering straw with patriarchal hierarchies briefly being put aside as men and women build together. For a time, frontier life stripped away the rules of everyday society as people came together to focus on what was necessary to survive. In this image, a woman has cut off the long sleeves of her kimono with a knife to stop them getting in the way of her work. A more romanticized picture can be seen in 'Cultivation Begins' which depicts the first day a hoe is put to work. Colonizers worked 16-hour days, getting up while the stars glimmered in the sky and laying down to rest only once the moon had shown its face. In 'Cultivation Begins', as they work to cut down the primeval forest, Date Kunishige proudly looks on.

Following the success of the first round of colonization Date's people received an increasing amount of government assistance, such as procuring a government ship to take the settlers to Hokkaido during the second round of migration. The third wave of immigration of Date's retainers came in September 1872 when the Meiji government formally abolished the class system that had existed under the Shogunate, a class system under which the samurai held the highest standing. Following this, the samurai who made up 7% of the population, lost their status and became ordinary civilians. Unlike the Daimyō who could transfer their position and privilege into political positions in the new government, lower ranking samurai lost their stipends and with it their livelihood. The colonization of Hokkaido was one means of escape, and thousands followed the precedent set by Date on the northern frontier. From 1872 to 1874 the Development Commission supplied them with supplementary rice, salt, and miso and in 1877 William S. Clarke (1826-1886) the President of Sapporo Agricultural College advised going beyond subsistence farming by raising cattle and sugar beet to profit from the land. Following Clarke's advice in 1880 a sugar beet factory was established. After the abolition of their social class, samurai from across Japan moved to Hokkaido. If contemporary Japanese regions and prefectures are applied to the former domains, it is possible to understand where these colonizers came from.[58] All these former samurai to Hokkaido bought local cultures and customs from across the country. In total around 6,300 made the move and cultivated 2,300 hectares of land. These numbers were tiny compared to the mass migration organized under the Hokkaido Government in the following decades, but it marked the beginning of Hokkaido as a melting pot of various cultures.

Many of the former samurai who immigrated to Hokkaido came as a new class called the *Tondenhei*. This word roughly translates to 'colonization soldier' and as their name suggests the *Tondenhei* were both soldiers and farmers. Under the government's reforms many samurai who had lost their stipends struggled to re-adapt themselves to the life of a merchant or farmer. The resentment this caused particularly among young and unemployed samurai became a societal problem.

The target of many of these young samurai's rage was the foreigners whom they blamed for destroying the feudal class system. Such incidents happened particularly in the port cities opened to foreigners under the Shogunate. In Hakodate such an incident occurred in 1874 when Ludwig Haber (1843-1874) an acting consul of Germany was murdered in what is now Hakodate Park by Tazaki Hidechika, a young former samurai of Akita domain. Tazaki had not targeted Haber for any specific reason other than that he symbolized the foreign influences that he resented. Tazaki had been waiting in the area for a foreigner to pass by, and Haber happened to be his unfortunate victim. Tazaki was later executed for the murder. Perhaps if young samurai such as Tazaki had believed they had better prospects in the new Japan they might not have resorted to such measures. The murder of Ludwig Haber was not an isolated incident, there had been a number of attacks on foreigners in the years before the Meiji Restoration. In 1861 the Dutch secretary and translator Henry Heusken (1832-1861) who was serving under the U.S diplomat Townsend Harris was killed by an unknown swordsman, in 1862 the Englishmen Charles Richardson was killed by a samurai from Satsuma domain near Yokohama and in 1863 the U.S legation was torched by arsonists. During the final days of the Shogunate these anti-foreign sentiments were roused with the rallying cry, "restore the Emperor and expel the barbarians". Yet, under the new government it seemed as if the notion of expelling the barbarians had been tossed to the wind. The politicians of the new government further aggravated matters in 1872 with the abolition of the class system much to the dejection of the samurai who now found themselves lacking a means to make a living. But one man saw an opportunity to give a life of meaning to the young samurai and to develop the nation: Kuroda Kiyotaka of the Development Commission and later the second Prime Minister of Japan. In 1873 Kuroda proposed that former samurai of the Tohoku region become *Tondenhei*, the agricultural soldiers who would colonize the northern frontier while protecting from any invaders who dared enter Japan's northern borderlands. Developing Hokkaido gave them a sense of purpose, and their martial training acted as a bulwark should Russia threaten Japanese territorial claims. In July of 1874 the first *Todenhei* were recruited from men between the ages of 18 and 35 in Akita, Miyagi and Sakata. They bought their families with them and left behind their homes, making a new life for themselves on the frontier. Upon their recruitment, the *Tondenhei* were given a blue military jacket, hat and trousers. Each *Tondenhei* was also issued with a gun; as former samurai many brought ancestral swords with them. Thus, the first *Tondenhei* became iconic figures of Hokkaido. While they held onto their regional culture and martial values, they accepted that the past was never going to return and that they must be the products of a new age. By becoming *Tondenhei*, they could build a society for their nation while developing the northern frontier. Since the men spent a great deal of time conducting military drills, much of the cultivation under the *Tondenhei* system fell to the wives of these men.

From 1890, the *Tondenhei* system was widened to allow for applicants beyond the Tohoku region of northern Honshu, and the system was further broadened to encompass men not from samurai households. Within the *Tondenhei* from the first commoner backgrounds, 90% were from the prefectures of Hyogo, Wakayama, Okayama and Tokushima in western Japan. At the closure of the *Tondenhei* system, 37 villages had been established throughout Hokkaido totaling 39,911 people with 74,755 hectares of land under cultivation.

Though the *Tondenhei* were both warriors and farmers, they spent most of their time on the latter, but they did see combat in 1877. Tensions amongst samurai in the former Satsuma domain, who had united under Saigō Takamori (1828-1877) in Kagoshima, erupted in an eight-month skirmish with the new government on the island of Kyushu and they employed *Tondenhei* from Hokkaido to fight against the Satsuma rebels. As Japan's army was modernized, *Tondenhei* were incorporated into the Imperial Japanese Army in 1882, but the passing of conscription laws in 1889 made the need for recruitment obsolete. Most of the Tondenehei were recruited into the army's seventh division which saw combat during the Sino-Japanese war (1894-1895). With Hokkaido's development progressing and the formation of a centralized army by 1904 it was no longer necessary to recruit *Tondenhei* and the system was finally abolished.

The *Tondenhei* was not the Development Commission's only means of attracting colonizers to Hokkaido. Throughout the late 1860s and 1870s, a number of laws were passed encouraging Wajin immigrants to venture north. In November 1869 the Immigration Assistance Act was passed providing farming tools, pots, futons, financial incentives and a three-year supplement of rice and miso, for any family that undertook the challenge. Later laws attempted to broaden the appeal.[59] In 1874 a law was passed that stipulated that if the concerned could support themselves the land they cultivated became their property after three years of work and in 1877 land in Hokkaido became even more accessible with the Development Commission beginning to sell state land. However, all this land had once been the living space of the indigenous Ainu for hundreds of years before it was claimed as property of the state. Under the Development Commission, Hokkaido's population soared to unprecedented levels. At the dawn of the Meiji era there were about 20,000 Ainu and 40,000 Japanese in Hokkaido. By 1885, just before the abolition of the Three Prefecture system the population swelled to around 290,000. Most of these pioneers immigrated to Hokkaido because they saw an opportunity to make a future for themselves on a frontier full of possibilities. However, not all who were brought to Hokkaido came by choice.

During winters at the small fishing village of Abashiri on Hokkaido's north coast, it is extremely cold and a harsh wind routinely blows down off the Sea of Okhotsk. Under both the Development Commission and the Three Prefectures System, remote land such as Abashiri had remained largely undeveloped. Most of the Wajin who immigrated to Hokkaido chose the established Wajin areas around Hakodate and those with a more adventurous inclination settled for the region around Sapporo. Few were audacious enough to brave the real wilderness far from the towns. Yet, soon the population of this tiny village rose into the thousands. One day in 1890, 50 men arrived clad in orange with their hands and feet bound, and their wardens ordered them to cut down trees to build temporary lodgings. The next month, a further 50 arrived and built their lodging. This continued until there were over 1,000 prisoners, enough to make what had once been a small fishing village into a sizable town. These men were the inmates of Abashiri prison and from the viewpoint of the wardens, their lives were worth little more than livestock. If they should happen to die during their labor that was to be their punishment, and many died from the cold, overwork and malnourishment. When a prisoner succumbed, he was hastily buried in an unmarked grave dug into the cold earth. The prisoners soon named such graves 'mounds of chain'.

As with the *Tondenhei*, prison labor in Hokkaido served two functions: the first was to develop land that very few Wajin settled of their own accord and the second was to reduce the pressure of the burgeoning prison population of the modern Japanese nation state. Crimes such as theft, fraud or illegal logging resulted in imprisonment in Hokkaido and a more modernized state saw a need for places to imprison some of the population. Reminiscent of the penalty of exile used under the Kamakura Shogunate, those who opposed the state also became fodder for forced labor in Hokkaido, with little distinction made between common-law and political prisoners. This included former samurai who rebelled against the new government including the Saga rebellion in 1874, the Satsuma rebellion in 1877 and even those who participated in the Freedom and People's Rights Movement of the 1880s. Sentences were typically long and in Abashiri one third of prisoners received life sentences with the remainder serving 12 years or more.

During the 1880s and 1890s, five prisons were built on Hokkaido. The first was Kabato north of Sapporo, which became the third largest prison in Japan after Tokyo and Miyagi. Before the prison was built, Kabato had only 18 residents. Three years later, this population had expanded to 1,800 with a town established to support the services of the prison. At Kabato, prisoners were worked to death to cultivate parts of Hokkaido no one else was willing to settle in. In just the autumn of 1891, over 200 inmates died. In 1882, two more prisons were built in Sorachi, not far from Sapporo, and Kushiro on Hokkaido's south coast.

In 1890, Abashiri was constructed followed in 1896 by Tokachi jail, west of Kushiro. In 1885, there were 3,000 prisoners in Hokkaido and by 1893 this had risen to over 7,000. The type of forced labor that prisoners were subjected to varied with each prison. Labor at Kabato focused on lumber and road building, whereas Sorachi consisted primarily of mining coal. Regardless of the type of work, the prisoners were tied to one another by chains around their ankles or waists to prevent any escapes. Prison labor constructed vital sections of Hokkaido's infrastructure with over half the roads of this period built by the hands of inmates, including the road that runs between Mikasa and Asahikawa. Prison labor, which was effectively slave labor, eventually came under public criticism and the practice was abandoned in 1897.

Life in the prisons followed a strict routine. In Abashiri, this began with the prisoners waking at 6:40 am, inspections at 6:55 followed by breakfast between 6:50 and 7:10. By 7:40, the day's labor began and lasted until 16:20. During the workday prisoners received two small breaks of 15 minutes and a 30 minute lunch break. The prisoners' day then concluded with a meal at 17:00 and lights out by 21:00. Prisoners repeated this monotonous routine throughout their extensive sentences.

Among Hokkaido's prisons, Abashiri has become the most famous, created in a unique design to allow for the near-constant surveillance of the prisoners. Abashiri was a panopticon composed of a central nucleus with five separate corridors stretching out containing the prison cells. From this central position, guards could survey the entire inmate population from one fixed location. Prisoners who feigned illness in an attempt to break the routine risked being locked in solitary confinement. Among the 13 offenses that could result in a stretch in solitary confinement were: disobeying orders, possession of tobacco, use of foul language, gambling, injuring oneself on purpose and attempting escape. While prisoners received a few hours to rest in the evening, there was also the immense cold of Hokkaido's winter to contend with. In Abashiri, temperatures could drop as low as -20 celsius (-68 fahrenheit). Due to the isolation and harsh winters along the Sea of Okhotsk, Abashiri appeared to be the most secure prison in Japan.

But there was one man who successfully broke out of Abashiri, Shiratori Yoshie (1907-1979). Arrested at the age of 25 on charges of armed robbery and homicide, Shiratori escaped from four separate prisons throughout his life. This began with

Aomori prison in 1936, Akita prison in 1942, Abashiri prison in 1944 and finally Sapporo prison in 1947. Shiratori became known as the 'Escape King' and on one occasion he threatened a warden by saying "Please give me another blanket. If you don't, I'll break out." In Aomori prison, Shiratori escaped from solitary confinement by using the short period of time prisoners were given to empty their latrines to bend a wire he had found into the shape of a key. Shiratori achieved this by making an imprint of the lock by repeatedly shoving his finger into the keyhole. After breaking out, he was on the run for three months. In Akita, Shiratori escaped by sawing through a rusty grate in the ceiling of his cell with a piece of tin plate and a nail. As with his escape in Aomori, he carefully timed his escape to coincide with the wardens changing shifts. Even though Shiratori had escaped from these prisons, surely he could have no success in Abashiri. And even if he could successfully escape, he only had the wilderness of Hokkaido to greet him. In Abashiri, Shiratori was thrown into solitary confinement with manacles and leg binds with only a light blanket suitable for summer, yet even this failed to stop the Escape King. In Abashiri, Shiratori succeeded in corroding the lock on his cell door by repeatedly retching miso soup onto it. On August 19, 1944 after the lock had sufficiently corroded, he removed the bar of his cell, dislocated his shoulders, arms and knees and slipped through a small window running down the ceiling in the corridor outside of his cell.[60]

Despite the abolition of prison labor in 1897, forced labor continued in Hokkaido under what came to be known as 'Tako Builders'. The Tako Builders came to Hokkaido under six-month contracts beginning in the 1920s and continuing until shortly after Japan's defeat in the World War II. Over this period about 30,000 indebted men, mostly from Tokyo and Osaka came to Hokkaido. The labor was semi-forced and though a meager wage and food were provided, builders were prohibited from leaving the tiny Takobeya, or 'Tako Lodgings', on the construction site. There are two possible origins of the name Tako Builder. In Japanese one meaning of "Tako" is octopus – and just as a starving octopus will eat its own tentacles so too would the Tako Builders be worked to death to pay off their debts. Another meaning of the word "Tako" is kite just as how a kite drifts when its string is cut, so too the Tako Builders - fleeing at their first opportunity. Similar to the prison labor, Tako Builders were treated as sub-human and dispensable. Those who survived their sentence went into cities such as Asahikawa and Hakodate generating protests from the local people. The Tako Builders were treated as pariahs.

One piece of infrastructure that captures the brutal nature of the Tako Builder's work is the Jōmon tunnel built between March 1912 and October 1914. In a two-year period over 100 Tako Builders perished during the tunnel's construction. In some cases, those who refused orders were beaten to death with shovels by the foreman.[61]

While prison and indentured labor was utilized to develop Hokkaido, the island was never a prison colony. The first governor was Iwamura Michitoshi (1840-1915) of the former Tosa domain who was a proponent of free immigration to Hokkaido. In 1875 the Hokkaido Government passed a law stipulating that government land was to be provided to anyone who submitted a plausible plan for the development up to 100,000 Tsubo (330,578 m²) at a price of 1 yen per Tsubo (1 Tsubo being roughly 3.31m²).[62]

Land provided a great incentive to immigrate north. One could leave the more densely populated towns of Honshu, Shikoku and Kyushu and potentially make a fortune as a pioneer. An 1891 Hokkaido Government pamphlet emphasized that freedom from conscription and cheap land could be found in Hokkaido.[63] In addition to this, the 1886 act included freedom from taxation for the first 20 years with the exception of the already developed land in the south centered on Hakodate, Matsumae and Esashi. Tax exemptions were not limited to land, and those who immigrated to Hokkaido could expect tax exemptions when purchasing vehicles, soy sauce, sweets and alcohol, additionally general tax rates in Hokkaido were already 2.5 times less than the mainland. Alongside such incentives came a desire to build a new life and family in Hokkaido or escape troubles at home. In 1911 crop failure throughout Tohoku prompted mass migration to Hokkaido. Under the Hokkaido Government there were three peaks of immigration, the first was in 1897 following the Sino-Japanese war, the second in 1908 and third in 1919 following the First World War. Immigrants to Hokkaido came from all over Japan, the prefectures with the highest levels of immigration to Hokkaido were Ishikawa and Toyama from the Hokuriku region and Aomori in Tohoku. By 1926 the total population stood at 2,430,000 however this was only around 80% towards the Hokkaido Government's goal of 3,000,000. Regardless of this, over a half century Hokkaido's population swelled from a few thousand to a few million.

Despite the incentives to immigrate to Hokkaido much of the island was still frontier territory bringing with it the dangers of living in isolation, exposure to the elements and attacks from wild animals. The Tomamae-Sankebetsu Incident is one such case of the dangers of life on the Hokkaido frontier.

The bear had first made its presence known on a November night in 1915 when it awoke the Tomizō household in the night. Seeking the advice of two Matagi (traditional hunters of Tohoku region) who informed him that the bear must be an "Anamotazu", a bear that has failed to go into hibernation and lurking the land. After the bear fails to make a reappearance, the Matagi suggested that perhaps the bear had at last gone into hibernation after all.

But this was not the case. The next attack was on the Ōta house at the upper courses of the Sankebetsu River in December. When some of the men of the village visit the scene, they surmise that the bear was likely eating the ears of corn hanging from the eaves when it was startled by Mayu, the Woman of the houses' scream causing it to crash through the window in a wild rage.

In the following days, 30 of the village men organized a search party, those with guns brought them, those who did not brought hoes, should they encounter the beast. After advancing 150 meters they encountered the bear. It was larger than a horse, weighing 340 kilograms and with a length of 2.7 meters with a white stripe running down its breast giving it the appearance of wearing a Kasaya. Five of the party shoot the bear, but it flees into the forest. It is here they discover the remains of Mayu buried beneath a Sakhalin fur and take the remains back to the village, something that only prompts the bear to attack again, going on to kill five children and a pregnant woman. By the twelfth the Hokkaido Government had arranged a volunteer party of locals to take down the bear, including Ainu, members of the army and the police. On the following day, it was the Russo-Japanese war veteran, the 57-year-old Yamamoto Heikichi (1858-1950) who singlehandedly took down the bear. Yamamoto shot the bear close to the heart, even this failed to kill the beast. As the furious bear advanced closer towards him, he released another shot into the bear's head finally putting an end to the nightmare that had plagued the settlers. When the rest of the party found Yamamoto and the bear, those who were furious with the horrors this monster has bought upon them began kicking the bear's corpse until someone at last yelled "Banzai". With the bear now dead the cries of 200 men yelling Banzai echoed throughout the forest.

In the latter half of the 19th Century the English naturalist and resident of Hakodate, Thomas Blakiston (1832-1891)

Inside of a frontier house – photography taken at Historical Village of Hokkaido by the author

noticed that the animals and fauna differed upon crossing the Tsugaru Straits from Honshu to Hokkaido. Blakiston came to realize that a zoogeographical boundary separated Honshu and Hokkaido with wildlife in Honshu being related to South Asia, while wildlife in Hokkaido was part of a Northern Asia ecosphere. The Hokkaido wolf (now extinct) was more closely related to North-American wolves than those in South-Asia and the largest living species of owl, the Blakiston's fish owl, is also more closely related to birds further north. Both these creatures are considered *Kamuy* (gods) in Ainu mythology with the former known as *Horkew Kamuy* (hunting god), and the latter as *Kotan Kor Kamuy* (god that protects the village). Blakiston published his findings in the *Asiatic Society of Japan* in 1883. Even before this ecological line was scientifically proven, Wajin had known for centuries that the climate of Honshu and Hokkaido were worlds apart. To develop land in Hokkaido, Japanese agricultural methods were not guaranteed to work and the Development Commission looked to Western countries as a model, employing 45 Americans, five Russians, four British, four Germans and one Frenchman between 1869 and 1879. Kuroda Kiyotaka who was the second in command of the Development Commission saw the rapid development of the American west as a design that could be applied to Japan's north. Kuroda believed that agricultural knowledge, techniques and machinery used in America, particularly in the more northern states could be adapted to the comparable climate of Hokkaido. Kuroda proposed the Development Commission employ the American experts to bring their wealth of knowledge to Hokkaido.

With his proposition approved Kuroda left for America with several students in January 1871. During his time there, Kuroda met Ulysses S. Grant (1822-1885) and was introduced to Horace Capron (1804-1885) who became the first of Hokkaido's pioneering American agriculturalists. At the time of Kuroda and Capron's meeting, Capron was the Commissioner of Agriculture and was just the man to bring modern methods of farming to Hokkaido. Capron was born in Attleboro, Massachusetts and had managed a cotton cloth factory and ranch during his younger years. In 1862, at the age of 58 he had fought on the side of the Union in the Civil War and was promoted to cavalry officer. Kuroda first met Capron when he was in Boston and was soon convinced that Capron's knowledge would bear fruit if applied to Hokkaido. When Capron was invited to Japan as an advisor by the Meiji government, he accepted the offer arriving in Yokohama in 1871 at the age of 67. Over his roughly four-year term as an advisor, Capron provided his expert opinion and advice to the Development Commission. Capron contributed his ideas to a number of issues including infrastructure, land management, immigration, livestock, fisheries, and industrialization with the Development Commission carrying out most of Capron's suggestions. To introduce Western agriculture to Hokkaido, Capron began by importing livestock, seeds, and machinery from abroad to a training area in Tokyo's Aoyama neighborhood, which later was moved to locations throughout Hokkaido. At Capron's training areas the youth of Japan came to learn Western farming techniques. Capron encouraged the raising of crops such as barley, wheat, onion, beet, and haricot as well as dairy farming, which he believed was well suited to Hokkaido's humid continental climate. Kuroda respected Capron as an expert and the two continued to exchange letters throughout their lives, although they did not agree on every aspect of Hokkaido's development. Capron believed that the encouragement of the immigration of self-employed businessmen was necessary, Kuroda was very much of the belief that state-led development, not private capitalism, was the most suitable way to develop Hokkaido. Upon Capron's return to America, he was fond of showing off Japanese curiosities he had collected during his tenure in Hokkaido, including elaborately carved pieces of ivory, gold lacquerware and paper *Koinobori*, large paper carp that are hosited in the spring, now held by the Smithsonian Museum. In Hokkaido Capron is commemorated through a statue that stands in Ōdori Park in Sapporo.

One year after Capron left Japan, another New England agriculturalist arrived in Hokkaido to leave behind an enduring legacy, William S. Clarke (1826-1886). Clarke was born in Easthampton, Massachusetts, rose to the rank of Colonel in the Union Army before becoming a state legislator in 1864. Clarke studied at Amherst University becoming professor there in 1852. In 1867 Clarke became the dean of the newly constructed Massachusetts Agricultural College (currently the University of Massachusetts Amherst). Nine years after becoming dean in March 1876, Clarke was invited to take up a similar role at

Sapporo Agricultural College in June of the same year, Clarke arrived in Japan in time for the college's opening in August.[64] The Sapporo Agricultural College aligned with Kuroda's vision that a new generation of Japanese would learn Western agricultural methods to modernize Hokkaido. The Development Commission paid the tuition fees of the students and in return each student was duty bound to work for the Development Commission for at least five years after graduation. Upon the opening of the Agricultural College, 24 students enrolled in Agricultural Science. Bringing new forms of agriculture required diligence and determination: the college's program put the students through a rigorous education, only 13 students successfully graduated the four-year course in 1880.

Clarke introduced his students to contemporary techniques in farming, fishing and animal husbandry, bringing a model farm and barn to Japan for the first time. These barns resembling their American counterparts can be found throughout Hokkaido today. All this was done in his eight-month term in Hokkaido. He also took the view that practical skills alone were not enough to bring Hokkaido into modernity and believed, that the word of Christ was a necessity for development. Clarke was a pious Christian and gave a copy of the Bible to each of his students. Upon admission to the college, Clarke encouraged each student to make a vow to abstain from alcohol and tobacco. over his time in Hokkaido, he formed a tight bond with his students that continued long after he left Japan. Clarke bade farewell to his students in April 1877 at what is now Kitahiroshima City where he purportedly told them, "Boys, be ambitious! Be ambitious not for money or for selfish aggrandizement, not for that evanescent thing which men call fame. Be ambitious for the attainment of all that a man ought to be."[65] Clarke had handed down his knowledge to these young men, and it was now up to them now to transform Japan.[66]

While Clarke spent less than a year in Hokkaido, upon his return he continued contributing to Hokkaido's future. When the Development Commission requested fertilizer, seeds and livestock from America, Clarke acted as an agent to obtain them. Like Capron, Clarke also maintained close ties with Kuroda, in one case sending him a pair of binoculars during the Satsuma rebellion of 1877 to which Kuroda thanked him by sending him sea otter pelts. Clarke was particularly interested in the growth of his former students and was so keen to receive letters from them that he opened and read them before he had even left the post office. Clarke was particularly delighted when some of his students informed him of their baptism. Upon Clarke's death his students sent an elm tree from Sapporo to be planted by his grave at Amherst. Thus, a piece of Hokkaido marks the final resting place of the island's most distinguished foreign advisor.

Not all developments involving Western technology took place under the instructive gaze of foreign advisors. One significant case is the development of Hokkaido's beer industry. Before the advent of the Meiji era, Murahashi Hisanari (1842-1892) was one of 17 young samurai who absconded from Satsuma domain despite the *Sakoku* policy in order to study abroad. Murahashi went to the United Kingdom in 1865 and returned in 1868, the year of the Meiji Restoration. In 1872, Murahashi joined the Development Commission and during his tenure, noticed the similarity between the climate of Hokkaido and England. As hops grew well in Hokkaido and with the abundance of water and snow for use in distilleries, it seemed logical to build a brewery. Construction for the first distillery began in 1876 with Nakagawa Seibei (1848-1916), who had studied beer brewing in Germany, as the beer master to oversee its construction.

Japan's first beer brewery opened under the Development

Commission, and it was eventually reborn as Sapporo Breweries after the state sold the operation to private buyers in 1886. The star symbol which endures as the Sapporo Breweries logo comes from a Satsuma flag; as officials from Satsuma were so prominent in the Development Commission, Sapporo was often jokingly referred to as "Satsuporo" during this period.[67]

Alongside agriculture, foreign advisors played an essential role in the development of infrastructure. Under the American A.G Warfield, construction of the 180-kilometer highway stretching from Hakodate to Sapporo, via Mori, Muroran, and Tomakomai, was completed in 1873. The road was the first in Japan purpose-made for horse and cart.[68] Unlike Capron and Clarke, Warfield lost favor with the Development Commission and was dismissed following a drunken incident when he shot an Ainu's dog in February 1879.

In addition to roads, the development of the railways formed an integral part of the country's modernization. Japan's first railway began carrying passengers in 1872, between Sakuragichō in Yokohama to Shinbashi in Tokyo. The American surveyor Benjamin Smith Lyman (1835-1920) suggested the route for Hokkaido's first railway and construction linking the area from Mikasa in Horonai to Temiya in Otaru was completed in 1882, forming the Horonai railway. The route stretched about 90 kilometers and two steam trains were imported from America to be used on the track. The foreign advisors of the Meiji era played a key role in the agricultural, architectural and cultural evolution of Hokkaido and the wider country, a legacy still felt today.

8

THE COLONIZATION OF SAKHALIN

JAPAN'S NORTHERN frontier did not stop at Hokkaido but continued further north still across the Sōya Straits to Karafuto, the Japanese territory on southern Sakhalin. While today Japan is an island nation with no land bordering any other state, there was a 40 year period were Japan shared a border with Russia on the island of Sakhalin.

During this period, the Japanese term for Sakhalin was Karafuto (in this book the term Karafuto will be used to refer to the Japanese territory, while the term Sakhalin will be used to refer to the island itself). Those who moved north to Karafuto faced a winter significantly harsher than that of Hokkaido. Winters in Sakhalin are characterized by snowfall that lasts for days on end and frozen rivers, even the seven-kilometer stretch of ocean in the Mamiya Strait separating Sakhalin from the Eurasian continent freezes over. In Sakhalin the winter is considerably colder than Hokkaido. It is not until March that the sun begins to melt the snow, and this slow process continues throughout April and May. In April hibernating animals awake and flowers begin to increasingly appear throughout the island. During the colonial era, alongside the awakening wildlife itinerant workers would make their way to Karafuto, from Hokkaido they crossed the Sōya Straits, which they named "the salty river".

Much of the work in Karafuto was impossible to perform during the colder months, such as loggers working in the burgeoning lumber industry; logs felled in the winter had to wait for the river ice to thaw to transport them downstream. When the herring made their way along the coast of Karafuto to spawn in spring, a rush of fishermen from the mainland swarmed to capitalize on the abundance of the catches. The awakening of spring fades into summer in July with purple firewood's blooming in the fields. In the early 20th century, during the summer season, tourists from across Japan came to Karafuto to escape the southern humidity. In addition to the pleasant climate, tourists were drawn to Karafuto for its air of exoticism; Russians who had chosen to settle in the Japanese territory sold bread by the station. Summer is fleeting and by early September the long winter begins once again to grip the island.

Today, a flight from Hokkaido's Shinchitose airport to Sakhalin will fly over Cape Sōya, the most northern tip of Hokkaido, after about 40 minutes and a further seven minutes later over Cape Crillon, the southern tip of Sakhalin. Hokkaido and Sakhalin are so close that on a clear day the outline of either island is in view of the other. As with Hokkaido, Sakhalin spans the Sea of Okhotsk and the Sea of Japan. The island is slightly smaller at 76,400 km^2, making Sakhalin the 23rd largest island in the world.

Although Wajin had been active on Sakhalin under the Tokugawa Shogunate, the southern half of the island (Karafuto) only became Japanese-ruled in 1905. The name Karafuto seems to have entered Japanese from an Ainu phrase *kamuy kar put ya mosir*, which can be translated as "the land the gods created at the mouth of the river", a reference to the Amur River on the neighboring continent. The Hokkaido Ainu often referred to the island as *Karapto*, which became Karafuto in Japanese.

Anthropological and archeological research shows that the

Ainu moved into Karafuto during the 13th Century and by the time the island became a contested territory between the great powers of Japan and Russia, there were three indigenous groups of people on the island, the Ainu occupying the south, the Uilita peoples to their north and the Nivikh peoples further north still. The Matsumae clan first sent samurai to Karafuto in 1679. During this period, the Matsumae did not even have comprehensive control over Hokkaido, and by 1684 even this faint Waijin presence on the island had come to an end.

With Russian expansion south, the Tokugawa Shogunate took an increasing interest in Sakhalin, and from 1861-1864 samurai clans from Tohoku received orders to guard the southern portion of the island. In 1855, the Treaty of Shimoda agreed to joint Japanese and Russian ownership of the island with no fixed border being delimitated. The Development Commission encouraged colonizers to move to the island, albeit not on the same scale as to Hokkaido. After 1875, Japan surrendered claims to Sakhalin after Enomoto Takeaki, the former leader of the army that resisted the Meiji Restoration and now a diplomat, concluded the Treaty of Saint Petersburg. This treaty gave Russia full jurisdiction over Sakhalin in exchange for full Japanese jurisdiction over the Kuril Islands. But when the Russo-Japanese war ended with a Japanese victory, the country once again claimed Karafuto from its new position of strength. The 1905 Treaty of Portsmouth agreed to set the Japanese-Russian border at the 50th parallel north, aligned with cities such as Vancouver, Paris, and Seattle. Japan now controlled about 48% of the island, creating a territory roughly the size of Taiwan. For five years between 1920 and 1925, Japan controlled the entirety of the island — Japan entered the Russian civil war between the communist Red Army and the coalition of anti-communist forces under the banner of the White Army. But control over the southern portion of the island continued until

1945 when the Soviet army took Sakhalin and the Kuril Islands in their entirety, which together now form the Russian province of Sakhalin Oblast.

During the Japanese intervention (1918-1922), Japan, much like America and the United Kingdom, supported the white army in the Far East. From 1856 to 1922, Japan occupied the Russian coastal province of Primorskaya Oblast. During the war, an incident occurred at Nikolayevsk-on-Amur, on the Eurasian continent just west of Sakhalin; a Russian general attacked and murdered civilians who had already surrendered to the Russian forces. In retaliation for the incident, Japan occupied the north of Sakhalin, bringing the island fully under Japanese control. Many veterans who survived this tumultuous period made a home for themselves in Karafuto, where stories of their experiences of Russian brutality spread through the populace. In 1925, after Japan and the Soviet-Union normalized relations through the Soviet-Japanese Basic Convention, the status of the Sakhalin territory reverted to that laid out in the 1905 Treaty of Portsmouth.

Before Karafuto became a Japanese territory, over 35,000 Russians were living in southern Sakhalin and most of these were exiles, as Russia had used the island as a prison colony. After the territory exchanged hands, only 227 Russians remained by 1906.

In 1905, there were close to 2,000 people living in Karafuto, most of them indigenous Ainu. The few Russians mostly left or were removed when the territory came into Japanese hands. As a colony, Karafuto's population quickly rose with Wajin alone numbering 10,806 the following year. By 1910, Karafuto's population had increased to 30,000 and by 1921 as many as 40,000 had settled there. Among these immigrants, one-third came from Hokkaido with the remainder originating from elsewhere in Japan. It was not until 1908 that the Karafuto government began to change Russian place names throughout the territory to Japanese equivalents: Vladimirovka became Toyohara and Korsakov becoming Ōtomari.

Development of Sakhalin in the Far East had not been a priority for either imperial or soviet Russia. As a result, when Karafuto became a Japanese territory in 1905, the land was still largely in a pristine state of nature. As with Hokkaido, the Japanese government was convinced that it had the necessary ability and population to develop Karafuto too.

Though southern Sakhalin had become a Japanese territory, this did not lead to the complete disappearance of Russian inhabitants. Like all frontiers, Karafuto was isolated and difficult to get to from the urban centers of Japan. During this period, the only way to Karafuto was by boat. On August 21, 1905, a 746-ton mail boat imported from the United Kingdom began plying the Hokkaido-Karafuto route: stopping at Hakodate, Otaru in Hokkaido and finally Ōtomari in Karafuto.

As with the Hokkaido frontier, many people moved to Karafuto to build a new life for themselves and over time, a generation of Japanese people native to Karafuto were born and raised there. By 1940, Karafuto had established itself as an integrated part of Japan with populous settlements equaling those of some towns in Honshu in size and population. In 1940, Toyohara (now Yuzhno-Sakhalinsk) had a population exceeding 38,000. With such a large Japanese population, Karafuto was officially declared by the Japanese government as being part of mainland Japanese territory in April 1923.

The acidic soil and long winters meant there was not much chance for vegetation to become compost over the more temperate seasons. Although it was possible to farm in Karafuto, the land was less fertile than the more southerly Hokkaido. On Karafuto, the short farming season began in April as the snows thawed, seeds were planted in May, the harvest brought in throughout August and September, and by October the snows had returned and the winter set in. In Hokkaido, the backbone of the economy was farming, while in Karafuto it was the exploitation of natural resources through fishing, lumber, and mining.

Frontier territories have always offered individuals a chance to dramatically change their fortune, and the same was true of Karafuto, with Japan's jobless and poor flocking to a territory they coined "treasure island". As with all frontiers, while there were riches to be made, there were no guarantees that one might not return empty-handed or even survive. In Karafuto, if one were to fall sick, there was no compensation. And then there were those who despite working all year, squandered their money away on gambling and drink.

The spring fishing season on Karafuto was particularly busy, from the end of May until June when herring spawning off the coast of the island turning the ocean white. Since Japan's first treaty with Russia, fishermen from Hokkaido and as far away as Honshu, made their way to Karafuto for this annual event. Fishing in Karafuto was strictly seasonal, unlike the more fixed logging industry, and during the spring and summer, Karafuto's population dramatically increased as a result. In 1911, the summer population of Karafuto was around 57,000, the winter population was almost half that at 36,725. When the herring arrived to spawn, settlers ran to neighboring villages to tell the fishermen that the herring had come at last. People gathered on the beaches and seagulls gathered overhead, anticipating the castoffs of the fishermen. Miura Rihichi who began working the fishery in Karafuto during his 30s recalls,

"It became terribly busy during the herring season
[...] Some even slept on board the boats ten days

before the herring came [...] rather than going to fish at a fixed time, we had to be ready to work as soon as the herring came."[69]

By 1927, overfishing had led to a decline in fish stocks, but there were other bounties to be found in Karafuto. The Ezo spruce and Sakhalin fir trees that covered 80% of the island away from the ocean provided another natural resource. The historian Nozoe Kenji (1935-2018) recalled how, when he was a child, in early winter nearly all the men of his village in Akita Prefecture left to work in Karafuto's lumber industry. The primary destination of this timber was paper mills, with the first opening in 1913. By 1933 numerous companies' mills had been consolidated into the Ōji Paper company. During an economic downturn during the Taishō era (1912-1926), many came to Karafuto to try to earn a living in this emerging industry.

One of these individuals who was attracted to Karafuto was Sasaki Keisuke who recalls that "during the depression we could make about five yen a day, there were rumors that if one went to Hokkaido or Karafuto one could make as much as one thousand yen."[70] Others left for more personal reasons, such as Fujita Yogorō who departed for Karafuto at the age of 21, not wanting to be a farmer like his father. When Fujita arrived in Karafuto, he entered a bunkhouse like many single men who worked in the lumber industry. These bunkhouses provided a place to stay close to the worksite but were often isolated from other settlements. Smaller bunkhouses could house 50 people, and most had space for 80 to 100 men.

The standard layout of the bunkhouses consisted of a sleeping area around the sides of the building with an area for eating in the center. It is in the bunkhouses that Fujita had his first experience of the workers called 'Jako'. These were men who had no place to call home, no wife or children. What characterized a Jako was the aimlessness of their existence; they bounced between different places and jobs, never staying anywhere too long. Instead of saving their wages, they tended to spend them on gambling and drinking. Fujita recalls how serious some of the fights among the Jako could get. "The jokes became too real, and they'd start fighting [...] they would brandish knives, stab each other and slash at each other's wrists."[71]

It was not just the restless Jako who characterized life in the bunkhouses. Winter on Karafuto was so cold that even *sake* could freeze and skis were necessary to cover the distance from the bunkhouses to the worksite. The isolation coupled with the frigid weather meant that even those who died often did not have their bodies properly dealt with until early spring. Sasaki recalls:

> "Sometimes people would get injured and then die suddenly. During that time, we notified a doctor and the police. Since it was too cold to go to town, we would dig a hole in the snow and bury the body there. They'd freeze and then would be carried into town by horse sleigh once the snow began to thaw."[72]

In the bunkhouse where Sasaki stayed, this number was usually five or six each winter. In addition to the Ōji Paper Company, vast amounts of Karafuto's forest were owned by Kyoto, Hokkaido, and Tohoku Universities. Kyoto University alone owned 3,000 hectares of forest on Karafuto. In the winter, trees were cut down for sale and in summertime agricultural science students came to the forests to take measurements and create nurseries.

As was the case with Hokkaido, not all those who came to Karafuto came of their own accord, and the climate was not the only hardship to be confronted. In 1910, following the acquisition of the Korean Peninsula, the Japanese Empire reorganized farmlands, causing many to lose their property. As Koreans were now viewed as citizens of the empire, many went to Karafuto to ease the labor shortage. In some cases, Koreans were sent forcibly. By the end of World War II, there were approximately 23,000 Koreans in Karafuto.[73] Koreans in the labor force faced frequent discrimination, with wages lower than their Japanese counterparts, and they were often forced to do work many Japanese refused. From 1939 to 1943, there were approximately 32,000 deaths in coal mining, and many Koreans were made to work in the claustrophobic and fragile mines.

While Korean men might be worked to death in coalmines, the women often found themselves driven into prostitution, some as young as ten years old. Edo Yasohachi recalls the number of Korean prostitutes in Ōtomari: "When I asked why so many Koreans had come to Karafuto, they told me they were lied to about jobs. The Japanese lied to Korean women. I think it's a terrible thing the Japanese did."[74]

As with all empires throughout history, the subjects in the Japanese empire were by no means equal.

9

FORCED MIGRATION

FROM THE LATE 17th Century onwards, the Ainu of Sakhalin and the Kuril Islands were caught between Russia and Japan. Some of the most northern of these Ainu had adopted Russian names and converted to Orthodox Christianity, but the land these Ainu lived on came into jeopardy with the 1875 Treaty of Saint Petersburg between Russia and Japan.

In the treaty, Japan agreed to relinquish territorial claims to Sakhalin in return for full jurisdiction of the Kuril Islands. The territorial shift brought with it fears that the Sakhalin and Kuril Ainu might potentially aid the Russians in a war between the two empires, and there was a forced migration of the Sakhalin Ainu to Hokkaido, carried out under the Development Commission (1869-1882). Meanwhile, there was a forced migration of the northern Kuril Ainu to Shikotan Island off the coast of Hokkaido under the jurisdiction of the Nemuro Prefectural Government (1882-1886) and later the Hokkaido Government.

Both groups of Ainu found themselves in an unfamiliar climate where they were pathologically vulnerable and were expected to replace traditions of hunting with agriculture. Early contact with the Russians and Japanese also exposed the Ainu to what Alfred Crosby has termed the "virgin soil epidemic". The isolated indigenous populations such as the Ainu were immunologically weak to the diseases that accompanied the colonizers. Between 1767 and 1769, early Russian contacts in the northern Kuril Island of Paramushir exposed the indigenous people to smallpox, and the results were devastating. It must have seemed to the Paramushir Ainu that death incarnate had come to the island, and during this time, Paramushir gained the nickname *Nūpe Mosir,* the island of tears.

One hundred years later, the northern Kuril Ainu who were moved to Shikotan again succumbed to pestilence, with Shikotan also gaining the same unfortunate nickname, *Nūpe Mosir.* Like the Trail of Tears in 19th Century America, the forced migration of the Sakhalin and Kuril Ainu is a tragic story that shows how such policies, justified at the time in terms of modernization, have the potential to wipe out such peoples and with them their histories, cultures and languages.

With the implementation of the Treaty of Saint Petersburg, the Ainu of Sakhalin were given the choice of either moving to Japan within three years, or staying and becoming citizens of the Russian Empire. Since the Ainu around Aniva Bay in the south of Sakhalin had long been under the Matsumae's contract merchant system, they were familiar with Japan, and if they had to move, the Sakhalin Ainu desired to move across to Cape Sōya on the northern tip of Hokkaido, allowing them to live in an environment similar to that of home.

Kuroda Kiyotaka, believed that Cape Sōya was too close to Sakhalin should war with Russia break out. Kuroda instead opted to move the Sakhalin Ainu further south to the outskirts of Sapporo where they could reform their way of life as agriculturalists. Even before the plan was instigated there were voices of deep protest from within the Development Commission. Matsumoto Jūrō (1840-1916) was sympathetic to the Ainu, at times, Matsumoto even donned an *Attus,* an Ainu garment made from the fiber of elm trees, gifted to him by an Ainu. Matsumoto was adamant that the Sakhalin Ainu should be moved to Cape Sōya were they might continue fishing for their livelihood. At Cape Sōya there was both a suitable climate and a profession that they understood. When Kuroda ignored Matsumoto's advice, he furiously resigned from the Development Commission, returning to his home prefecture of Yamagata.

Following the 1875 Treaty of St Petersburg, only some of the Sakhalin and northern Kuril Ainu chose to become new citizens of Japan. In Sakhalin, one third chose to move, in the belief that the Development Commission would provide for them. A total of 841 Sakhalin Ainu were moved to Wakkanai at Cape Sōya, but the following year they were moved again to what is now Ebetsu, just outside Sapporo. The Sakhalin Ainu were given rice, salt and materials to construct housing. By the Ishikawa River, an area was designated for them to catch salmon and trout and a school was built for the children. This brief spell of optimism amongst the Ainu was soon wiped out with an outbreak of smallpox in 1886 which persisted for four years, killing around 300 of the 841 Sakhalin Ainu. The Ainu who survived the ordeal longed for their homeland and traditional way of life, and by the end of the Russo-Japanese war in 1905, most of the Sakhalin Ainu had either gained employment as fishermen in Sakhalin or fled home. Only 27 chose to remain in Hokkaido.

The forced movement of the Sakhalin Ainu to Ebetsu ended as Matsumoto had predicted. Those who survived were still close enough to return home, something impossible for the northern Kuril Ainu.

While Hokkaido and Sakhalin are separated by the 40-kilometer Sōya Straits, the northern Kuril Islands are a considerably greater distance from Hokkaido. From north to south, the Kuril Islands are about the same length as Honshu, and just as the climate of Aomori Prefecture (average temperature of 8.3 celsius/46 farenheit in April) at Honshu's north and Yamaguchi Prefecture (average temperature 13.9 celsius/57 farenheit in April) in Honshu's south have a considerably diverse climate, so do the northern and southern Kuril Islands. If overlaid over the islands of Great Britain, the Kuril Islands stretch almost from the most northern point of Scotland to England's south coast just off France, being only about 100 kilometers shorter.

The northern Kuril Islands descend from the Kamchatka Peninsula, creating a passage from mainland Eurasia to Hokkaido. North of the Kuril Islands and east of the Kamchatka Peninsula, there is the Aleutian Island chain which connects Eurasia to the American continent. The northern and southern Kuril Islands have a distinct climate and ecology. The most northerly of the Kuril Islands is Shumshu, which is so close to Kamchatka, it almost appears to be part of the peninsula when viewed from space. Other major northern Kuril Islands include Paramushir, Onekotan and Matua, all of whose names have their origin in the Ainu language.

The southern Kuril Islands are made up of the two major islands of Iturup, Kunashir, and the considerably smaller Shikotan and Habaomai islands. The northern Kuril Islands are characterized by a deep mist from mid-April caused by warm damp air meeting cooler air. Their high northern latitude means that night last only a few hours in the summer, and the same is true for daylight in winter. Spring begins as the snows gradually melt away in March and April, and by May the ice on the frozen rivers cracks and thaws as water fowl flock to the islands for the mating season. Though there are no trees on the northern Kurils, bushes and moss thrive and arctic raspberries bear fruit as the sockeye salmon make their way upstream to spawn in June. As with Sakhalin, summer is brief and flowers wilt as early as April and September sees the arrival of light rains that soon turn to snow come October. As the year draws to a close, temperatures in November hover around 1 or 2 degrees celsius (33 farenheit) and daylight in December lasts only six hours.

Under the supervision of the Development Commission and its successor in Nemuro Prefecture (from 1884 onwards), the Ainu of the northern Kuril Islands were uprooted and relocated to islands in the south of the island chain, to prevent them developing further relationships with the Russians. Unlike the Ainu of southern Sakhalin, who had a historical relationship with the Japanese, the Ainu of the northern Kuril Islands had a history of contact with the Russians which went back as far as the 1700s. With the increasing influence of the Russians in the region, most of the northern Kuril Ainu had converted to Russian Orthodox Christianity, and the Russian Alaskan Company had also set up a base on Shumshu Island and even brought Aleutians to the northern Kurils.

With the 1875 Treaty of Saint Petersburg, the northern Kuril Island Ainu found themselves in a predicament. Choosing Russia meant losing their homes, while choosing Japan meant losing their livelihood. No matter what choice an individual was to make, there were friends and family who might choose the alternative. The northern Kuril Ainu were given three years to make their decision. The Aleutians and Ainu who had converted to the orthodox faith on Urup Island decided to move to Russia. Although there had been tensions between the northern Kuril Ainu and the Russians, they were at least an enemy they understood.

On Shumshu Island, there was less unanimity, and on August 1878 the *Genmu*, a steamship that had departed from Hakodate, arrived on the island with Development Commission officials to assess the island to ascertain which citizenship the Shumshu

Ainu desired.

The Development Commission had surveyed Shumshu Island in 1877 and recorded around 70 Ainu living on the island, but with most having chosen Russia, only 22 remained behind. From the northern Kuril Islands, a total of 97 Ainu opted to become Japanese citizens. Unlike the Ainu of Sakhalin, who had been moved to Hokkaido, an island visible with the naked eye from Cape Sōya, the distance between the northern and southern Kuril Islands was too great to easily return, being around 1,300 kilometers. The archaeologist Kitakamae Yasuo (1919-2020) has discovered the burnt remains of Ainu dwellings on Shumshu, either torched by the Ainu themselves knowing they could never return, or by visiting officials.

Finally, in 1884 the Ainu of Shumshu, Paramushir and Rasshua Islands left their homes behind and moved down the island chain, to the flatter verdant islands in the south. The Development Commission and regional successor body Nemuro Prefecture, believed that the Ainu of the northern Kuril Islands would be able to adapt like the Ainu on Iturup, who could speak Japanese and, in some cases, bore children of mixed Wajin and Ainu descent. However, the Ainu of the southern Kuril Islands had the advantage of centuries of contact with Wajin, an experience their northern counterparts lacked. On the way to Shikotan, the new home of the northern Kuril Ainu, the ship stopped at Iturp Island to show them exemplar Ainu. The baron and politician, Yasuba Yasukazu (1835-1899) exclaimed, "It is impossible to distinguish the aboriginals of this port with the mainland Japanese!"[75] Four Ainu alighted at Iturup with the remaining 93 arriving at Shikotan in the early morning of the July 11, 1884. The Ainu on Shikotan were provided with two cows, a calf and fishing and farming equipment. The Ainu celebrated their new home by drinking, dancing and thanking the officials. Once the festivities were over, with the exception of one translator, a doctor and a prefectural bureaucrat, the Nemuro officials returned to Hokkaido.

Although Nemuro Prefecture had created a ten-year plan for the development of the Ainu on Shikotan, centered around agriculture, fishing and cattle, they did not take into account the fact that the northern Kuril Ainu were used to a very different climate and it was difficult to suddenly leave their way of life behind to become farmers.

By October, 1884 the Ainu on Shikotan had built houses in the Japanese style with the help of builders from Nemuro. The Ainu were given rice and attempted to adapt to their new way of life on the island. Yet, within only two months both young and old within the community began to fall ill and die. By 1885, 12 had passed away from disease and malnourishment. The optimism that the Ainu had about starting a new life were soon dashed.

Following an assimilation policy that was carried out throughout Hokkaido, the young of Shikotan were to be reeducated to become more similar to the Wajin. On August 3, 1884, two children aged ten and 11 were sent to Nemuro, and by early December their education began on Shikotan in the office of the Nemuro official.

Despite making efforts to become more like the Wajin by 1889, 22 men and 27 women had passed away in a period of only five years. The deaths of the Kuril Ainu in Shikotan were recorded in the official history as being the result of going from the carefree life of hunting to a well-regulated life of farming, coupled with a lack of exercise, making them vulnerable to disease. The northern Kuril Ainu were vulnerable to endemic diseases that they had had little contact with, and this coupled with constant malnutrition and a lack of knowledge, made life on the island a constant struggle. As with the Sakhalin Ainu, it proved to be a costly mistake to forcibly relocate the northern Kuril Ainu and expect them to adapt well.

The northern Kuril Ainu left behind no records of their experience on Shikotan Island, but there were Europeans who caught glimpses of their life. In 1889, the Englishman Henry James Snow (1848-1915) who was poaching sea otters, recorded that the Ainu on Shikotan longed for their homes and were used to a diet of meat rather than rice and fish. One native of Ushishir Island told Snow that Shikotan was no good for them. Ushishiri Island, on the other hand, was excellent as it had ample sea lions, sea otters and birds.

Another visitor to Shikotan was "Nikolai of Japan", the Russian missionary who had first come to Japan following the opening of Hakodate. He was accompanied by two other clergymen of the Orthodox Church: Metropolitan Sergius and the priest Ignatiy Kato. Their journey to Shikotan is recorded in an account of their Hokkaido travels written by Sergius in 1903.[76] Nikolai, Sergius and Kato visited Shikotan in August of 1898. During this time, the Shikotan Ainu still possessed their Russian names, which they did not renounce until 1910. Sergius recorded that many of the Ainu had tuberculosis and had been cut off from their former homes as well as from the nearby Japanese. Sergius wrote:

> "A Japanese missionary spoke in tears as he told us he saw a great deal of faith in the hearts of these men. They have become spiritual orphans. They are isolated in their village, while most of their relatives have moved to Russia. There are no inhabitants on the neighboring island and what is worse is that there are no Japanese close by either, so that they have no partners to trade with [...]they live in a narrow world and have no

choice but to make do within their village."[77]

While on Shikotan, the three men of faith prayed with the Ainu who were upholding their Orthodox faith. That night, as their boat pulled away from the shore, the three heard cries of "Proshchay!" (farewell). Sergius wondered if the Ainu would be able to survive long on Shikotan Island.

Eventually the Hokkaido Government (from 1886 onwards) could no longer ignore the fact that the resettlement of the northern Kuril Ainu had been an abject failure, and in 1901, a report was published chronicling the affair.[78] There were some voices in the Hokkaido Government which called for the northern Kuril Ainu to be allowed to return, but the dominant opinion was that this would be a step backwards, arguing that hunting was no longer a sustainable means of living and the young had become accustomed to eating a diet of rice and would be unable to readjust to life in the northern Kurils.

Photograph of Kuril Ainu taken in 1903 by the anthropologist Torii Ryūzō (1870-1953)

In 1892, Wajin settlers moved to Shikotan and the combination of the Japanese assimilation policy and a relatively small population meant that the culture of the Kuril Ainu was largely lost to the world over the coming generations. Yet traces still remain. In March 1992, a letter arrived at the Ainu museum in Shiraoi which claimed to be written by the descendants of the Ainu who chose to leave Shumshu island for Russia in 1881. Through the generations, they moved from Shumshu to nearby Petropavlovsk-Kamchatsky and then on through the Russian Empire. This particular family ending up in Poland in 1945. In this way, to a far greater extent than the Hokkaido Ainu, the northern Kuril Ainu and Sakhalin Ainu became scattered to the further reaches of the world.

10

'FORMER ABORIGINALS':
THE AINU IN COLONIAL HOKKAIDO

THE MEIJI restoration transformed Japan from a feudalistic society of samurai, farmers and merchants into a modern industrial power. Like the world's first industrial nation, the United Kingdom, modernization in these islands at the edge of Asia had profound consequences for the neighboring continent. In the United Kingdom, industrialization also brought with it a certain pride, a belief that there was something inherently special about the country. Japan experienced the same shift in sentiments.

With pride came the desire to display the nation's new-found progress, both at home and to the world. Beginning in 1887, a number of exhibitions were held to display the transition of Japan into a modern nations-state. The first of many National Industrial Exhibitions was held in Tokyo in that year, and the exhibition attracted 49,000 attendees. Those that followed became even more popular, attracting growing audiences. Japanese visitors believed they had much to be proud of, that by the end of the 19th Century their relatively small island nation had caught up with the foreign powers who had once threatened them with gunboat diplomacy. As with the industrialized countries of Europe, modernization led to colonization and this, too, was something celebrated in Japan. The Japanese defeat of the neighboring Qing empire and the acquisition of Taiwan in 1895 extended the Japanese sphere of influence further into Asia, and also marked a crucial step in Japan's move onto the world stage as an imperial power. The fifth National Industrial Exhibition attracted over 4,300,000 attendees and took place in Osaka's Tenōji Park. In contrast to the prior exhibitions, Osaka showcased not only industrial developments of the age such as a huge fountain illuminated in five different colors and the Obayashi Tower fitted with an elevator, something many were seeing for the first time, the exhibition also drew crowds to experience the budding jingoism of a nascent empire. Taiwan was not Japan's first colony — the development of Hokkaido can also be seen as a colonial endeavor. But Hokkaido was arguably not Japan's only colony, with the Ryukyu Kingdom having been annexed in 1872 and declared a prefecture in 1879. The kingdom's last king, Shō Tai (1843-1901), was exiled to Tokyo, and thus, a kingdom with its own unique language and culture became part of the Japanese state. While some members of the former Ryukyu court resisted colonization, Japan's defeat of the former superpower in the region, the Qing empire, solidified many Okinawans' opinion that they had a brighter future as part of the region's new superpower.

By the time of the Osaka exhibition, the indigenous peoples of Hokkaido, Okinawa and Taiwan had all become Japanese citizens. The Japanese empire followed the established paradigm of racial hierarchy long espoused in Europe and the Americas, with many Wajin looking down on the 'less civilized races' of the colonies. The Osaka Exhibition featured an anthropological display which was a materialization of such colonial attitudes: living exhibits of Chinese, Korean, Javanese, Indian, Turkish, indigenous peoples of Zanzibar and those closer to home, the indigenous peoples of Taiwan, Hokkaido and Okinawa.

Amongst the thousands of visitors to the Osaka Exhibition,

there were Okinawans who had come to see the success story of their country. Instead, they were shocked to discover that their mainland countrymen did not even view them as true Japanese. This news soon made its way to Okinawa and on the 11th of April a local paper argued, ironically, that the Okinawans should not be placed on the same lowly rank as the savage aboriginals of Hokkaido and Taiwan.

While many Okinawans of the day resented Wajin distinguishing them as a separate minority group, no such protest was forthcoming from the Ainu who attended the exhibition. Unlike the majority of Okinawans, the Ainu had a long history of discrimination from the Wajin and had no expectation of being treated or viewed as their equals. The 12 Ainu who traveled to Osaka were promised funds for the building of a new school in Tokachi. While Okinawans of the era would have balked at being placed on the same social level as the Ainu, but the groups shared many commonalities. Both had been forcibly incorporated into Japan and were made to adjust to life as minorities in the modern nation-state. Many Okinawans had proactively worked to become more 'Japanese' and the Okinawan reaction to the Osaka Exhibition showed how the image of the Ainu as a barbaric and backwards race had even permeated the most southern islands of the Japanese archipelago.

But even during an era in which discrimination was the norm, there were individual human interactions showing people realized their shared humanity. In March of 1825, the Okinawan historian, Iha Fuyū (1902-1929), often referred to as the father of Okinawa Studies, gave two speeches at the Tokyo Ainu School, where he met the Ainu activist Iboshi Hokuto (1902-1929). Like many Wajin, Iha had viewed the Ainu as a primitive people, but he soon realized the error of his ways after meeting Iboshi. He introduced the great work of Okinawan poetry the *Omoro Sōshi* which has much in common with the Ainu epic tales, the *Yukar*. Iha wrote:

"I was deeply moved after hearing Iboshi's lecture. I was told that the Ainu could not even count to five, but my prejudices have been shattered [...] I shook Iboshi's hand and I told him that even though I am from the polar opposite direction of his homeland. Coming from Ryukyu, I understand his feelings more than anyone [...] just as the ancestors of the Ryukyuan's left behind the *Omoro Sōshi*, the ancestors of the Ainu left behind the *Yukar*, both of which are beautiful collections of poetry."[79]

Yet, while Iha was recognizing the uniqueness of the Ainu, the Japanese government was pursuing a policy of assimilation.

While the Tokugawa Shogunate had tried to integrate the Ainu into the Wajin populace, the reforms were lackluster and the Shogunate never really attempted to create a unified Japanese identity amongst the Wajin, yet alone the Ainu, and during this era regional identity with the Daimyō would supersede the Shogunate. It was not until the Meiji Restoration that a modern Japanese state with allegiance to a figurehead, the Emperor, carried with it a national identity as Japanese. Meiji era reforms meant that all Japanese citizens were educated in the same kind of school system, spoke a standard version of Japanese, trained in the same conscript army and read the same newspapers. The Wajin of this era were themselves undergoing tremendous changes, they were becoming more and more aware of themselves as citizens of the Japan nation-state, more modern and more Westernized.

If the Wajin of the Meiji era were being transformed, the Ainu were undergoing all the more change. Under the assimilation policy, beginning in the Meiji era and continuing until 1945, the Ainu were expected to cast aside the supposedly barbarian ways of their ancestors and become more like the Wajin. Under this assimilation policy, the Development Commission quickly set about banning the supposedly barbaric customs of the Ainu. In 1871, *ninkari* earrings and the practice of tattooing were strictly prohibited. In the same year, the Ainu custom of burning the house of the dead to send it to the afterlife along with the deceased was also banned, although this practice had been declining even before 1871. In 1872 came a ban on *Iomante*, the religious festival in which bears were sacrificed to be sent to the realm of the gods.

Laws prohibiting such behavior at first failed to wipe out centuries of traditions, and there is a recorded case of a house burning ceremony being reported to the Shizunai police as late as 1900. In some cases, Ainu culture was even encouraged despite the assimilation policy. In 1885, five Sapporo Prefecture Officials attended an *Iomante* ceremony of bear sacrifice at Chitose, despite the practice being banned by the government, who was employing these very same officials. A sign of the differences between law and practice during this time.

The dissonance between wanting the Ainu to become more like the Wajin, and the desire to preserve parts of Ainu culture as a curiosity were consistent throughout the assimilation era. As with discrimination throughout time and place, it is very rarely, if ever, logical.

Isabella Bird (1831-1904), who visited Japan in 1871, was one of the first Westerners to see the reforms in action. She was generally supportive of the Development Commission, commenting:

> "'Mr. Von Seibold thinks that the officials threaten and knock them (the Ainu) about; and this is possible; but

I really think the [Development Commission] means well by them, and besides removing the oppressive restrictions by which, as a conquered race, they were unfettered, treats them far more humanely and equitably than the US government [...] treats the North American Indians."[80]

Bird's account also provided an insight into how the Ainu in Biratori reacted to the reforms imposed by the Development Commission, on banning of tattoos:

"They expressed themselves as very much grieved and tormented by the recent prohibition of tattooing. They say the gods will be angry, and that the women can't marry unless they are tattooed."[81]

Meiji era reforms went further by changing the very status of the Ainu within society. In 1872 the national family register reclassified the Ainu as commoners along with 97% of the Japanese population. The family register did away with the feudal hierarchy that had existed under the Shogunate, creating a relatively more meritocratic society.

On paper at least, this reclassification of the Ainu should have given Hokkaido's indigenous people a status equal to that of the majority of Wajin. In reality, the Ainu were designated as a subclass within Japanese society with regulations issued by the Development Commission referring to the Ainu as "former aboriginals", a term that had its historical roots in the era of the Shogunate. Prior to increasing contacts with Westerners, the Ainu had been referred to as either "Ezo", "Ezojin" or "Ijin". With the arrival of Matthew Perry and Russian expansion south, the Ainu came to be referred to as "aboriginals", a term which was explicitly chosen to stress that the Ainu were a people inherent to Japan, and not a foreign people that could be annexed.

The family register also gave Japanese citizens surnames, a privilege not granted to prior generations of no rank, but in this, too, there was a difference between the new surnames of Wajin and the Ainu. The officials visited the Ainu *kotans* and assigned Ainu arbitrary names. For example, all the Ainu in Nukibetsu received the surname Kurokawa (黒川) which is a combination of the Chinese characters for "black" and "river", since the corresponding place name in Ainu, *Nupki Pet* means "muddy river". Often the Meiji officials could not distinguish between male and female Ainu given names and so took to writing the men's name in the hiragana script and the women's in katakana.

While never to the extent of the Sakhalin and north Kuril Ainu, many Ainu in Hokkaido were also forcibly moved from land their ancestors had inhabited for centuries. Under two laws in 1872 and 1877, the entirety of land in Hokkaido was designated as being "ownerless", in others words owned by the state.[82] The Ainu's right to land became even more fragile with a law in 1886 which made the "ownerless" land of Hokkaido available for next to nothing for nobles, businessmen with political ties and capitalists.[83] When it was convenient, settlers to Hokkaido drove the Ainu off the most fertile land. Kushiro, Abashiri and Asahikawa are just a few places from where Ainu were moved, a process that was entirely legal under the laws of the era.

In the Hidaka region along the Niikappu and Shizunai rivers, Japanese colonizers seized Ainu settlements 'in the name of the Emperor', on the grounds that they were now imperial domains. Along the Saru river, the Ainu could do little to resist the declaration and were made to move upstream into the mountains of Nukibetsu, 40 kilometres away. They were forced to make do with inferior land to build new homes and attempt to reestablish a livelihood. The ancestors of the Ainu going back to the Jōmon had chosen rivers as locations for settlements precisely because of the natural resources they provided, the ability to use the river to travel and the relatively temperate climate. Higher up in the mountains of Nukibetsu, there is a slower onset of spring and an earlier autumn. Frost arrived two weeks earlier than at their former homes along the Saru river. High in the mountain rivers, no salmon came to spawn and the Saru Ainu were deprived of a vital food source.

Giichi Nomura (1914-2008) the head of the Ainu Association of Hokkaido from 1964 to 1996, reflected that "by 1899 the Ainu had lost all fertile and flat land. The land the Ainu were given in its place was swamps, valleys and mountains [...] in such places how could the Ainu lead lives of stability?"[84]

For the Hokkaido Ainu who were not forcibly relocated, laws which banned hunting and fishing were in many cases a death sentence, and throughout the Meiji era Hokkaido's indigenous people found their means of living gradually becoming outlawed. In 1873, harpoons for catching salmon, *mareks*, were banned, and in 1875 traditional Ainu fishing nets were also prohibited. These laws banning traditional fishing methods made it difficult for the Ainu to live off the land and in 1878 a final blow was dealt when salmon fishing itself was entirely prohibited across all of Hokkaido's rivers. On land, hunting was made increasingly difficult with legislation in 1876 designating that all deer in Hokkaido were off limits with the exception of 600 hunters who were to be given licenses. As with fishing, traditional Ainu means of hunting were banned, with poison arrows being banned the same year and the bow spring trap used to hunt bear, foxes and deer called *amappo* also banned in 1876. These measures made it harder for the Ainu to live through hunting, but failed to stop the practice all together. The bans on hunting and fishing served two purposes, the first was a pretext to civilize the Ainu and encourage their integration into Japanese society. The second was to preserve natural resources, such as fish, which had been decimated by the overfishing of the Wajin. While in Biratori, Isabella Bird wrote:

"Up to about this time the [Ainu] have obtained [meat] by means of poisoned arrows, arrow-traps, and pitfalls, but the Japanese Government has prohibited the use of poison and arrow-traps, and these men say that hunting is becoming extremely difficult, as the wild animals are driven back farther and farther into the mountains by the sound of the guns."[85]

However, the Ainu talking to Bird also remarked that "the eyes of the Japanese Government are not in every place!"[86]

In this new climate, money became an increasingly necessary commodity to survive, and even Ainu who wished to remain apart from capitalism found it difficult to avoid in a modernizing Hokkaido. Laws targeting traditional Ainu means of livelihood in the name of reformation, had deleterious consequences on the Ainu population. The Development Commission banned salmon fishing in the upper stream of the Saru river in 1883, and the following summer many of the Ainu of the Tokachi region suffered from malnutrition and starvation. This man-made disaster caused many Ainu to die, and an influx of Wajin immigrants brought diseases such as gonorrhea, syphilis, trachoma and tuberculosis to the Ainu, who remained particularly vulnerable. As with cultural customs, new laws alone were not enough to prevent them, and what had for centuries been hunting now simply became poaching. When the first Ainu politician in the Japanese Diet, Kayano Shigeru (1926-2006) was a child, he witnessed his father Seitarō being arrested in 1932 for illegal salmon fishing. Kayano records this traumatic experience in his memoir, *A Monument of the Ainu*.[87]

One day a constable arrived at the family home and said only, "Shall we go?" Seitarō sternly replied, "Yes, let's go", his voice remaining firm as he attempted to not let his anxiety be seen by his wife and children. Seitarō had been fishing for salmon and knew precisely why the constable was there. A young Kayano, not fully understanding the situation cried out, "Don't go father! What will we eat if you are gone?" Seitarō turned to his son and attempted to reassure him "Don't worry, I'll be back soon, so don't cry". Despite these words, it was Seitarō who was crying, not the young Kayano. As his father was escorted away, Kayano followed him as far as he could. Seitarō kept looking over his shoulder until his son was out of sight. Kayano stood crying on the road until his mother and the neighbors came to carry him home. Kayano's grandmother and mother of Seitarō said "the *Sisam* (Wajin) didn't create the salmon, my son caught the salmon to offer to the gods and to feed his children, how dare they arrest him."[88]

Following his father's arrest, every day the young Kayano went outside to look in the direction of Biratori, where his father had been taken. There was no sign of his return. After a few days, Kayano turned to his mother and asked "when will father come home?" She did not know, and avoided answering the question. Kayano's father eventually returned home, but this event was certainly traumatic for the young Ainu.

Many Ainu chose to break the new laws banning the catching of salmon, in order to continue to provide for their families. Such laws placed blame on the Ainu for declining fish stocks, yet it was in fact the Wajin who had overfished the salmon. Kayano later reflected: "The *Shamo* (Wajin) who created the law banning fishing were saying to the Ainu, 'die', it was such a law [...] it was as if a mother bird carrying food to her chicks had been beaten to death."[89]

By the late 1880s, it had become evident that the Wajin colonization of Hokkaido had been devastating for the indigenous people. The legislation that was enacted to try to remedy the situation firmly adhered to the belief that the best thing for the Ainu was that they assimilate to the point of being indistinguishable from the majority of Japanese citizens.

In 1899, the Hokkaido Former Aboriginal Protection Act was passed, with the seemingly noble intention of bettering the lot of the Ainu.[90] But this betterment entailed throwing away the traditions and customs of their ancestors. The crux of the Former Aboriginal Act was that the Ainu were to be educated in state schools, learn Japanese and take up farming.

This was not the first time the government had attempted to create a generation of Ainu farmers. An 1871 ordinance stated that the Development Commission would give tools to any Ainu who wished to take up farming, and in 1885 the Ainu of Abashiri were given horses and cows. The 1899 act went further, offering each Ainu family a maximum of five hectares of land on loan from the government. Under this scheme 9,656 hectares were given to Ainu families, but the scheme was not without its shortfalls. It was stipulated that if the land was not successfully cultivated, it was to be returned to the Japanese government. By 1909, only about 45% of land remained in Ainu possession and by 1960, there were very few Ainu farmers. Social Darwinist ideas, that the Ainu were lower on the scale of races and might be cheated out of land if it was given to them, persisted. Ainu also had to obtain permission from the Hokkaido government to sell or purchase land. This made the potential to profit from landownership far more difficult for the Ainu.

Social Darwinist ideas in the Former Aboriginal Act shaped the education for the Ainu, too, and this education changed how a younger generation of Ainu thought about themselves. Many adults were resistant to changing their way of life, but children were far more malleable, and from the viewpoint of the Meiji government, it was vital to create a generation who accepted national norms from a young age. Education was the key.

With the dawn of the Meiji era, education across Japan changed for the Wajin as well as the Ainu, with standardized topics of study, a standardized way of speaking (that of Tokyo) and a rise in nationalist fervor through the 1890 Imperial Rescript on Education. The Imperial Rescript on Education declared that the citizens of Japan:

> "...advance public good and promote common interests; always respect the Constitution and observe the laws; should emergency arise, offer yourselves courageously to the State and thus guard and maintain the prosperity of Our Imperial Throne coeval with heaven and earth."[91]

In short, the aim of national education was to make citizens loyal to the nation-state and induce in them a consciousness as Japanese citizens. Children were expected to memorize the Imperial Rescript on Education and it was read aloud during important days during the school year and national holidays. Modern education began with the establishment of a Department of Education in 1871 and an education system established the following year. In 1880, the Code of Education made education compulsory for three years and in 1886 compulsory education was extended to four years. This education system was extended to Hokkaido in 1892, and Japanese and Ainu were then assigned to the same state schools. However, the tendency was for schools to be built far from *kotans* and there was a reluctance on the part of many parents to send their children to Wajin schools operated by a state they distrusted, so Ainu attendance remained low. The Former Aboriginal Act marked a turning point with Ainu and Wajin children being separated with schools being established exclusively for the Ainu. Education consisted of ethnic culture, Japanese, arithmetic, exercise, and sewing for girls and farming for boys. History, geography and science taught to Wajin children were excluded. In the Ainu-focused schools, the students were to learn and speak in Japanese, and through history, the Ainu could learn about their exploitation and their inferior status. Science and geography were unnecessary as the Ainu were destined to be agricultural laborers who cultivated land in Hokkaido owned by Wajin. It was simply not necessary for them to learn to think critically about the world.

Protests by Wajin teachers working at these schools eventually resulted in Ainu children being allowed to also study previously prohibited subjects from 1908 onwards. The education in the Ainu schools also followed the Imperial Rescript on Education, including the placement of a portrait of the Meiji Emperor called a *Goshinei* before which the children were to pledge allegiance every day. The portrait was often housed in a special building separate from the school called the *Hōanden*. In 1901, under the provisions of the Former Aboriginal Protection Act, a ten-year plan was created which culminated in the building of 21 schools for the Ainu by 1912, with the first being built in Biratori in 1901.

The study of the Japanese language was the cornerstone of the Ainu schools curriculum, and for the first generation it was a struggle for them to learn such a foreign language. In some cases, when Ainu children failed to perform adequately in their memorization of Japanese, the frustrated teachers would yell "*bakamono!*" (idiot), to which the struggling student attempting to copy the teacher's Japanese returned "*bakamono!*" serving only to further infuriate the teacher. Kayano, whose father underwent such an experience, remarked that one could not help but laugh at such a story, even when one knows there was nothing humorous about the educational practices in such segregated schools.

The assimilation of the Ainu via education was of such great importance that the government committed to building a new school every year, providing that the village where the school would be built had at least 30 or more eligible children to attend. Despite the government's zeal, many Ainu parents were still understandably reluctant to send their children to the schools and only about one third of eligible children attended. To remedy this situation, in 1916, four years of elementary education were made compulsory for Ainu children. Social Darwinist views persisted and the compulsory four years was still less than the six years of elementary level education for Wajin children.

The Japanese government viewed the policy as a success. In 1901, the Hokkaido Government recorded only 44.6% of Ainu children attending school, but by 1910 this number had shot up to over 92%. As the schools were founded on the principle that the Ainu were inferior beings, criticism came from not only the Ainu community but also from many Wajin teachers who worked within the schools, culminating in the *de jure* abolishment of segregated schools in 1922. Regardless, it took until 1937 for the education of Ainu and Wajin children to become fully integrated throughout Hokkaido.

Despite the general view that assimilation was best for the Ainu, there was a dissonance within such ways of thinking. It was expected that the Ainu would embrace the Wajin ways in their language, eating habits and customs, but there were also acknowledgements within Japanese society that there was value in preserving parts of Ainu culture. This contradiction can be seen in the memoir of one Wajin, Mr. Iwano who travelled Hokkaido with officials from the Hokkaido Government in 1909. Seeing the assimilation policy as not going far enough, he wrote:

"The policy of the Hokkaido government is wrong. Since the Ainu are living things, it is all right to give them a piece of land for a living. Why should anyone waste his effort on an inferior race whose extinction is marked? What is the purpose of educating them? Even though a few of them may achieve something, it is not desirable to have them mix with Wajin to produce hybrids. In my opinion, it is sufficient to keep them alive like livestock [...] however, we must preserve the things that the Ainu race need to leave behind [...] (the) language the Ainu speak and the literature the Ainu have. Although Greece and Rome perished, their literature has been preserved."[92]

While not all Wajin took such a discriminatory approach to the preservation of Ainu culture, this way of thinking remained the trend until the post-war era. Discrimination from wider society led some Ainu to place further value on their heritage, and others to try and cast it off. Others still, would go through both these phases.

In the face of discrimination, numerous Ainu women had little choice but to integrate into Wajin society in Hokkaido, many marring Wajin men. Some Ainu men also sought to hide their backgrounds for fear of discrimination. Tsukamoto Kenichi, who was born to an Ainu father and Wajin mother in the Taishō period (1912-1926), recalled how his father, who had tried to keep his own identity secret, descended into alcoholism when his Ainu background was discovered by his wife and never recovered. Tsukamoto's father, Hashimoto Kenichi had paid off the debts of his wife's family in Aomori, and her older sister had also come to Hokkaido. It was during a wedding reception for her sister many years later, that a classmate from his school days recognized

Hashimoto and called him an "Ainu bear", just as the Wajin children had teased during their school days. When Hashimoto responded angrily, the former classmate said only: "Why are you getting angry, you are an Ainu bear aren't you? What's wrong with me saying it."[93]

With his father's secret discovered, Hashimoto's wife abandoned her children and left him, saying, "If I knew you were an Ainu I would have never married you."[94]

Tsukamoto's mother returned to Honshu and his father's descent into alcoholism resulted in him and his younger sister being entrusted to their grandparents.

Tsukamoto, like other Ainu of this time, would experience discrimination throughout his life. For Tsukamoto this led to resentment of his grandparents, particularly while he was at school, although his sister would defend them. Seeking a chance to escape, when Tsukamoto and his sister were offered work on a neighboring farm owned by the Suzuki family, he jumped at the opportunity. Tsukamoto's grandfather protested, saying the land the Suzukis owned was stolen from the Ainu. Regardless, Tsukamoto and his younger sister began working there, he performing manual labor and she caring for the younger children. This period came to an end for the siblings when the Suzuki's son stole some money and placed the blame on Tsukamoto. The truth was later revealed, and the Suzuki's offered Tsukamoto a chance to resume his employment. But after being treated as so expendable, Tsukamoto balked at such an insult. Around this time, he began listening to his grandfather's stories about hunting and, captivated, urged his grandfather to teach him. As his grandfather was bed-ridden, he began hunting with a friend of his grandfather's.

However, the customs of this generation of Ainu would not be enough to help the standards of living for the current generation of Ainu. On one occasion, the friend's daughter, Kazuko, and later Tsukamoto's wife, told him that he had to study to get ahead in the world, and urged him to move to Sapporo and take up an apprentice role in a shop she operated.

Tsukamoto, able to speak from his own experience, replied, that "even if the Ainu study they will just be used by the Wajin, I don't want to work below a detestable Wajin. Being a hunter is much better."[95]

Kazuko explained to Tsukamoto that the world had changed and what was possible for his grandfather and her father's generation was not possible for them. Kazuko told Tsukamoto of Ainu who had made a success of life in Wajin Hokkaido, giving the example of an Ainu soldier, a private first-class who would come to the shop. His Wajin subordinates would have to ask permission to drink tea or eat sweets that had been provided, and it was they who left the shop carrying the goods for the Ainu commander. This provided impetus for Tsukamoto to study and he would later work numerous jobs in Hokkaido, before heading to the Japanese colony of Manchukuo (Manchuria, northeast China).

With Japan's opening up to the world, Westerners also began to take an increasing interest in the Ainu, in some cases based on the misconception that the Ainu were a Caucasian race and therefore worthy of protection, a theory that was later debunked. Individuals such as Isabella Bird, who wrote about travels in Hokkaido in her 1880 book, *Unbeaten Tracks in Japan*, the Anglican Missionary John Batchelor (1855-1944) and Scottish physician Neil Gordon Munroe (1863-1942) all wrote extensively about the Ainu, highlighting their existence to a wider world. The observations of these writers contained plenty of misconceptions, but their books played a significant role in increasing global knowledge of the Ainu people. But while numerous Wajin and Westerners saw value in preserving Ainu culture during an age of assimilation, it was the Ainu themselves who did the most to preserve their culture.

On a number of occasions, members of the Japanese royal family visited the Ainu in Hokkaido, including the head of the new nation-state, the Meiji Emperor (1852-1912) in 1881. Yet these visits took place against the backdrop of the state's policies actively discouraging the Ainu from continuing their traditions. The Meiji Emperor visited the town of Shiraoi, not far from Muroran, south of Sapporo, and witnessed a faux *Iomante* ceremony, in which the ceremony was adapted so that no bear was killed. At the time of the Emperor's visit, Shiraoi was a small town of 655 residents, 498 of whom where Ainu. The Emperor's visit took place 13 years after the Meiji Restoration and before the instigation of the Former Aboriginal Act. Most of the Ainu in Shiraoi had grown up during a period when it was not necessary or even desirable to speak Japanese and at the time of the Emperor's visit, many of the Shiraoi Ainu could only understand their mother tongue. They were the last of their kind, with successive generations of Shiraoi Ainu speaking Japanese in daily life as a result of the assimilation policy.

Part of the nation building of the Meiji oligarchs involved publicizing the Emperors official visits across the nation, and reporting on the Meiji Emperor's visit to Shiraoi made the town and its Ainu inhabitants known throughout the country. Other members of the imperial family followed, with visits to Shiraoi in 1911 from the chamberlain of the Taisho Emperor (1879-1926), in 1918 from Prince Kanin Nomiya, Princess Kikuko Takamatsu (1911-2004) in 1928, Prince Takahito Mikasa (1915-2006) in 1932 and Prince Nagahisa Kitashirakawa (1910-1940) in 1934. Like everywhere throughout Hokkaido, the Wajin population over these years had dramatically increased, and by 1932, of a population of over 6,000, the Ainu only made up 860. Regardless of rising Wajin immigration, Shiraoi maintained its reputation as the place to go to see traditional Ainu, and by the end of the 1920s until 1935, *Iomante* ceremonies were being explicitly held for tourists. During the early Showa era (1926-1989), many Ainu men from Shiraoi went to work away from home as fisherman between June and September. But they still struggled to make ends meet as they had to bear the expense of renting boats and fishing equipment from Wajin owners. For the Ainu of this era, it was difficult to turn to farming since what had been deemed uncultivated land had been given primarily to Wajin colonizers. The Shiraoi Ainu took to providing for themselves and their families by growing daikons in the summer and cutting ice from Lake Poroto in winter.

In the midst of these financial hardships, tourism proved to be a welcome business opportunity. The Wajin headmaster of the Shiraoi Second Elementary School, Yamamoto Gisaburō, played a role in promoting Ainu culture during this period. Yamamoto was a member of the Shiraoi Aboriginal Society, formed in 1871 with the aim of providing the Ainu of Shiraoi with shared bath houses, street lights along the coast and a savings union.[96] Yamamoto had a central role in the organization and Ainu leaders and officials of the Shiraoi Women's Association frequently visited his office for advice. When royalty visited Shiraoi, it was Yamamoto who arranged for the school hall to be used for Ainu showcase dances. He was struck by the potential for a wider tourism business in Shiraoi, and he raised the possibility of further monetizing tourism. Ironically, Yamamoto, who supported the local Ainu and encouraged adults to display the unique culture of the Shiraoi to the upper echelons of Japanese society, also taught at a school which followed the assimilation policy. He reflected the many contradictions of the age, seeing value in the Ainu and at the same time working for a state which sought to gradually assimilate them so that they would be indistinguishable from the Wajin.

11

WESTERN ENCOUNTERS WITH THE AINU

THE LATE 19TH and early 20th centuries were also a time when many Westerners outside of Japan were first introduced to the Ainu. The 1904 Louisiana Purchase Exposition in St Louis and the 1910 Japan-British exhibition in London were an opportunity for ordinary British and Americans to meet Ainu for the first time. Through the aid of the British missionary John Batchelor in Hokkaido and the Chicago University anthropologist Fredrick Star (1858-1933), it was arranged for four Ainu men, three Ainu women and two baby girls to visit St Louis, and a traditional Ainu house, a *chise,* was transported and rebuilt there. Like Japan, the United States was also eager to show off its new colonies. The US had acquired the Philippines in 1898, and the exposition included 'Philippine villages' of ethnic groups in the Philippines such as the Igorots and the Moro people. The Ainu at the exhibition spent their days creating handicrafts, with men making carvings such as spoons and tobacco boxes and the women weaving. The Ainu handicrafts sold very well to the American visitors. Some of the curious Americans trampled over cultural boundaries, as when one barged in to the Ainu *chise* without permission to gain a closer look at the Ainu. One Mr. Alison who was looking after the Ainu attempted to usher them out. A woman exclaimed that she wanted to see what the Ainu were doing, to which Mr. Alison curtly replied that the Ainu had come to teach the Americans some manners.

The Ainu were met with a similar degree of curiosity in London. The 1910 Japan-British exhibition was held from May 14 to October 29 to celebrate the 1902 Anglo-Japanese Alliance. Japan made use of the event to show off the various peoples in its colonial empire, erecting Taiwanese, Korean and Ainu pavilions in London. Three *chise* were reconstructed and ten Ainu were sent — four women, five men and one baby. Unlike in St Louis, the *chise* constructed in London were only loosely based on reality. Two thatched towers ran between the two *chise*, something never seen in any Hokkaido *kotan*.

The Ainu and Taiwanese villages were part of a larger Japanese exhibition which included a Japanese garden and women serving tea. The Ainu village occupied about 3,000 square meters while the Taiwan village occupied about 10,000 square meters. British newspapers described the Ainu as "Tolstoyesque", and as having occupied a similar historical position with the Japanese as did the Britons to the Saxons. The first was likely a reference to Tolstoy's long beard as well as his asceticism and spiritualism. The second reference to just how the Anglo-Saxons had displaced the Britons, pushing them further into Great Britain's interior, the Japanese had displaced the Ainu.

The Daily News described the Ainu as a "vanishing people", comparing them to the Native Americans. As with the Native Americans, this was by no means an inevitable process, however. The views of contemporary papers reflected the views of the time and an empire that saw its own, stronger races as dominating what it deemed the lesser peoples of the world.

The difference between the British and Japanese reporting also reveals much about the two nations' way of thinking about the Ainu. When English materials were translated into Japanese, sections describing the Ainu as "the indigenous people of Japan" were deleted. A *Daily News* piece had called the Ainu "the politest people on earth", but when it was translated for the Japanese magazine *Taiyō*, it was rewritten as , "the most *obedient* people on earth." It was all part of the assimilation and nationalization policy which saw the Ainu as merging with the Wajin with a subservience to the state under the figurehead of the Emperor.

The Ainu in London became even more famous when Queen Mary (1867-1953) and King George V (1865-1936) visited the Ainu village. Additionally, in 1910 a baby was born which the papers proclaimed was "the first Ainu baby born in Europe".[97]

While both the Americans and British viewed the Ainu with a degree of ignorance, the curiosity of the visitors sparked a brief interest in the history and culture of the Ainu and led the Ainu who had participated in such exhibitions to re-evaluate their culture in a period when their home country's assimilation policy encouraged them to cast it aside.

There were also Europeans who tried to better the lot of the Ainu within Hokkaido, most notably the Church Mission Society, which was founded in London in 1799. Almost a century after the Mission Society's foundation, missionary work began in Japan and Reverend George Ensor was the first missionary sent, arriving at Nagasaki in 1869. In Hokkaido, the first missionary was Reverend Walter Dening (1846-1913) who arrived in the summer of 1874. Dening saw an opportunity that other Western nations had largely neglected: the conversion of Hokkaido's indigenous Ainu. In 1876, Dening received permission from the Church Mission Society to study the Ainu language and he departed for Biratori where the Ainu chief Hiramura Penriuk (1833-1903) cordially greeted him, offering Dening the opportunity to stay in his *chise*. Dening spent a month at the Ainu *kotan* in Biratori where he tried to learn the fundamentals of the Ainu language in order to propagate the Anglican teachings.

Penriuk was conscious of the difference between the wealthier Europeans and the plight of the Ainu, when Dening told the chief that there was only a single all-powerful god, Penriuk replied, "If the God who made you made us, how is it that you are so different – you so rich, we so poor?"[98]

The visit to Biratori was a success for Dening. This, in turn, led others in the Church Mission Society to realize the opportunity of proselytizing to the Ainu, such as the young missionary John Batchelor who later opened the first Ainu school in Porobetsu. By 1906, the society had over ten schools for the Ainu throughout Hokkaido. The Hakodate Ainu Training School was exemplary as it aimed to teach Ainu how to preserve their traditions and heritage for the future, something that was in dire need due to the Meiji government's colonialist policies, displacing the Ainu from their lands and encouraging them to adopt Japanese customs.

The Hakodate school opened its doors in 1893 with Charles Nettleship (1858-1928) taking up the mantle as the school's headmaster. Nettleship was born in Stratford, London and came to Japan via New Zealand. He worked as an English teacher in Tokushima in Shikoku before moving on to the Ainu mission at Porobetsu. With the opening of the Hakodate school, Nettleship baptized 14 children to be admitted to the school, though Nettleship received criticism from some within the society as he had never received a formal education at a seminary. The Hakodate school filled an important education gap: there were no state-run schools for Ainu in this period. The school had considerable success and by 1898, 60% of Anglicans in Hokkaido were Ainu.

Despite the Mission Society's good intentions, when the school officially opened in 1893 there was no building, land, stationary or food for the students. Donations from the Japanese,

British and even from some Ainu were collected which allowed the school to become a reality. The curriculum was intense, offering more than contemporary schools of the period. Students were woken at quarter to six in the morning to begin morning prayers and finished their day at nine at night. A typical week at the school included three hours of studying the Old Testament, five hours studying the New Testament, two hours of prayer books, ten hours of Japanese study, three hours of Ainu language study and five hours of mathematics. This book-based learning was coupled with the study of botany and practical skills of raising crops.

The school offered Ainu youth a chance to better themselves through education and students came from as far away as Kushiro, some 300 miles away. Other students came from Hakodate as well as other locations where the Church Mission Society was preaching throughout Hokkaido. By 1895, the school had 21 students of whom 19 were boys, and two were girls. Of this number, 14 had been baptized into the Anglican church. Of particular note is the student Matsu Kannari (1875-1961), a storyteller of *Yukar* (Ainu epics of the gods) who later went on to adopt the daughter of her sister Chiri Yukie (1903-1922). Chiri went down in history for creating the *Ainu Mythology*: the first book in the Ainu language, written in the Roman alphabet alongside Japanese. The school played a role in preserving the Ainu cultural legacy, but this came to an end to an end as a result of an 1899 ordinance by the Meiji government which forbade religious teachings in schools, and the discriminatory Hokkaido Former Aboriginals Protection Act which created separate schools for Ainu, forcing the school to close by 1906.

Of the British who came to Hakodate through the Church Mission Society, the aforementioned John Batchelor left a particularly enduring legacy. He was the first to establish a school for the Ainu and a forerunner in preserving Ainu culture. He at times was known as the 'The Father of the Ainu', and his work encouraged many Ainu to take pride in their culture and heritage.

Batchelor was born in 1854, 19 days before the signing of the Convention of Kanagawa, in the English county of Sussex, the sixth child of an 11-brother family. In his early 20s, Batchelor was working as a gardener when he happened to meet a missionary returned from India. This missionary spoke about the rewards of his work and adventures in India. The young Batchelor was entranced by tales of exotic lands and by the chance to live a life of purpose. With six other zealous youths, the 23-year-old Batchelor set sail for the British colony of Hong Kong on September 22, 1876. After 50 days of traversing the Atlantic, Mediterranean and Indian oceans, Batchelor arrived and enrolled at St Paul's College to begin his missionary training. Misfortune soon struck him: in the sub-tropical climate, Batchelor fell ill to malaria, forcing him to suspend his studies. It was while bedridden, sweating in the humid weather, that he caught word of northern Japan's temperate climate. Someone even told him the Hokkaido climate resembled that of the British Isles. After his recovery, Batchelor quickly left Hong Kong on May 31, 1877 and arrived in Yokohama a week later. In Yokohama, Batchelor spent ten days with the Church Mission Society before leaving aboard a freight ship on July 16, bound for Hakodate. Upon his arrival in Hakodate, the Church Mission Society assigned him to the senior missionary Walter Dening, so that he might learn the ropes of missionary work in the recently-opened port city. Batchelor settled in Motomachi, which had become the city's foreign settlement, and he began diligently studying Japanese.

Within his first year in Hakodate, Batchelor's Japanese had improved enough for him to make friends with locals his own age. One particular event during this time changed the course of the young Englishman's life. Walking through Hakodate, Batchelor happened to cross paths with two Ainu, who had come to sell bear hides and meat in the city. Amongst the cosmopolitan and increasingly Westernized Hakodate residents, these Ainu seemed to hark back to a lost age: they carried bows, wore boots of deer hide and had long hair down to their shoulders. It was Batchelor's first encounter with Ainu culture. The Ainu told him they were from Biratori *kotan* and since he was asking so many questions of them why did he not visit Biratori himself? The young Batchelor, clean-shaven and dressed in a suit, would have made sharp contrast with the two Ainu in the streets of Hakodate, although in his later years and after decades of dedication to improving the lot of the Ainu, Batchelor too grew a long beard not dissimilar from the two Ainu he first met in Hakodate.

Batchelor took the Ainu up on their offer, and left in search of an Ainu *kotan*. Biratori remained too far into Hokkaido's interior for Batchelor to access with his current means, but he soon departed by horse-drawn carriage for Mori *kotan*, 40 kilometers north of Hakodate. Much to his disappointment, he arrived to discover that most of the Ainu in Mori had already adopted Japanese customs. Unknown to Batchelor, hundreds of Ainu there had died due to their low immunity to diseases carried by Japanese migrants to Hokkaido. The period 1807 to 1854 saw the biggest decrease in Ainu in the southern Kuril Islands and Hokkaido, with an estimated 74% decline in the Ainu population.

Batchelor traveled further north to Otoshibe *kotan* where he was delighted to find 107 Ainu who still held onto many of their traditional customs. During that visit, he learnt his first Ainu words, father (*Mici*), mother (*Unu*), house (*Chise*), and woman (*Menoko*). Even here, it was evident to Batchelor that the Ainu's culture was rapidly fading away, with Japanese outnumbering the Ainu four to one. Longing to go to Biratori *kotan*, Batchelor succeeded in persuading the elder Dening to take him along to Biratori upon his return to Hakodate. In the early spring of 1879, Dening and Batchelor set off from Hakodate and about halfway to Biratori stopped at Usu *kotan* where Batchelor met Mukai Tomizō. Mukai became a close confidant of Batchelor, so much so that Batchelor went on to adopt his daughter, Yaeko, later in life. After nearly three months at Usu *kotan*, Batchelor had improved his proficiency of the Ainu language and the pair left for the final leg of their journey.

In the 19th Century, on his way to explore Sakhalin, the explorer Mamiya Rinzō passed through Biratori, and reported there were 140 Ainu households with roughly 1,500 Ainu living there. Today, Biratori is 40 kilometers from the port city of Tomakomai and has one of the highest concentrations of Ainu in Hokkaido. When the two missionaries arrived in Biratori, chief Penriuk warmly greeted them. The chief was so delighted with Batchelor's enthusiasm that he kissed his hands. Batchelor soon made a reputation for himself amongst the Ainu of Biratori, from chief all the way down to the children. As Batchelor and Dening had come to the Biratori *kotan*, the Ainu children mischievously ran around shouting " *hūre-sisam*" (red foreigner). The fact that both the young Batchelor and Dening were clean-shaven made them stand out amongst the great bearded Ainu men.

Batchelor soon acquainted himself with the Ainu children, on one occasion pulling out a red handkerchief and saying in Ainu "Do you say *hūre-sisam* because my face is as red as this?"[99]

The children were startled that he could speak Ainu and Batchelor successfully won them over with his humor. Batchelor built a cordial relationship with Penriuk to the extent that the chief even allowed him to build an annex onto his *chise* to use for missionary work.

Due to Batchelor's popularity and his success at making inroads with the Ainu of Biratori, the Church Mission Society made Batchelor a layman and granted him a salary in 1879, two years after his arrival in Hakodate. Batchelor's greatest missionary breakthrough came on June 17, 1893 when Chief Penriuk agreed to allow himself, his wife and his daughter to be baptized by Batchelor. Since Penriuk was held in high regard as Biratori's chief, this paved the way for further baptisms and in the same year, 132 Ainu women were also baptized. While many Ainu men did not convert, they had no qualms about allowing their wives or children to do so.

With an increased number of Christians in Biratori, the Ainu began talking about the possibility of establishing a church. At first, Batchelor petitioned the Church Mission Society to allocate funds for the building of an Ainu church in Biratori, but the Society informed him that no funds were available. Batchelor concluded that his only choice was to provide the money himself and took out a 400 dollar loan (equivalent to over 10,000 dollars in 2020) to finance its construction. After Batchelor secured funding, the local Ainu cleared the land of trees and Japanese constructors built the church. The first Ainu Anglican church was completed in 1894.

Batchelor's missionary and social work touched the hearts of many of his contemporaries but it was not his only legacy— his research on the Ainu language is also a rich academic record. In 1889, after years of practicing Ainu and particularly with the help of chief Penriuk, Batchelor published 'An Ainu-English-Japanese Dictionary and Grammar', a 20,000-word introduction to the Ainu language, the first of its kind. It was a success and a second edition was published in 1905, a third in 1916 and fourth in 1938. With each edition, Batchelor revised his work, creating a more comprehensive volume.

Batchelor's fascination with the Ainu language came at a

crucial time in history when the Ainu were being encouraged to forget their own language and learn Japanese instead. Batchelor prompted academic interest both in Japan and abroad, and the numerous schools he founded throughout his life encouraged Ainu to take pride in their native language.

While Batchelor's Ainu dictionary was the first of its kind, it was not without its flaws. One scholar of the Ainu language, Nakagawa Hiroshi, has commented that Batchelor mixed up words from the Saru and Porobetsu dialects in his compilations. There are differences in the dialects not reflected in Batchelor's work, which is therefore not considered comprehensive. For example, the word for Gods (*Kamuy*) is the same in all Ainu dialects, but the word for wind is *Rera* in all Ainu dialects except for the Karafuto dialect, which is *Reera*. In particular, colors have a large degree of variation across dialects. In the majority, blue is *Siwnin*, in the Saru dialect, the word *Ōhopetiro* (meaning: the color of a deep river) can be used alongside *siwnin*, but in the Bihoro dialect the word *suynin* is used for blue (meaning: the color of the sky and ocean). Nevertheless, the work, examined within its historical context, is commendable as a forerunner in the research of Ainu language. As for Batchelor's proficiency in the Ainu language, the granddaughter of the chief of Kawakami *kotan*, Sunazawa Kura remarked:

> "since my grandfather was chief, many foreigners came to visit him and Batchelor always visited when he came to Asahikawa [...] Batchelor understood the spirit of the Ainu, and he spoke Ainu as good as any Ainu. I've met many researchers studying the Ainu language, none could speak as well as Batchelor."[100]

Following his success in Biratori, Batchelor continued to

conduct missions throughout the Ainu *kotans*. By 1896, he had established Anglican churches in Biratori, Porobetsu, Usu, and Sapporo. In these four churches, Batchelor added signage saying 'Ainu Church' in addition to 'Anglican Church'. This infuriated some Japanese Anglicans who believed that the Ainu should be assimilated into Japan's Wajin majority. In a petition presented to a Hakodate Church Mission Society meeting in August 1896, the accusers condemned Batchelor, arguing that there was no such thing as Ainu since all people in Japan were Japanese subjects. Furthermore, it was an insult to the government of Japan to say that Ainu was a living language, let alone write a version of the Bible in Ainu, as Batchelor had done. Batchelor responded that if the Ainu language was dead, why did the Tokyo Imperial University teach courses in the language? And why on his passport had the Japanese government granted him status as a researcher of the Ainu language?

On January 2, 1892, he moved to an old two-story printing shop in Sapporo that happened to have been built on the location of the last Ainu chief of Sapporo before he was driven out.[101] For Batchelor, Sapporo was a more convenient location than Hakodate, being closer to numerous Ainu *kotans*. From summer to autumn 1891, the 29-year-old Batchelor toured the *kotans* of Chitose, Kurshiro, Abashiri, Akkeshi and Usu to preach about the danger of alcohol abuse — a blight on many indigenous communities around the world. Wajin had for centuries used alcohol as one of the main products of trade with the Ainu and the difficulties of adapting to a changing world led many, men in particular, to turn to alcohol.

On the land next to Batchelor's home, he commissioned the construction of a *chise* as the Ainu Hospital Rest House. Since Batchelor lacked experience as a clinician he relied on clinicians in Sapporo volunteering. On the institution's opening, five

Ainu were admitted and the head of Sapporo Hospital, Sekiba Fujihiko, conducted the examinations of the patients. By 1896, Batchelor had hired a nurse to work in the institution. The good work of the institution was such that news soon spread and Ainu came from far and wide to be diagnosed and treated. Batchelor had funded the Ainu Hospital Rest House out of his own pocket but in May 1896, he convinced the Church Mission Society to fund the upkeep of the institution.

Following its opening, around 2,000 Ainu visited the institution in Sapporo and Batchelor came to realize that the alcohol problem must be solved for the Ainu to increase their standing within Japanese society. On February 4, 1892 he held a lecture on the Ainu in which 400 people participated. During the lecture a domestic employee of Batchelor, Parapita, held a performance about the origins of the Ainu and their customs and why alcoholism was causing a decrease in the Ainu population. Parapita spoke in Ainu with Batchelor translating into Japanese. Batchelor concluded the lecture with a speech about the life of the Ainu, their language and the impetus to protect them. For many of the attendees, this was something they had simply never considered.

The event was such a success that a second lecture was scheduled the following week. Between March and April of 1892 Parapita, Batchelor and his wife held ten lectures throughout Tokyo, Osaka and Kobe which over 4,000 people attended. While the lectures were a success, Batchelor was eventually forced to close the Ainu Rest Hospital in spite of its increasing popularity, when the Russo-Japanese war broke out in 1904, the cost of supplies soared and even the Church Mission Society could not keep the operation afloat.

In 1906, Batchelor adopted a 22-old girl, Yaeko (1884-1962), who he had baptized at the age of eight. Yaeko was the daughter of the Ainu Mukai Tomizō and Hutchise. When her father Mukai passed away when Yaeko was 11, Batchalor took up the responsibility as her carer. There were no laws to register adoption at the time and even in Batchelor's home, the United Kingdom, such laws were not introduced until 1926. But an adoption contract was signed at the Anglican church in Sapporo with Yaeko's mother in attendance. The Batchelors treated Yaeko as if she were their own flesh and blood, and she accompanied the couple on trips to preach at Ainu *kotans* and even on a tour of Karafuto in 1912, the Japanese territory in Sakhalin following the conclusion of the Russo-Japanese war.

In the spring of 1909, Batchelor, Louisa and Yaeko left Hokkaido for a yearlong sojourn in England. On the day of their departure the *Hokkaido Shimbun* newspaper ran the headline "World famous scholar of the Ainu, John Batchelor goes back home for the first time in 30 years." They sailed from Otaru port to Vladivostok and then rode the Siberian railway to Europe and on to London. Having arrived in the UK, Batchelor received a letter from his friend and Hokkaido University Professor, Miyabe Kingo (1860-1951) saying that the Meiji Emperor had bestowed upon Batchelor the Orders of the Sacred Treasure for his long years of service researching the Ainu language and culture. Batchelor received the order at a ceremony at the Japanese embassy in London. The bestowing of the order on Batchelor once again captured the dissonance of the age — on one hand, the assimilation policy encouraged the Ainu to forsake their past and culture and on the other, Batchelor was recognized precisely for his work in attempting to improve the conditions of the Ainu people and prevent the loss of their unique cultural heritage.

Their time in London brought to light some interest in Hokkaido's indigenous people. At Lambeth Palace, the Archbishop of Canterbury designated Batchelor Arch Deacon for the Anglican Church in Hokkaido, making Batchelor the only Anglican Deacon in Japan. The Archbishop also took the hands of Yaeko and placed them upon her head, saying: "May God bless the Ainu". Batchelor and Yaeko also embarked on a speaking tour to educate the British people about the Ainu. Yaeko spoke in Japanese and Batchelor translated. On occasion, members of the audience were bought to tears with mothers hugging their children after listening to the plight of the Ainu people. Like her father, Yaeko continued the work of preserving Ainu culture, publishing a collection of poems entitled *"For the Young Ainu"*.[102] After one year in England, the group returned to Japan in April of 1910.

By the mid-1930s, tolerance within Japanese society for any form of criticism was in sharp decline. With the fog of war, Batchelor began to notice changes in Japanese society. In an entry in his journal on the August 30, 1938 Batchelor lamented how unjustified the Japanese invasion of China had been. With war on the horizon, Batchelor concluded that the world was descending into chaos: "Lord help us clear the skies. Every country seems to be falling into darkness."

Batchelor was astounded to find that Japanese people, from schoolteachers to Christian pastors, were calling Japan's aggression in Asia a "holy war". In an increasingly censored environment Batchelor could do little to speak out, as any form of criticism was deemed unpatriotic. Also in 1938, Batchelor was compelled to make two radio broadcasts on June 6 and October 15, in which he said that Western powers criticizing Japan's war in Asia simply did not understand the matter and that Japan had no need of Western "reason" or "morals". Batchelor's journal entries show he believed none of this.

Gradually, all the missionaries of the Church Mission Society returned to the UK, leaving Batchelor and his niece Florence.

Sensing the situation might deteriorate even further, they left Sapporo on November 17, 1940 and the following month boarded the *Ajia-Maru* at Yokohama, bound for Vancouver.

Even in such dire circumstances, the 87 seven-year-old Batchelor intended to return to Japan once the war died down, but his hopes were dashed when in 1941 Japan attached Pearl Harbor, forcing the US into the war, with the UK also declaring war on Japan, and Batchelor reluctantly made his way to England. He passed away one year before the conclusion of the war, and was buried in his hometown of Uckfield in Sussex.

Despite his passing, Batchelor was not forgotten and remains a popular figure often remembered fondly as the "Father of the Ainu". In 1974, a fund-raising campaign was started in which Ainu from Biratori contributed tens of thousands of yen to establish a monument to Batchelor in Uckfield.[103]

After spending 64 years of his life working for the betterment of the Ainu, increasing militarization prompted Batchelor to leave those who had become so dear to him and the place that had become his home.

PART 3

1945 to the Present Day

HOKKAIDO

12

Hokkaido and World War II

By February 1945, Japan's prolonged war in Asia had led to hundreds of thousands sacrificing their lives for the empire. The propaganda line utilized to justify the war was that the Japanese Empire was building an Asia Co-Prosperity Sphere and freeing oppressed Asians from their European colonizers, but in reality, the Western hierarchical structures remained, with Japanese ranked higher than their new colonial subjects.

While the Japanese offensive began with numerous successes, from the attack on China in 1937, through the occupation of most of Southeast Asia and the Pacific in late 1941 and 1942, an expensive war dragging out over the years took its toll on Japan proper. As the war raged on, rations began to dwindle on the home front and air raids leveled cities, killing thousands of civilians and making tens of thousands homeless.

In 1944, the Americans captured Guam and Saipan and began a campaign with local guerillas to recapture the Philippines. At home, there was a shortage of young men to send to the front lines and a shortage of able workers within Japan. Recruitment for the armed forces was of the utmost importance to the preservation of the Empire, and one February day in the final year of the war, a representative from the Imperial Japanese Army arrived in the Ainu village of Nibutani in northern Hokkaido.

The villagers gathered outside in the snow to hear the announcement: "Japan needs new weapons," he paused, his eyes surveying the young men of Nibutani. "You will clutch bombs in your hands and charge at the enemy [...] Each one of you will become a new weapon. Those who can, raise your hands."[104]

Such a speech aimed to encourage the young men to take up arms and if need be, capture the spirit of *Gyokusai*, a word in which the characters mean 'smashed jewel' – signifying an honorable death without surrender. *Gyokusai* propaganda reached such a peak in 1944 that the military administration announced the "death of the one hundred million", requiring civilians to commit mass suicide or fight to the death against any hostile invaders who dared to venture onto Japanese soil. *Gyokusai* cast a long shadow over the final months of the war. Infamous examples are how they drove their aircraft into Allied ships and the battles of Saipan, Iwo Jima, and Okinawa where many soldiers chose to take their own lives rather than surrender to the Allied forces. *Gyokusai* even extended to civilians. The wartime propaganda machine perpetuated the impression that the enemy would rape and brutally murder every civilian woman and child and surely death by one's own hand was better than such a humiliation. This propaganda led to some soldiers forcing civilians to commit suicide alongside them to avoid what they believed to be a far worse fate. During the battle of Saipan in 1944, a precipice on the island gained the moniker "Suicide Cliff" as hundreds of civilians jumped, or were forced to jump, to their deaths. Those who refused to commit suicide were mercilessly killed by Japanese soldiers to prevent their surrender to the Americans.

The needless deaths resulted from a combination of colonial ambitions, wartime propaganda, and delusions about Japan's military power. During its height in 1942, the Japanese empire extended as far west as Burma (Myanmar), south to the Dutch

East Indies (Indonesia) and eastwards far into the Pacific. But Japan had begun its imperial ventures closer to home, decades earlier with Hokkaido and the Ryukyu archipelago. At the dawn of the Meiji era both Hokkaido (1869) and the Ryukyu Kingdom (1872) were integrated into Japan, and in both cases, the indigenous people of Hokkaido and Ryukyu (Okinawa Prefecture from 1879) were given little say in the matter. This set a precedent for the Japanese expansion into Asia decades later. The expansion began in 1895 when the Treaty of Shimonoseki concluded the First Sino-Japanese War and formally assimilated Taiwan into the Empire. Territory further expanded north after the Russian defeat during the Russo-Japanese war of 1904-05, and the Treaty of Portsmouth (1906) integrated southern Sakhalin into Japan, as Karafuto.

The Treaty of Portsmouth also gave the Japanese rights in southern Manchuria in northeast China. The region fell under the Japanese sphere of influence, justified in accordance with the treaty, although there was no formal announcement of Manchuria as a Japanese colony. Like other Japanese colonies, some Ainu migrated there with hopes of a better life, although generally what they found was more of the same. Just as colonization and development was the official line for Hokkaido, a similar approach was used in Manchuria which fell into Japanese hands in 1934. Tsukamoto Kenichi, the son of an Ainu father and Wajin mother had moved there in the hopes of saving some money as well as avoiding the experience as an Ainu in Japan. In Manchuria, he witnessed children picking up pieces of food that settlers had discarded, reminding him of the poor life he and his younger sister had to live in Hokkaido. In a letter to his sister from 1942 he wrote:

"When I saw these two Manchurian children, it reminded me of [you] and when we were younger […] we would survive by taking the potatoes unwanted by the Wajin […] In the Meiji Period, the Wajin came to Hokkaido and took the land from the Ainu, condemning them to a lowly form of existence. Now it has become the Shōwa era, and the Wajin are doing the same in far away Manchuria. When I think about this […] I want to return to Hokkaido."[105]

Like many young Ainu of the era, Tsukamoto was sent to all corners of the empire to fight for Japan. In 1910, Korea was declared a protectorate, the frontiers of the empire advancing ever further. Going beyond the Treaty of Portsmouth, the Mukden Incident, on the night of September 18, 1931, provided a pretext for a formal invasion of China — an explosive was detonated on the Japanese-owned Southern Manchuria Railway, the Japanese claimed Chinese militants were sabotaging Japanese property and launched a full-scale invasion of China. By 1932, Manchukuo had been established in Manchuria as a Japanese puppet state with the 26 year old Pu Yi (1906-1967), the last Emperor of China, as Emperor of Manchukuo.

Japan hurtled towards total war, and on July 7, 1937 the Marco Polo Bridge Incident triggered the Second Sino-Japanese War (1937-1945). A National Mobilization Law was passed by Prime Minister Fumimaro Konoe (1891-1945), allowing the government to exercise complete control over the empire's economy.[106]

America and her allies condemned Japan's war of aggression but did very little in response. Then on the December 7, 1941 the Japanese navy conducted its sneak attack on Pearl Harbor, and the Japanese military successfully captured British Malaya (Malaysia and Singapore), the Philippines and most of British

Burma and the Dutch East Indies (Indonesia). The Navy had hoped to take the U.S fleet out of the Pacific war with its attack on Pearl Harbor; Japan had employed a similar tactic in the Russo-Japanese War. But the attack had the opposite effect, spurring the Americans to join the war.

The Pacific was not the only potential theatre of war. The Japanese military was wary of an American attack from Alaska, with enemy forces having only to move south through the Aleutian Island chain to bring them to northern Japan. As a preemptive measure in 1942, the Japanese occupied the western Aleutian island of Kiska followed by the neighboring island of Attu in 1943. The United States Congress had declared war on Japan the day after the Pearl Harbor attack and over the following two years, Japan struggled to hold territory gained thus far. In the middle of 1943, American forces expelled the Japanese from Attu and Kiska, marking the first significant Japanese losses in the war.

The American reclamation of the two Aleutian Islands allowed for the launching of air raids on Karafuto and the Kuril Islands. The American air force could now strike targets on Japanese soil. On July 18, of the same year, six American B-24 bombers attacked ships between the northern Kuril Islands of Paramushir and Shumshu Island marking the first air raids by American forces.

But the cities of Hokkaido never experienced the intense air raids that targeted Tokyo, killing over 100,000 civilians, nor atomic bombings as in Hiroshima and Nagasaki. Hokkaido also saw no land battles. Karafuto, the Kuril Islands and Okinawa, however, were far less fortunate.

Hokkaido did not completely escape the costs of war, as the young and able were sent to fight and those not conscripted were duty-bound to support the war economy. By 1943, conscription had taken all men over the age of 20 and the economy at home was suffering labor shortages. One means to remedy the problem was the forced labor of the empire's colonial subjects. In particular, Korea and China shouldered the burden. During 1944, Prime Minister Hideki Tojō (1884-1948) passed a motion in the Diet to import workers from China to solve the labor shortage at home. Throughout Japan, 38,935 Chinese workers bolstered the Japanese wartime economy, 16,282 of whom where assigned to Hokkaido. Of these, 3,047 died, a staggering death rate of 18.7%. In Hokkaido, one of the most common jobs was the back-breaking work of coal mining.

Liu Lianren (1913-2000) was one of the thousands of Chinese forced to labor for the Japanese empire; he was brought to Japan against his will in 1944. Liu escaped in July of 1945 and spent many years hiding from the authorities throughout Hokkaido. Not knowing that the war had ended in September of 1945 he remained on the run for 13 years.

Liu was one of a group of 80 men seized by Japanese troops near his home in Shandong Province, and they were shipped to the town of Numata, not far from Asahikawa in Hokkaido. He was assigned to work at the Meiji Mining Industry Mines. Towards the end of the war, in April 1945, the workers of the mine consisted of 515 Japanese, 584 Koreans, 64 students and women volunteers and 195 Chinese. Living conditions were abysmal and Chinese workers were treated with particular contempt. Liu wrote in his memoir how life in the mines was a living hell. By the end of October, there was frost and snow. In places the snow would pile up to over 30 centimeters. The wooden cabin where he was forced to live was full of holes through which the wind and snow would blew in. Food was little more than a gruel consisting of acorns, sawdust, and moldy corn.

The death rate for captured Chinese was particularly high

as their captors considered them as expendable, forcing them to shovel coal for hours on end. Unsurprisingly, given these circumstances many wanted to escape. On July, 16 days before Japan's surrender, Liu and five others fled into the wilds of Hokkaido. Following weeks at large, the group disbanded. Liu ended up on his own and for the next 13 years remained in hiding throughout Hokkaido, almost always on the move. During this time, he traveled to the fringes of towns and cities including Wakkanai, Kushiro, Asahikawa, and Sapporo, constantly paranoid of capture and assuming a likely death sentence if he was caught. Liu was eventually found on February 8, 1958 in a mountain in Tobetsu on the east coast of Hokkaido. The Japanese authorities initially suspected Liu was an illegal immigrant, though they soon realized he was a victim of the wartime forced labor program. In April 1958, he was shipped home to China.

He had years stolen from his life and on three separate occasions in 1991, 1995 and 1998 he visited Tobetsu and Numata to campaign for reparations. Like many others, his attempts were in vain. The Tokyo District Court upheld his case and ordered the government to compensate him in 1996, but this ruling was later overturned. As for many others in countries that had suffered both war and colonialism, there was to be no formal compensation. He died in the year 2000 at the age of 87, but the people of Hokkaido did not completely forget his suffering. In September 2002, a monument was erected in Tobetsu's Wakaba district to commemorate his life, a symbol of thousands of unfortunate victims of the empire, forced to leave their homes to toil in a foreign land.

Hokkaido's Ainu and Wajin were sent to every corner of the empire to fight for the Emperor, chance to reassess their own place within Japan, as well as to consider their similarities and differences with the empire's other colonial subjects. On July 24, 1944, Tsukamoto Kenichi entered an Asahikawa battalion and on August 31 was dispatched to Okinawa, which would be the site of one of the most brutal battles of the Pacific War. With his experience of working as a cook in Manchuria, Tsukamoto took up a similar role in Okinawa. Tsukamoto's time in Okinawa opened his eyes to the parallels between Okinawa in the south and Hokkaido in the north. Both were semi-integrated colonies and had indigenous people with a different culture from the Wajin. In a letter to his sister written on September 12, 1944, Tsukamoto wrote,

"I thought in Okinawa Japanese would be used, but I discovered that the elderly don't understand it at all. It's just like when [you] couldn't understand the Ainu language spoken by our grandmother and grandfather. But the difference in Okinawa is that the elderly speak with their grandchildren in Okinawan with no restraint. When [I] look at Okinawans, I regret that I didn't treasure Ainu words, like the Okinawans do their own language."[107]

It is thanks to this reflection that Tsukamoto began adding Ainu words into descriptions in his wartime journal.

Before Okinawa became a battlefield in April 1945, Tsukamoto had the chance to interact with everyday Okinawans. Tsukamoto often bought vegetables from local women, and as many of them did not understand standard Japanese, he tried using the few Okinawan words he had picked up. On one occasion he called an elderly women "Ayā", she laughed and called over someone Tsukamoto assumed was her daughter. The daughter explained to Tsukamoto that the word "Ayā" was used by nobles in the

Ryukyu Kingdom to refer to their mothers and taught him a more common word. Tsukamoto reflected that even in Okinawa, which is so small compared to Hokkaido, there are regional and class distinctions among the people.

When the allied assault on Okinawa began in earnest, Tsukamoto was injured and took refuge with an Okinawan woman, "Matsuko-san", whose husband was working in the Philippines, and her two children, Tokuichi and Kana, and two elderly grandparents.[108]

Tsukamoto quickly became close with the family, entertaining the two young children while they hid in the family tomb. Graves in Okinawa, known as turtle-back tombs, are large stone edifices in which the bones of family members are enshrined. They are so large that when Perry's crew first visited Ryukyu, they assumed these were the local peoples' houses. These turtleback tombs with their thick stone walls provided protection for many civilians during the battle. The Okinawan family assumed that Tsukamoto was the same as any other mainland Japanese soldier, gave him an Okinawan outfit, as it was better for his injured leg than his military fatigues, she remarked that he physically resembled an Okinawan.

"*Obāchan* (title for older women), I am not a Japanese soldier, I am an Ainu from Hokkaido," he replied with Matsuko translating. Tsukamoto explained that only one hundred years ago, the Ainu were not Japanese, although now he was Japanese. She replied that Okinawa was the same, and that since he as an Ainu had traits resembling Okinawans, surely the Ainu and Okinawans shared common ancestors.

Tsukamoto and another injured soldier spent just under a month living in the tomb with the family, during which time both the grandfather and grandmother were killed. They suspected they died at the hands of Japanese troops, who shot anyone on sight who did not repeat a password unknown to civilians. By mid-May, the Allies had overwhelmed the base of the Japanese forces at Shuri Castle, and Ushijima Mitsuru (1887-1945), the general commanding the forces in Okinawa, made the fateful decision to move the Japanese forces south towards the coast, herding thousands of civilians ahead of them. They were forced to hide in caves with their backs to the sea and nowhere left to retreat to.

It was in a cave in Yonabara that Tokuichi began playing a *Mukkuri* that Tsukamoto had earlier made for him while they were still hiding in the tomb. The *Mukkuri* is a traditional Ainu instrument made from bamboo similar to a jaw harp. Other children in the cave asked for a *Mukkuri* and Tsukamoto spent an entire day carving around eight *Mukkuri* for them, and then spent more time teaching them how to play it. As the battle raged on outside, the *Mukkuri* became a source of comfort for the children.

On June 17, American planes dropped fliers ordering the remnants of the Japanese army to surrender and implored them not to harm civilians. The former group, those who remained were mostly elder Okinawans who could not read Japanese, and young children.

Writing in his journal, Tsukamoto worried how his family would be treated and if Wajin soldiers would slaughter his wife and children in Hokkaido just as they had in Okinawa. On June 23, General Ushijima committed suicide, but without issuing an order of surrender to the remnants of the Japanese forces. The fighting and massacre of civilians continued in Okinawa's south. On the 23rd Tsukamoto wrote in his journal:

> "I'm sick of war, if I can return alive, like the Okinawan people I will throw out my chest and proudly speak the Ainu language. Whether its soldiers, or Okinawans,

when they are dying on the battlefield, it is not the name of the Emperor they call out, but the names of their mothers and wives [...] I absolutely won't die for the Emperor and country. I must return alive and hold my baby in these hands."[109]

Tsukamoto would never get to meet his child. On June 25, an elderly refugee came to the cave and told the people the Americans would not harm civilians but would furnish them with provisions. It seemed the people in the cave knew this man and were convinced they should surrender. But as they began to leave the cave, the Japanese soldiers opened fire with machine guns and grenades, killing all but two, including the soldier who was in the tomb. This soldier, called Kawakami, found Tsukamoto's body outside the cave. He was taken to a civilian internment camp, and six months later returned to the Japan mainland.[110]

During the war, men in Hokkaido deemed fit to fight on the front lines were dispatched across the Empire. Kayano Shigeru, was one of the young Ainu men who raised his hand on that day in February, 1945 that began this chapter. He was assigned to a military support role at Muroran on the Hachichōdaira runway, south of Sapporo where he witnessed the American attack on Hokkaido as Japan lurched towards defeat. One month before the Japanese surrender, American gunships began bombarding Muroran, and Kayano recalled:

"It was a cloudy day just after eight in the morning when I heard this thunderous sound [...] of bombs ripping apart as they exploded. At first, I didn't know what I was hearing. Sergeant Kasamatsu told me the sound was shells from gunships."[111]

The Muroran bombardment was part of the larger American offensive on Hokkaido, including aircraft carriers and aerial bombing attacks on Kushiro (killing 183), Nemuro (killing 369) and the cities of Hakodate, Otaru, Obihiro, and Asahikawa. The offensive resulted in over 2,000 deaths, most of them civilians. Sapporo, the biggest city in Hokkaido, miraculously suffered only a single death despite being targeted by the American forces.

During the Allied offensive on Hokkaido, the soldiers at Muroran were instructed to hide in narrow foxholes in the ground dubbed 'octopus pots' in Japanese, due to their similarity to the long, jar-like ceramics used by fishermen to trap octopi. In these narrow holes, two men sat with blankets around their heads, the shells exploding above.

Occasionally, soldiers would stand up from the holes, fire a few rounds, often in random directions, and then duck down again. During the naval bombardment of Muroran, over 860 shells were fired, killing over 400 civilians.

A month later, the war ended. After listening to the Emperor announce Japan's defeat on the radio, the second lieutenant announced, "Japan has lost the war." All propaganda and talk of fighting to the last man evaporated with the Emperor's broadcast. In the immediate surrender, no one knew what the Allies would do once they arrived in Japan, prompting a mass burning of documents: valuable sources that have been lost to history.

This elimination of evidence was not restricted to military documents. Soldiers were ordered to burn even their journals as they might "create trouble once the Americans arrived." Kayano obeyed and burned his journal of four years, which for Kayano "was more of a shock for me than losing the war."[112] Shortly after the surrender and release from duty, Kayano returned to his hometown, the Ainu village of Nibutani,

"I saw the after-effects of losing the war on the *kotan*. Many had died, fathers never returned home, husbands vanished. Those left behind had tremendous hardships to face."[113]

Despite a number of war deaths Hokkaido avoided the merciless and repeated bombings of industrial cities experienced by Tokyo and Osaka in the final year of the war. In just one day, March 10, over 88,000 Japanese were killed and over one million people in Tokyo became homeless. To address the damage from the war, between 1946 and 1950, tens of thousands of people who had lost their homes during the bombings were permitted to relocate from central Japan to Hokkaido, to start a new life, thereby continuing the tradition of the colonizers of the Meiji era. Yet while the war had ended in Hokkaido the battle raged further north.

13

NŪPE MOSIR: THE BATTLE FOR KARAFUTO AND THE KURIL ISLANDS

FOLLOWING THE Aleutian Islands conflict in 1942, the Japanese armed forces suffered further defeats including the battle of Guadalcanal in 1943 and Operation Hailstone in 1944, which saw the Japanese lose further islands throughout the Pacific. The U.S successfully captured Guam and Saipan, the capture of which gave the Allies a base to launch air raids on the Japanese mainland. On June 16, 1944 the first aerial bombing by a B29 took place over the city of Kitakyushu. The tide had turned and at this point, Japan had little chance of winning the war in the Pacific.

Yet, the Japanese military administration forged on with increasingly ferocious propaganda and began to make plans for a final battle against the allies on the home islands. In the final months of the war needless massacres followed. In April, the Battle of Okinawa began and dragged on for over two months, leading to the deaths of thousands of civilians.

On July 5, Germany surrendered unconditionally. Allied war efforts were now focused entirely on Japan, which vowed to continue fighting despite the increasing likelihood of defeat. On August 6, the U.S air force dropped an atomic bomb on the city of Hiroshima, the world's first nuclear attack on an enemy target. The immediate blast and firestorm killed over 70,000 people.

Three days later, with the Japanese government still wavering, a second atomic bomb was dropped on Nagasaki.

The Soviet Union, which had been reluctant to engage with the Japanese while still fighting the Germans to the west, now saw an opportunity to take over the Sea of Okhotsk in its entirety, a Russian dream for hundreds of years. On August 8, two days after Hiroshima and three days before the Japanese surrendered, the Soviet Union declared war on Japan, and on August 11, the Soviets invaded Karafuto – the southern half of the island of Sakhalin. They also invaded the Kuril Islands on the August 18 and fighting continued in Karafuto until August 25.

Hokkaido avoided any land battles, but Karafuto and the Kuril Islands were quickly brought under the control of the Soviet Army. Huge numbers of Japanese citizens fled south to Hokkaido in a desperate attempt to outrun the invading Russians. Not all succeeded. Some were caught in what had become a war zone, others took matters into their own hands and committed suicide.

Those who failed to evacuate Karafuto before the Soviets established control now found themselves living in a foreign country. Many were gradually repatriated back to Japan's main island in the following years, but others, for various reasons decided to stay in their homes in former Japanese Karafuto, now once more Russian Sakhalin. They and their descendants continue to live in Sakhalin today.

This chapter looks at wartime Sakhalin and the Kuril Islands. Its title, *Nūpe Mosir*, is the Ainu word for island (or land) of tears, which captures the tragedy. Like the diseases of the previous century, outlanders from the north and south had brought war and violence, leading to tragic consequences for the peoples here.

At the time of the Soviet invasion, of the 400,000 Japanese citizens in Karafuto, approximately 100,000 escaped to Hokkaido before the Soviets closed the border. Most of them were Wajin, followed by Koreans as well as a number of Ainu, Nivkh, and Uilita peoples native to Sakhalin.

Japanese citizens who were born in Karafuto still fondly remember their childhood homes. Kanehiro, born in 1934 at Shisuka (Poronaysk in Russian) dreamt about the Karafuto even after having left — smoke rising from the fifteen-meter tall chimneys of the paper factories, primeval forests of pine covering the mountain in a carpet of deep green and ice fishing on the Poronay river. Kamata Nami, born in Karafuto in 1927, told Nozoe Kenji in 2009 how she yearned to return to her childhood home, but added, "At this age and in weak health I know I'll never go back."[114]

During wartime, there was a general belief that it was impossible for Japan to lose the war. After all, Japan had won numerous successful campaigns against China, Korea and even Russia, who were Europeans. Japan had also signed the Soviet-Japanese Neutrality Pact (1941) with the Soviet Union, which declared both sides would not declare war on one another. As late as 1944, it did not seem remotely possible that Japan might lose Karafuto. But while the possibility of Karafuto becoming a battleground seemed far-fetched, it did not escape the realities of the wartime economy.

In the final six months of the war, Kasahara Ichizō was one of the individuals conscripted from Hakodate to work in the Mitsubishi Mines at the Japanese-Russian border. He recalls feeling "nothing more than a slave," of the wartime economy. Propaganda also penetrated Karafuto with miners having to thank a picture of the Prime Minister Hideki Tōjō for food before they started eating and after finishing a meal. Not everyone blindly believed the wartime propaganda, and Kasahara questioned why he was made to go through such a routine. But he knew that any protest would only bring a harsh punishment and kept his thoughts to himself.

During the final year of the war, the atmosphere in Karafuto began to change. Air raid shelters were constructed and practice evacuation drills were carried out. Money became little more than scraps of paper and metal as there was little available to buy. Wearing luxuries such as new clothing could bring about a scolding from neighbors as displaying a lack of patriotism and a trivial attitude towards the war effort.

On March 24, 1945, the 88th Army Division was formed from 20,388 men in Karafuto, and alongside it the Karafuto Volunteer corps. While volunteer corps had been created throughout Japan, only in Okinawa and Karafuto did these civilian soldiers see combat.

Despite the optimism regarding avoiding a war with Russia, before 1945 there had already been signs that a war with the Soviets was imminent. As early as 1944, the number of Soviet troops had increased at the border and by spring 1945, smoke

Headquarters of the 88th Army Division in what was the Museum of Karafuto at the time and is the now the Sakhalin Regional Museum. The museum was built in the Imperial Crown Style (teikan yōshiki) which began in the 1930s

rising from the forests on the Soviet side, signaled their increasing numbers. One Japanese border guard reported: "The number of Soviets is increasing, they are amassing supplies, it appears they are planning for an invasion."[115]

Despite such signs of an imminent Soviet invasion, the wartime administration gave no orders for civilians to evacuate. The possibility of war coming to Karafuto remained far from the majority of the population's minds.

In 1942, at the Second Moscow Conference between the Allied Powers, Stalin remarked to Averell Harriman, who was representing President Franklin D. Roosevelt, that Japan was an "old enemy of Russia" and that "the defeat of Japan would only benefit Russia." Stalin's ambitions solidified during the Yalta Conference in early February 1945, in which both President Roosevelt (1882-1945) and British Prime Minister Winston Churchill (1874-1965) agreed that if Russia joined the war against the Japanese, they could claim Japan's northern territories but with the important exception of Hokkaido. Stalin agreed to enter into the war against Japan with the condition that it wait until a few months after Germany had been defeated.

The agreement at Yalta declared that:

"The former rights of Russia violated by the treasonous Japanese attack of 1904 shall be restored", a reference to the Japanese victory in the Russo-Japanese war, and that "the southern part of Sakhalin [...] will be returned to the Soviet Union", and finally "The Kuril Islands shall be handed over to the Soviet Union."

During the early hours of August 8, 1945, the Soviet Union declared war on Japan. The following day, Soviet troops rushed into Manchukuo. The Soviet offensive had begun. On that same misty morning, Soviet soldiers attacked local police stationed on the Japanese side of the 50th parallel, which marked the divide between Soviet Sakhalin and Japanese Karafuto. A few hours later, at nine o'clock, a second skirmish began which culminated in the Soviet capture of a guard tower at Handa along the Russo-Japanese border. On the morning of August 11, two-thousand Soviet soldiers crossed the border, outnumbering the Japanese soldiers three to one, and the civilians of Karafuto began to panic.

Miners carved spears out of bamboo and hid in air raid shelters, as they prepared to defend themselves against the Russians. Others attempted to head south while they still had time. Some boarded small motorboats and headed for Hokkaido, few successfully. Most were intercepted by Soviet bombs and torpedoes. On the 9th, Soviet air raids began to target Japanese settlements close to the 50th parallel and hundreds of civilians began to move south. On the twelfth, the governor of Karafuto, Ōtsu Toshio (1893-1958) finally gave orders for civilians to evacuate from Karafuto's north, the following day this order was extended to Karafuto in its entirety. Thousands of Japanese citizens made their way to the ports of Maoka (Kholmsk) and Honto (Nevelsk) in the southwest and Ōtomari (Korsakov) on Salmon Cove to the southeast.

First to leave were the elderly, women and children who boarded trains heading south. Some of the men left behind worked at destroying anything the Soviet's might use. Miura Kenji who worked in Karafuto's timber industry recalls: "We didn't want the Soviets to use our land, so we set many things on fire. We didn't consult anyone, it was based on our feelings. During that time, I went into a lumber factory and poured out gasoline. Then I set it on fire."[116]

On August 15, the unthinkable happened; Emperor Hirohito's (1901-1989) radio announcement declared that Japan had surrendered. But in Karafuto, the war raged on.

Stalin was all the more determined to capture the islands of the

Sea of Okhotsk: Sakhalin, the Kuril Islands, Hokkaido — all had the potential to become part of the Soviet Union. On August 16, the Soviets crossed the Mamiya Straits, separating mainland East Asia and Sakhalin, to attack Esutoru (Uglegorsk). Throughout the Soviet invasion, Japanese soldiers continued fighting. If they could at least slow the Soviets down, they could protect the civilians of Karafuto and prevent an attack on Hokkaido.

The day after the surrender of Japan, General Douglas MacArthur (1880-1964), who was soon to become the Supreme Commander of the allied forces in post-war Japan, called for an end of the Soviet offensive. The Soviets ignored him.

On August 19, additional Soviet forces crossed the Straits of Mamiya to land at Maoka (Kholmsk). Emperor Hirohito's announcement had done little to erase the years of wartime propaganda. Many believed it more honorable, or less painful, to commit suicide than surrender to the Russians, and probably be tortured. Kishi Hiromu (born in 1933), who was a middle school student at the time recalls the voices of fellow Japanese he heard as he hid from Russian soldiers: "The enemies have landed, we have no choice but to die." Kishi, who had been raised amid *Gyokusai* propaganda, thought he too had no choice but to take his own life; until he was told: "Japan lost the war because of its inferiority in science, we need the young to study science to rebuild Japan, so don't you think about dying!"[117] Kishi survived, but hundreds of others were not as fortunate.

The Soviet invasion of Karafuto reached its climax when 1,600 Soviet troops landed in Ōtomari (Korsakov) on August 25. Following an order issued on August 18 to stand down, the 3,400-man Japanese garrison at Ōtomari surrendered, as did the troops at Toyohara (Yuzhno-Sakhalinsk), the seat of Karafuto's government. Ten days after the formal Japanese surrender, with over 2,000 civilians dead and over 60% of Japanese settlements burnt to the ground, the Soviets had captured the entire island of Sakhalin.

During the Soviet invasion, evacuees used any means possible to travel south. The fastest method was aboard freight trains. Space was limited and the waves of evacuees unending. Many of those who could find space in the freight carriages abandoned their luggage, leaving mounds of discarded suitcases outside the railway stations. Inside the carriages, the evacuees were crowded into cramped cattle carriages, akin to the animals which they had formerly transported, though the evacuees hoped for a happier fate.

Kanehiro, who was at Shisuka (Poronaysk) at the time of the Soviet invasion, evacuated with his mother, brother, and sister. His father, like all healthy men under 50, was ordered to stay behind by the local government. Kanehiro and his family took the train to Ōtomari (Korsakov). Their troubles did not end at the port; they encountered lines of women and children in their hundreds to Hokkaido. Eventually, Kanehiro and his family managed to board a ship bound for safety. Aboard the ship, Kanehiro witnessed a traumatic scene: a woman screaming as she hurled other passengers' luggage into the ocean. The crowd was furious, the woman had clearly lost her mind. As Kanehiro looked on, the woman attempted to throw the baby she was carrying overboard. Another passenger managed to take hold of the child and prevent the woman's deed. After the boat arrived in Hokkaido, Kanehiro saw another woman carrying the baby. What became of the mother or the baby he never found out. For Kanehiro, like many who were born in Karafuto, the Japan he had heard about as a boy was a world away from the war-torn reality that was about to become his home:

"When I was a child in Karafuto, I had an image of

Japan as a country of abundance. After I came to Japan,
there were many days where I couldn't eat anything.
I thought: is Japan such a poor country? And why did
I have to leave Karafuto to come to this impoverished
Japan?"[118]

The period of evacuation from Karafuto to Hokkaido lasted
only 13 days, ending on August 28 when the Soviets declared
that all Japanese citizens were to return to their homes. The
thousands who were waiting at the port to evacuate had missed
the small window to make it to Hokkaido. Under the Soviets,
Japanese citizens were eventually permitted to return to Japan.
Kanehiro's father finally rejoined his family three years after
being separated from his wife and children in Karafuto.

The Japanese citizens left behind spent the next few years
living in the Soviet Union's Sakhalin. Of the Japanese population,
the Soviets rounded up 13,000, beginning with the governor of
Karafuto, judges, police, leaders of industry and finally military
men, and sent them to internment camps in Sakhalin, Siberia,
Nakhodka, and Khabarovsk. Civilians were free but had to deal
with an improvised war economy. Money fell out of use and
bartering became the prime means of exchange and lines for
bread became common sights.

On August 27, the Soviet army ordered all civilians to resume
work and most returned to the same jobs they had held when
Karafuto was Japanese territory. If one could not find work,
there were other means of surviving. In the immediate aftermath
of the war, stealing became increasingly common for Russians
and Koreans as well as the Japanese partaking in the practice.
The frigid climate of Sakhalin meant that a cold snap could
shatter thin window glass, making it easier for thieves to sneak
into stores and houses. But when thieves were caught, there

was little justice. Despite being wartime enemies, the Japanese and Russians in southern Sakhalin now had to coexist, but for the majority of Sakhalin's Japanese population, this period of cohabitation was to be short-lived and apart from the Japanese who chose to stay in Sakhalin and thousands of Koreans who had lost their Japanese citizenship, most returned to Japan through Hokkaido before the close of the decade.

As early as September 22, 1945 the Japanese government had been ordered by the Supreme Command for the Allied Powers to begin preparing for Japanese citizens to return to Japan from its former colonies. Following this order, on December 4, the Ministry of Health and Welfare set up an office in Hakodate to process repatriates from Karafuto. The first official repatriation began on the December 2, 1946 when the *Ōsumi-Maru* left Maoka bound for Hakodate with 1,061 passengers aboard. Over the following two days, the *Unzen-Maru*, *Hakuryū-Maru* and the *Shinkō-Maru* also departed for Hakodate. Due to engine failure aboard the *Ōsumi-Maru*, the first to reach Hakodate was the *Hakuryū-Maru* arriving on the evening of December 5. In the first wave of repatriation, 5,702 Japanese citizens returned from Soviet Sakhalin. Following this, a second and third tranche of repatriations took place in 1947, the fourth in 1948 and fifth in July 1949.

In total, 279,356 people, most of them civilians, moved from Sakhalin to Japan during this period. Repatriation was conducted with cooperation between the Soviet and Japanese sides, but returning was by no means simple: to leave one had to obtain a permit from the Soviet administration and once this had been received, repatriation still remained a haphazard process. One case is Kamada Nami who, with six members of her family, repatriated in 1947. "In July of 1947 the evacuation order came, and we were told to gather our things and prepare [...] we were told to rendezvous at a certain place, at a certain time, but no train came. We were then told that the repatriation had been canceled and we went home [...] the same process happened again and again, finally on the third time we left."[119]

Travelling from Shisuka to Toyohara, the fisherman Sugawara Yasuzō was crowded into a playing field with thousands of others. They filled out paperwork, waited and finally with 8,000 others were crammed aboard a ship leaving from Maoka, bound for Wakkanai in Hokkaido. In Sugawara's words:

"In 1948 at Honto, about 30,000 evacuees were crowded into a girls' school to be processed, and when boats arrived to carry them to Hokkaido, only 800 people at a time could be ferried across the waters."[120]

After being processed in Honto, he was evacuated to Hakodate where he was shortly sent to a fisherman's bunkhouse that had been re-purposed as temporary lodgings for repatriates. Those now safe in Hokkaido had to decide whether to go back to their hometowns or make a living for themselves in Hokkaido. Sugawara was one of the latter and the Hokkaido government provided him with a boat, encouraging him to contribute to the development of the fishing industry. Sugawara reminisced that returning to Japan three years after Karafuto had been lost did him no harm. But there were others who always longed for their childhood home.

Generally, historians view the Battle of Okinawa as the only battle fought on Japanese soil during the World War II. The Battle of Okinawa was a tragedy and the 82-day campaign led to tens of thousands of deaths. However, the battle of Okinawa was not the sole engagement fought on what was at the time Japanese territory; the Soviet invasion of Sakhalin and the Kuril Islands was the last stand for the Japanese forces and the final battle of the war. As Sakhalin and the Kurils are now no longer Japanese territories, they are frequently written out of Japan's history, but until the Soviet invasion, Sakhalin and the Kurils were viewed as being as Japanese as Okinawa. The government in 1918 even declared Karafuto as part of Japan's mainland.

At the outbreak of the war, the Japanese military administration were determined to maintain their grip on Karafuto, the Kuril Islands and Okinawa, yet by the end of the war Russia occupied Japan's former northern territories and America the southern islands. America eventually returned Okinawa to Japan in 1972, bringing Okinawa back into the national historical narrative. The northern islands, however, remain outside Japan's control.

To the east of Hokkaido and Sakhalin, the Kuril Islands were also the scene of a bloody battle, and Japan still claims the southern islands today. The most northerly of the island chain is Shumshu Island. This island is about 20 kilometers in width, with a surface area of about 380 km^2. It is only 11 kilometers away from Kamchatka effectively making it a gateway to Hokkaido. This small island became the scene of one of the fiercest skirmishes between the Soviet and Japanese forces. To the south, the Second Kuril Strait separates Shumshu from Paramushir Island: a narrow gap of 2.5 kilometers.

As professor Nakayama Takashi of the National Defense Academy of Japan has pointed out, the Soviet Union had prepared to occupy at least northern Hokkaido and the capture of the Kuril Islands and Karafuto were the initial steps in this plan. In the final year of the war, there were 8,500 Japanese soldiers stationed on Shumshu and 23,000 distributed along the Kuril Island chain. Japanese intelligence about Kamchatka had noted that a low number of Soviet troops occupied the area. Though it did not look like a Soviet invasion was imminent, there was the possibility of an American invasion of Japan from the north, especially after their recapture of the Aleutian Islands close to Kamchatka.

Life was difficult for the troops stationed on Shumshu Island: winters were cold and long. Even simple tasks, such as going to the toilet, could cost one's life. Soldiers reached the outhouse, which was a separate building from the soldiers' barracks, using a rope to guide them between the buildings. If one lost hold of the rope in the darkness, or wavered in the adverse weather, they were at the mercy of nature. Soldiers routinely perished fumbling in the dark only footsteps away from shelter.

When Emperor Hirohito announced Japan's surrender, soldiers of the 91st Infantry Division stationed on the island gathered around the wireless to hear the voice of the Emperor announce Japan's surrender.

The next day, Tsutsumi Fusaki (1890-1959) the commander of the 91st Division, had a difficult decision to make: should he order the men to lay down their weapons, or order them to hold out. After all, the Soviet's had not halted their attack on Karafuto.

On August 18, at 2am soldiers on Shumshu island received an alert that troops were advancing towards them; they were uncertain whether they were Soviet or American.

The ferocious battle that took place on Shumshu island has been referred to as "the Battle to Protect Hokkaido". The Soviets aimed to land on Shumshu's Takeda beach, but heavy Japanese fire effectively slowed their advance.

In the pre-dawn darkness, Soviet commanders ordered their soldiers burdened with up to 30kg of weapons, food and ammunition to jump into the ocean from their boats while the water below was still at least three meters deep. Many of these Russian soldiers sank to the bottom of the icy water burdened by the overwhelmingly heavy loads. When they did land, the

Soviet troops faced Japanese troops who were willing to fight to the death. The fighting was so fierce that the Soviet *Izvestia* broadsheet described The Battle of Shumshu Island as causing "far greater losses than Manchuko or the Korean Peninsula. The 19th of August has become a day that will sadden the hearts of the Soviet people."

Stalin had under-estimated the difficulty of capturing Shumshu because during the capture of Manchuko, the Soviet troops had met little resistance, and the same was expected in the Kuril Islands. But while the Soviets had a record of successful land attacks, the Soviet Navy had vastly less experience. Even the boats used on the attack on Shumshu were provided by the Americans. When the fighting ended, it was not because of negotiations between the two sides, but because imperial headquarters ordered the Japanese soldiers to formally step down.

It is thanks to the soldiers who fought at Shumshu that Soviet soldiers were prevented from reaching Hokkaido. Such an event may have established a very different cold war world in which Hokkaido, like Germany, might have been divided by the Allied and Soviets into separate halves. Today their bravery is remembered by Japan's Self Defense Force's 11th Tank Battalion, which paints 士魂 ('soul of the samurai') onto their tanks to honor the soldiers who fought on Shumshu to slow down the Soviet offensive south towards Hokkaido.[121]

The Soviet invasion of the Kuril Islands did not end at Shumshu, but the occupation further down the island chain was far less bloody and had a more direct effect on those living in Hokkaido.

About 17,000 Japanese citizens lived in the southern Kuril Islands; throughout August news reached Iturup of the battles in the northern Islands but the future of the islanders in the south remained unclear. On September 20, Soviet troops arrived in the village. The Soviets now had a strong grip on Japan's former northern territories and there was no fear of Japanese retaliation further south. The Russian general announced that the islanders on Iturup could carry on life as usual without fear of separation.

For the next two years the islanders were confined to Iturup, now living in the *de facto* Soviet Union, they were cut off from Japanese newspapers and radio. They did not face the shortages of food experienced in neighboring Sakhalin — their island had not seen combat, and they could still grow vegetables and catch fish. On August 30, 1947 the islanders were finally ordered to move to Japanese territory.

Leaving their homes behind was a sad experience. As the 150 islanders boarded the Russian cargo ships, their dogs ran after them, and as the boat drifted on the waves the islanders looked out to a home they never called their own again. A solitary dog jumped into the surf, swimming out towards his master before giving up and returning to the shore. The Japanese aboard the ship looked on tearfully.

Although the Japanese citizens who lived throughout the Kuril Islands lost their homes. A program between the Japanese and Russian government allowed former inhabitants to visit, and many made much use of the program. Today, the campaign for the return of the southern Kuril Islands to Japan forms part of the Northern Territory Dispute with Russia. On occasion organizations for the return of the islands of Iturup, Kunashir, Shikotan and Habomai protest outside stations throughout Japanese cities, and in Sapporo, the former Hokkaido Government Building houses a room dedicated to the education and return of the islands in the northern territory dispute.

Shohei Yamamoto, a resident of Iturup now in old age and having not having lived on his island for decades recognizes that Iturup will never be his home again, but he does wish for future generations of Japanese to experience his former home: "I want the government to negotiate with Russia even if it takes one hundred or two hundred years."[122]

14

Utari The Ainu's Fight for Recognition

The Ainu had been organizing and fighting for their rights and to preserve their culture from the 20th century. Beginning in the Taishō era (1912-1926), Ainu worked both at home and abroad, joining with minority peoples from around the world to campaign for the recognition of the rights of indigenous people. The Ainu realized that the discrimination they faced had parallels with the First Nation people of Canada, Native Americans, aboriginals of Australia and many other indigenous people across the globe. These pioneers fought against established narratives that sought to discard them to the wastebasket of history as anachronistic peoples soon to pass from this earth. It is thanks to these people that the National Ainu Museum within *Upopoy* became one of the few National Museums in Japan in 2020.

Growing up in the early decades of the assimilation policy, one teenage girl committed to paper the Ainu myths which had previously been only handed down orally. The result showed many Wajin and Ainu the common humanity they possessed. In an era in which many Japanese saw the Ainu as backwards aboriginals, this teenager showed that the Ainu too were human beings who breathed, dreamed and felt pain just as they did. Her name was Chiri Yukie, and she is one of the few women who continues to appear in school history textbooks throughout Japan.

Chiri was discovered by the linguist Kindaichi Kyōsuke (1882-1971) who met her when visiting the house of the Ainu missionary and poet Imekanu (Japanese name Kannari Matsu 1875-1961). Imekanu had worked as a missionary under John Batchelor and was Chiri's aunt. From a young age, she had learned from her mother the Ainu *Yukar,* epic poems about humans and the gods. Chiri had been living with her aunt since the age of six, and had grown up learning the Ainu myths and legends. Kindaichi, who spent his entire academic life researching the Ainu, recognized that the 17 year-old Chiri, fluent in both the Ainu and Japanese languages, had the potential to become a great Ainu scholar. In an era when many Ainu parents decided not to teach their children the ways of the Ainu, in the hopes that they would modernize and succeed in Japanese society, Kindiachi told Chiri that the *Yukar* had as much value to humanity as the Greek epic poems of the *Iliad* and *Odyssey*. After Kindaichi returned to Tokyo, he sent Chiri notes encouraging her to write down what she knew. After Chiri graduated from the Asahikawa women's vocational school, Kindaichi invited her to move to Tokyo to further the work.

In May 1922, she moved in with Kindaichi and his wife. During those early days in Tokyo, she taught the basic grammar of the Ainu language to Kindaichi who later in life worked with Kayano to record the Ainu language. Chiri had just finished writing 'A Collection of Ainu Mythology' when at the age of only 19, she suddenly died of a heart attack, robbing the world of a potential great Ainu scholar.[123] Chiri's writings proved to be of huge value for generations of scholars as she wrote the book in both Japanese as well as in the roman script version of Ainu.

Following her sudden death, *Ainu Mythology* was published by Kindaichi in 1923. As the preface played a key role in changing the perception of many Wajin towards the Ainu, it is worth allowing Chiri to speak in her own words:

"A long time ago in this spacious Hokkaido, our ancestors were free in this blessed land. Like innocent children, we were cradled by beautiful Mother Nature and lived carefree lives. It was as if we were her favorite child, what happy people we were. In the winter we would make our way through the thick snow in defiance of the frozen air, we would cross over mountains and hunt bears. When summer's breezes blew, we would swim amongst the green waves, with the song of the gulls as our companions we would build small boats like the leaves of trees and set them afloat to catch fish. When in spring the flowers bloomed, we would bathe in the gentle light of the sun, amongst the birds that would forever sing and we would gather *fuki* and mugwort. When the leaves changed color in autumn, we would split the ears of grain, and would fish for salmon late into the night as the bonfires burned along the banks. We would hear the cries of deer through the valleys and would dream under a full moon. Oh, what a wonderful life it was! Such a tranquil state of being has long been shattered, the land is rapidly changing, one by one the hills and meadows become villages and these villages become towns. The nature of ancient times has become but a pale shadow. Now, only a few of the people who once dwelt so happily in the fields and mountains remain. Those of us left behind can do nothing but stare in astonishment at a bygone age. Moreover, we see the beautiful spirits of our forefathers, who's every action held something spiritual, we have become burdened with unease, unsteady, unable to see the way, a wretched sight: something passing from this world. Such is our name and a sad name to bear it has become. For our contented ancestors surely it would be impossible for them to imagine that their native land would fall into such a wretched state. Time flows on and the world ceaselessly goes on changing. From our great defeat, there could someday emerge two or three leaders then perhaps we can catch up with the world. That is our sincere wish, for which we pray morning and night. The language we use to talk with our beloved ancestors has become worn, even its many beautiful words will be doomed to go the way of their users and disappear from this earth. Oh, what a tragedy, that such is already close to being lost."[124]

Yet the culture of the Ainu did not disappear from this earth and Chiri herself has not been forgotten: stories from her bestselling *Ainu Mythology* are taught in Japanese elementary schools and at the Asahikawa Hokumon Junior High School, which has been built on the site of her former school, and where a stone monument stands in her honor.

As long as there are individuals who identify with and seek to revive a culture and heritage, it is never truly gone.

Historically, Chiri is the most famous Ainu of the Taishō era and she inspired other Ainu in the same period. Iboshi Hokuto never met Chiri, but he came to know of her after meeting Kindaichi in Tokyo in 1925. Through conversations with Kindaichi, Iboshi's sense of identity as an Ainu grew. Eventually he committed himself to the goals of "Research about the Ainu by the Ainu" and "The revival of Ainu culture by the Ainu" and traveled to Biratori. At a meeting in the Ainu church with Yaeko

Batchelor, Iboshi came up with three ideas for the betterment of the local Ainu. First, planting a garden of 300 apple trees so that they might achieve a degree of financial independence, second, establishment of a kindergarten and vocational school for Ainu children and third, a magazine written by Ainu young people.

With this manifesto, Iboshi began a tour of the Ainu *kotans* and at Shiribeshi, Ishikari and Iburi called for Ainu self-reliance. From the autumn of 1926 to 1928, Iboshi had preached to the *Utari* (brothers and sisters) and his words rippled throughout the Ainu communities. But like Chiri, the life of young Iboshi was tragically cut short. In 1928, he contracted tuberculosis and passed away in January the following year aged 27. Iboshi's Ainu self-reliance movement was itself short-lived but his message persisted.

It was during the Taishō period that the word *Utari* was first used by Ainu to mean a wider concept of community. In 1927, Ainu in Tokachi formed an organization called the Tokachi Ainu Asahi Corporation which began to publish an annual magazine, *The Light of Ezo*.[125] While the magazine was published for only a few years, it aimed to serve as a place where "the valuable opinions of the Ainu could be exchanged."

This was not the only such movement of the Taishō era. In 1930, the Asahi organization was reorganized into the Ainu Association of Hokkaido, the first pan-Ainu group.[126] The Ainu also began to organize around issues that most affected them, particularly discrimination. In 1939, when a law in Asahikawa attempted to move Ainu off their land, a representative was sent to Tokyo to campaign against the measure.[127] By the mid-1930s, ultra-nationalism, which led Japan along the path to war, meant the authorities viewed any form of protest as a betrayal of the country, and this effectively put an end to Ainu campaigns for their rights. Like all Japanese citizens and regardless of their ethnicity, the Ainu had to fight for their country both overseas and on the home front. Japanese citizens fighting in the war were told that if they fell in battle, their spirits would be enshrined and worshipped at Yasukuni Shrine in Tokyo; Ainu, too, are enshrined there. When the Soviets invaded Sakhalin, Ainu and Wajin, alongside some Uilita and Nivkh, indigenous ethnic groups inhabiting the northern half of Sakhalin Island and the lower reaches of the Amur River, fled to Hokkaido.

With Japan's defeat in 1945 there seemed, for a brief spell, to be the real possibility that Japan might lose both Okinawa and Hokkaido. The Supreme Commander for the Allied Powers (SCAP), General Douglas MacArthur, and the U.S. army occupying force, were intent on making Japan a democratic state. In late 1945, Lieutenant General Joseph May Swing (1894-1984), invited influential members of the Ainu Assocation of Hokkadio to GHQ headquarters in Tokyo, including Chiri Mashiho, the younger brother of Chiri Yukie, to discuss with them their thoughts on Ainu independence. Although it was unlikely that the Americans would agree to the idea of creating an Ainu republic within Japan, Swing said that if the Ainu wanted independence now was their chance. But during the discussions, the Ainu expressed their desire to remain Japanese citizens, working for their rights within the nation-state.[128]

The post-war period saw a return of the early Ainu rights movements and a gradual increase in government support. Perhaps the most influential organization today is the Ainu Association of Hokkaido, established in the 1930s. By February 24, 1946 the organization had been granted official charity status by the Japanese government and in April 1961 it changed its name to the Hokkaido Utari Association. On April 1, 2009 it once again became the Ainu Association of Hokkaido.

The Ainu Association of Hokkaido held its first postwar

meeting in January 1946 at the Hokkaido Government building, with the support of the Hokkaido government. On February 24, an opening ceremony was held in Shizunai with officials from both the Hokkaido Government and Hokkaido University attending. The aim of the reborn organization was to foster education, promote Ainu culture, welfare and agricultural and fishing reforms. The word *Utari* in Ainu means "comrade" and the decision to change the organization name from "Ainu" to "*Utari*" stemmed from discriminatory use of the term Ainu. The organization strove to show to the masses of Japan that their culture deserved to exist and had value as something part of Japan. But the Former Aboriginal Act, enacted in 1899 to force the integration of the Ainiu into Japanese society, was still law.

In 1964, the Hokkaido Ainu Festival took place in Asahikawa. Ainu from across Hokkaido gathered to perform *Yukar* and dances, with academics such as Kindaichi giving speeches. The event became a forerunner of Ainu festivals regularly held in Hokkaido, and occasionally Tokyo, that continue today. Part of the motivation for the festivals was to attract tourists to Asahikawa, a relatively unpopular destination at the time and now Hokkaido's second-biggest city. Wajin became increasingly involved with the promotion of Ainu rights and in 1964. Wajin students from Tokyo went to work part-time in Akan with the *Peure Utari* organization (Young Utari organization) with the local Ainu. This organization, like many others formed in the 1960s and 1970s, continues to be active to this day.

In the post-war era Ainu individuals and organizations began working to increase the wider recognition and understanding of their people within Japan. It was not necessarily always a problem of racism that the Ainu faced from their Wajin compatriots, although this was also present, but more a general lack of understanding. Many Wajin had never even heard of the

Ainu, and since many had not been taught about this in school, they could not be blamed. One of these projects to foster wider understanding of the Ainu was the building of a museum in Shiraoi.

In 1947, tourism at Shiraoi involved a few girls doing Ainu dances while someone rode around on a bicycle to gather spectators. The spectators paid three yen to watch and through this, the girls could help contribute to their families. By 1951, the Shiraoi Ainu had established a horse and cart that ran between Shiraoi station and Shiraoi *kotan*. By 1962 on the way they stopped at the public hall, where a group gave talks about the Ainu. By the 1960s, tourists had increased and in 1964, 560,000 visited. By this time, the Shiraoi Ainu had created a tourist *kotan* near the station. As with tourists all over the world there were numerous occasions when visitors overstepped boundaries. To remedy this problem in 1965, the *kotan* was moved 1.5 km away to Poroto Lake, reopening in May of the same year.

A key figure in the founding of the Shiraoi Ainu Museum was Moritake Takeichi (1902-1976). Moritake worked as a railway porter at Shiraoi station from 1912 to 1923. During this time, the stationmaster often asked Moritake as an Ainu, to show tourists around the *kotan*. Moritake recalls:

> "I really didn't enjoy it, after we walked only a few steps I would start getting all sorts of questions from the tourists, 'Do the Ainu understand Japanese?', 'what sort of clothes do the Ainu wear? Etc. I'd hear hurtful things as well 'Is it true that Ainu men do nothing but drink while the women do all the work?' It's clear they didn't know that I was an Ainu."[129]

To fight back against the prejudice the Ainu faced, Moritake eventually left his job at the railway to found a small Ainu museum in Shiraoi in 1967, at the time Moritake was 65. Moritake worked to correct Wajin misconceptions about the Ainu, and gradually would begin to receive letters including the following, "If I hadn't met you when I came to Hokkaido, I would have gone on ignorant and with misconceptions about the Ainu." Such letters made Moritake proud and confirmed that there was value in teaching others about the Ainu. The small museum that he founded would go on to become the Shiraoi Ainu Museum and until 2018, it stood on the shores of Poroto Lake. At the age of 64, Moritake wrote the following poem:

"When I reached an age of discretion, I was unaffected. As I got older, I cursed that I was born Ainu. As I entered the prime of my life, I opened my eyes to being Ainu, and mustered my strength. Now, they call me an *Ekashi* (chief), and from the bottom of my heart I am glad to have been born an Ainu. For the word Ainu means human."[130]

While the Shiraoi Museum helped educate, over a decade later there was still much work to be done.

Although the revival and preservation of Ainu culture was important, the Ainu had also suffered economically during Hokkaido's colonization and the *Utari* organization worked to bring the standard of living for Ainu to the same level as their Wajin counterparts by providing scholarships for Ainu to study, and the construction of community halls and public baths. In 1974, the organization began a welfare measure providing personal provisions for entering school, work and living. The Ainu rights movement was not limited to Hokkaido, as many Ainu had moved to cities across Japan to work, particularly

Tokyo.

In 1972, Ukaji Shizue (born 1933) put an advertisement in the *Asahi Shimbun* newspaper calling for a meeting of Ainu, and in 1973 the Tokyo Utari Organization was founded and continues to be active. The organization's small exhibition room is only a short walk from Tokyo station, one of the world's busiest, and therefore provides an opportunity for anyone passing through Tokyo station to learn more about Ainu culture.

When discussing the Ainu rights movement, Kayano Shigeru is a figure impossible to overlook. Like Chiri, Kayano preserved and promoted Ainu culture and represented the Ainu on an unprecedented scale when he became the first Ainu member of the Japanese Diet. Like many Ainu, his grandfather had been forced to work under the Matsumae, his father was arrested for illegal fishing, and Kayano himself had served in the final days of the war when Hokkaido was bombarded by American ships. It was many years before Kayano even believed it was possible to correct the misconceptions of numerous Wajin towards the Ainu. In the post-war era, many researchers came to Nibutani to collect Ainu curios and assess Ainu for their research. These assessments involved taking photographs of individuals from all sides (resembling mugshots) and collecting samples of blood. This may have provided some spare money for families willing to partake, but it also sidelined the Ainu as a spectacle of sorts. In his memoir, Kayano recalls one individual he particularly despised, "Professor K":

> "He would come to Nibutani and take (Ainu) things; he would open the sacred graves of our ancestors and leave with their bones. He would take blood from the villagers and try to ascertain whether the Ainu really did have thick hair [...] I don't know how much blood

he took from my mother, sometimes she would come home dizzy."[131]

As with many Ainu households by the mid 1930's, Kayano's family had sold nearly all the Ainu objects they had possessed, with the exception of a few pieces of clothing. Following the war, Kayano worked for a time as the head of a lumberjack group, and it was during this time that he decided to dedicate his spare income to buying back Ainu objects purchased as curios by Wajin. He lacked the financial power that many Wajin buyers held and later reflected, "Most of what I collected was junk." Regardless, Kayano strived to rescue his culture from being confined to academies and museums. Kayano continued to expand his personal collection until an event on May Day in 1954 laid the seeds of his nascent activism.

On that fateful day, he was ploughing the fields in front of the family house when a man in his 40s approached. Certain that this was just another Wajin researcher, Kayano ignored him and continued his work. But the man, Sobu Tomio, went into the house and started talking to Kayano's father. They talked late into the night, and Sobu later proposed to Kayano that he arrange for Ainu entertainers from Nibutani to travel around Honshu performing in the elementary and middle schools. His goal, he said, was to correct Wajin misconceptions and show them that the Ainu speak fluent Japanese, and do not make their livelihood from hunting and 'primitive'means. After some discussion, Kayano agreed to put aside his reluctance to work with Sobu and decided to also sell Ainu crafts.

The first destination of their tour was Akita City where seven Ainu dances and songs were performed in May, 1954. After the performance had finished, Kayano's father provided an explanation and then Kayano offered the Ainu crafts for sale.

After only one week of the tour, Kayano had for the most part memorized his father's speech and on one occasion, he said, "Why don't you give it a go?" and handed him the microphone. Kayano was nervous at first, but the other members of the troupe encouraged him, and he gained in confidence and even began to get involved in the performances. Through the school tours, Kayano made more money than he had initially expected. Each child in the audience paid ten yen and there were a few hundred in each school. The Ainu crafts also sold far better than he had expected; there was evidently an interest in Ainu culture. Yet despite this interest, Kayano also began to realize how ignorant of the Ainu many Wajin were. Kayano was surprised by comments from teachers such as "Your Japanese is excellent!" and "The clothes you are wearing are just like those worn by Japanese!" only further enflaming Kayano's passion to preserve and teach Ainu culture. The popularity of the Ainu troupe in the schools led to newspaper reports followed by other schools requesting that they visit and after touring schools in Akita Prefecture, they also performed in schools in Yamagata and Fukushima Prefectures. But unfortunately, Kayano's initial suspicions about Sobu, turned out to be correct: he ran off with much of the money the troupe had earned. Despite Sobu's duplicity, the troupe's success inspired Kayano to set up his own organization, and he went on to perform in many other schools. Kayano wrote in his memoirs that the experience:

> "was a valuable lesson for me. It showed me that not just in Nibutani, but also around the world there were a variety of cultures, which I had been able to confirm with my own eyes. What's more, in each place I had seen the commemoration of historic sites and museums, and this broadened my horizons."[132]

In 1954, Kayano had begun learning the ancient art of Ainu carving, taking to it after work, even on rainy days in the woods in the bunkhouse. By 1959, Kayano was able to produce carvings with enough skill to sell them. Making more money than logging, even in a leadership role as the head of the Shigeru lumber group. Kayano even convinced some of his logging friends to try their hands at carving in the Ainu style. This was just in time for a tourist boom and subsequent interest in such goods.

Alongside his collection of Ainu objects, Kayano also realized that if no one stood up to preserve it, the Ainu language could be lost. By the 1950s, there were only three individuals around him who could fluently speak the Ainu language, Nitani Kunimatsu (1888-1960), Nitai Ichitarō (1892-1968) and Kayano's father, Kaizawa Seitarō (1893-1956). The trio frequently met and on one occasion Kayano overheared "out of the three of us, the one who dies first will be the luckiest, for the other two can conduct the Ainu ceremonies in the Ainu language and the dead will be able to go to *Kamuy Mosir*."[133]

Kayano was deeply moved by the idea of the Ainu language dying with those few who still spoke it. It seemed as if Chiri's predictions decades prior would be realized. The so-called luckiest of the three ended up being Kayano's father, who died in February 1956, with a funeral being held on the nineteenth of that month. About a year and a half after his father's death, Kayano met Chiri Mashiho (1909-1961) an Ainu researcher and the younger brother of Chiri Yukie. Chiri had come to Nibutani on a number of occasions but Kayano had always been away logging and had never met him. On this occasion, when he heard Chiri, who was working as a member of the ethnography museum in Tokyo, was in Biratori, Kayano rushed down to meet him. Kayano stayed in an inn in Noboribetsu with Chiri and recorded some of the Ainu language, and took Chiri fishing with the *Marep* along with other Ainu for Chiri's research. Kayano was pleased to meet an Ainu conducting research to preserve their own culture and they agreed to keep in touch. Unfortunately, a few years from their encounter, Chiri passed away.

After meeting Chiri, Kayano decided that he, too, should make more efforts to preserve the Ainu language and bought a tape recorder, an expensive piece of equipment in 1959. At the time, tapes held about an hour of audio and cost 500 yen each. In 1960, Nitai, the second of the three fluent speakers of Ainu passed away. Kayano knew that this was perhaps the last chance to record the Ainu funeral rites for posterity. The elders of Nibutani recognized the significance of the occasion and allowed Kayano to record the *ioytakkote*: the last rites of the deceased. Fully committed to obtaining Ainu curios and recording the Ainu language, Kayano began a summer job to save money for recordings in 1961.

The job was working as a 'tourist Ainu' in Noboribetsu. The Ainu *chise* attraction, where he and others performed songs and dances related to *Iomante,* each lasting about 30 minutes. Kayano took the job to fund his main aims, but he held a degree of reluctance: "It didn't please me to work as a tourist Ainu, lots of things were against what I had learned about Ainu culture and the Ainu mentality, but it was decent money." After each performance, Wajin tourists swarmed Kayano and the others with questions, "Your Japanese is great! Where did you learn?", "What sort of food do you eat?", "Do the Ainu go to the same schools as Japanese children?", "Do the Ainu pay taxes?"

At first, an irate Kayano answered these questions coldly. In time, he began to understand that most Wajin had no inkling whatsoever about the Ainu and could hardly be blamed for a culture that had not been taught to them. He began to answer their questions more cooperatively, trying to explain to them that the culture and language of the Ainu is on the verge of extinction.

Kayano worked in Noboribetsu, performing and selling carvings, for seven summers before leaving in 1967. In 1968, he began to sell his carvings in a souvenir shop off the national highway near Nibutani. He jointly owned the shop with four others from Nibutani, and their shop remained in business until 1975. Kayano had been preserving the Ainu culture on a personal scale, but he was slowed down with a run in with pleurisy in March 1970 which put him to the city hospital in Tomakomai. As he lay in bed, Kayano pondered what might happen to his recordings and collection of Ainu objects when he passed away. In the middle of June of the same year, he was discharged from hospital, leaving with a determination to build something for future generations.

Upon his return, Kayano decided to build a museum dedicated to Ainu culture, at his own expense. He decided on a 100-square-meter building in Biratori, for 3,000,000 yen (about 8,000 dollars at the time). The Hokkaido Utari Association caught wind of Kayano's project and started raising money to help build the facility, and donations also came in from the Biratori government, donating 2,700,000 yen (7,500 dollars), the Hokkaido Government donating 2,000,000 yen and the JKA Foundation (Japan Bicycle Promotion Association) donating 4,350,000 yen. Government funding for the Ainu museum, however, paled in comparison to their contribution to the Hokkaido Development Memorial Center (now the Hokkaido Museum), to which they donated 3,700,000,000 Yen.

By December 1971, Kayano's building was complete and on June 23, 1972 it opened as the Nibutani Ainu Culture Museum. Kayano's legacy continued with the municipal Nibutani Ainu Culture Museum opening in Biratori in 1992, to which Kayano donated much of his collection. In March 1992, Kayano's old museum reopened as the Kayano Shigeru Nibutani Ainu Museum, showcasing Kayano's personal collection of Ainu-related objects. Both museums can be visited in Biratori today, and Kayano's legacy continues.

Kayano began his political career in 1975, when he was recommended for the Biratori Town Council. He initially dismissed the idea, having no interest in politics, but he was convinced otherwise after learning that there would be not a single Ainu on the council if he did not run. He won the election, launching his political career and eventually leading to a seat in the national Diet.

Kayano also worked to preserve the Ainu language. In the 1980s, while an undergraduate at Hokkaido University, Honda Yūko attended a class held by Kayano, and she saw firsthand the positive impact it had. After graduation, Honda had wanted to continue on to graduate school to do further research into Ainu culture, but she failed the entrance exam, and wrote a letter to Kayano asking if she would be able to work at the Ainu language school he had recently established in Nibutani. Kayano agreed, and in the April 1983, Honda moved to Nibutani with the intention to work for a year and then reapplying for graduate school.

The language school, the first of its kind in Japan, opened on May 22, 1983. Kayano, then 57 years old, had set up the school not only help preserve Ainu culture, but as a means to revive it for younger generations. The first cohort of students were quick to pick up Ainu, with Kayano delighted to teach them the Ainu words of plants and animals. That summer, Kayano developed gallstones and was rushed to hospital in Tomakomai and Honda took over administration of the school. While Kayano was hospitalized, Honda traveled to the hospital, learning Ainu from Kayano and then teaching them to the children. She enjoyed instructing the children in Ainu, and by September she had dropped her plans for further study.

Honda spent more than ten years working at Kayano's language school and over that period saw a change in the children's attitudes towards learning Ainu. As a Wajin, Honda watched as a generation of Ainu became more confident, even proud of their culture, and also saw the ignorance amongst many Wajin, who believed that the Ainu had either been completely assimilated into the Wajin world or were still living the life of hunter-gathers distant from Japanese society. In May 1986, Honda and 18 of the school's children visited Canada to meet First Nation children. The children from Nibutani learnt about the indigenous peoples of Canada while teaching them about their own culture. Through sharing stories and experiences, they came to understand their own place in the world against a background of global colonization.

In September 1987, the Biratori-Nibutani Ainu Language Institution opened.[134] Unlike Kayano's school, a private venture for children funded by Kayano himself, the Biratori-Nibutani Ainu Language Institution was established by the Ainu Association of Hokkaido and received financial support from both the Hokkaido and National governments. The school was dedicated to the study and teaching of the Ainu language to adults as well as children. Ainu language studies and education took another step forward in July 1991, when a central body on the topic was set up and in 1993, the first common text, that aimed to produce a standard version of Ainu to study. Today, online resources produced by the Ainu Association of Hokkaido allow Japanese speakers, and English speakers to a lesser extent, to learn words, phrases and grammar of the Ainu language.

During her time when she was teaching, Honda herself was delighted to see young children's attitudes towards the study of the Ainu language evolve. Early on, she noticed that they often tried to hide that they were studying Ainu, the result of decades of assimilation policy that had created a self-loathing amongst many Ainu families. Some children stopped as soon as they entered middle school as they did not want their new classmates to know. Ten years later, she saw children openly saying, "Today I have Ainu language classes, and I can't be late!"[135]

But despite some positive changes, Honda was frustrated to observe the persistence of unenlightened views in society. Many failed to understand the existence of Ainu in modern society. In Nibutani, an old woman was employed in a *chise* built for tourists and spent her time making *Attus* for their amusement. Some of the Wajin tourists imagined her as a noble savage of sorts, with one Wajin asking questions such as "Don't you get cold living here?" and "Where do you sleep?" to which the good-humored lady pointed to a rafter, the tourist taken aback replied, "Don't you fall off?"[136]

In the 1980s, Honda noted that many visitors to Nibutani expected to see unchanged Ainu, displaying an ignorance of decades of assimilation policy.

One of Kayano's most significant political campaigns was bringing a lawsuit, with town councilor Kaizawa Tadashi (1912-1992), against the building of the Nibutani dam. The Hokkaido Regional Development Bureau commissioned the dam on the Saru River to supply water to the industrial area of Tomakomai, 30km west of the dam site. Later, the commission added hydroelectricity and flood control to the scheme. But the project would submerge land given to Ainu farmers under the Former Aboriginal Protection Act, meaning Ainu would have to exhume the remains of those buried there and relocate them. Two Ainu landowners refused to sell the land and in 1987, the Bureau forcibly confiscated it from them. What followed was a drawn-out legal battle, eventually won by the Ainu complainants in a classic hollow victory. In 1997, the Sapporo District Court of Hokkaido ruled that Bureau had illegally seized the Ainu's land under the Land Expropriation Act. But by this time, the construction of the dam was completed and the court ruled that it was not necessary to decommission it.

One surprising outcome of the ruling was that the court acknowledged, for the first time in jurisprudence history, that the Ainu were the indigenous people of Hokkaido and not "former aboriginals" or "minorities". Yet, while the 1990s saw recognition of the Ainu as indigenous people of Hokkaido, it was not until the following decade that this was extended to "indigenous people of Japan".

Before this ruling, a decade prior, a statement by the Prime Minister of Japan, Nakasone Yasuhiro (1945-2012) questioned whether the Ainu even existed in modern Japan. His comment, given below, was a slap in the face to generations of Ainu who had navigated discrimination and fought to preserve their culture within Japanese society. Fortunately, the backlash to Nakasone's statement prompted many Ainu to organize on an unforeseen scale.

The controversy started on September 22, 1986, when Nakasone made the following remark during a speech:

"Japan is a society of high levels of education. A considerably intelligent society, which has far surpassed the United States where there are many blacks, Puerto Ricans and Mexicans whose average levels are low."[137]

His words immediately met with a backlash from America, and on September 24, in an attempt to recoup, Nakasone held a press conference at the Prime Minister's Official Residence in which he said: "What I've said has been taken out of context. America has had huge successes with Apollo and SDI (The Strategic Defense Initiative). Because America is a multi-ethnic state there are places where it's hard to deliver in education, since Japan is a state of only one ethnicity it's very easy."[138]

In response to his statement, the Hokkaido Utari Association issued a statement: "To say Japan is a homogenous ethnic state ignores the existence of the Ainu." Then on November 13, 1986 a meeting was held in Tokyo by Ainu organizers during which they issued a proclamation:

> "Japan is not a homogeneous ethnic state. The Ainu have lived in Sakhalin, the Kuril Islands and the Japanese Archipelago since ancient times. But the Japanese nation-state since the times of the Yamato court has a history of invasion, oppression and discrimination towards the Ainu."[139]

Naklasone's comments offended both Japan's American allies and the Ainu citizens of Japan, but most particularly the Ainu, who had experience of both the pressures of assimilation and discrimination. To say that Japan was a homogenous ethnic state was a denial of the lives they, and their forebears, had lived.

Two such individuals were Ōtani Yōichi and Akibe Hideo (both born in 1960). Ōtani's great-grandfather had said to his descendants "I'll be the last Ainu, you become Japanese." Such sentiments were quite common for Ainu parents during the era of the assimilation policies. Ōtani left Hokkaido for Osaka at the age of 22 and following his great grandfather's advice, he diligently studied Buddhism and Shinto to become a "real Wajin". Ōtani had spent most of his life trying to hide his Ainu heritage, but when he heard Nakasone's statement, he was furious. After all the discrimination he and his ancestors had faced, how could the Prime Minister, of all the people in Japan seemingly deny their existence?

Ōtani moved to Tokyo and joined the Tokyo Utari Association, which was formed independently of the Hokkaido association by Ukaji Shizue. Having moved from Shizunai to Hokkaido, Ukaji sought to create an organization to help Ainu who were unfamiliar with the Tokyo environment, as well as to fight the poverty and discrimination Ainu faced both in Tokyo and Hokkaido. Historically, many Ainu received less education or dropped out of school early due to bullying, and subsequently often entered low-paying employment. Often Ōtani's three children went to school to the cries from some children of "*Gaijin!*" "*Gaijin!*" (Foreigner!). Ōtani describes such treatment as a baptism of sorts, and representative of the kind of everyday discrimination the Ainu faced. Collectively, the Tokyo Ainu had more influence to resist discrimination than single individuals did, and by the time Ōtani joined the Tokyo Utari Association, it had grown to about thirty members. As many members came from prefectures surrounding Tokyo (Kanagawa, Chiba, Saitama), the organization eventually changed its name to the Kanto Utari Association.

In response to Nakasone's statement, the Association sent a letter to the Prime Minister's office, but all they received in reply was a postcard stating that the media had manipulated the statement. Ōtani was further enraged when Nakasone said his body was on the quite hairy side, perhaps he had some Ainu blood himself, Ōtani felt this was making light of the matter.

At the time, Ōtani reflected that Nakasone's statement was an embarrassment to anyone who held Japanese citizenship, but he did not hold Nakasone solely responsible for his statement: many Wajin held similar beliefs and were simply a product of their cultural and educational environment.

To prove there were Ainu living in Tokyo as modern Japanese citizens, and not just a fading minority in the wilds of Hokkaido, in 1974 and again in 1988, the Association took an informal census of individuals they knew. The findings showed that at least 2,700 Ainu were living in Tokyo and the reason for coming to the city was, for 30% of respondents, to escape discrimination. The survey also found that, compared to 95% of Wajin, only 78% percent of Ainu in Tokyo had completed middle-school.

Even during the time of Nakasone's statement, there were undercurrents of change in Japanese society. With many Brazilian and other descendants of Japanese immigrants coming to Japan, there was a slight increase in foreign names in school classes and one of Ōtani's children using an Ainu name seemed less unusual than it had in decades prior. The Kanto Utari Association continued to push the study of Ainu culture, and a Wajin professor, an expert in the Ainu language, regularly lectured at the association. At first, Ōtani felt humiliated about learning the language of his ancestors from a Wajin, and was angry when other members of the association praised the professor's expertise. But over time, he became thankful.

Like Ōtani, Akibe also experienced discrimination growing up. Akibe recalls, "I didn't have a very good impression of the word *Ainu* when I was younger. When I began elementary school, a student in the third or fourth year said to me, 'you're an Ainu' and that's my first memory of being called an Ainu."

Akibe, like many Ainu children, was bullied at school, with children telling him that he smelled and ate strange food. Subsequently, Akibe lost interest in attending high school if it meant becoming the target of further abuse. He had heard that in the great metropolises of Tokyo or Yokohama, there were many Ainu, and they could hide their Ainu heritage from the world.

Akibe thought he could perhaps do the same. Yet Akibe's mother made him take the high school entrance examination and, much to Akibe's annoyance, he passed, and was enrolled at a high school in Akan.

During his time in high school, Akibe was introduced to a *Yukar* circle and for the first time he began to take pride in his own heritage, losing the desire to submerge his identity. During his first year of high school, Akibe was invited to visit Canada with ten Ainu students and ten Japanese academics. During their time in Canada, the First Nation People told the Ainu students that the problem was not what the Ainu would do about their situation, but how the Ainu could contribute to the world. This left a deep impression on Akibe and for the first time in his life he realized that fighting for the rights of the Ainu alone was not enough. As with Kayano, he reached the conclusion that wider education about the Ainu was also necessary. With new-found confidence in his Ainu heritage, by the end of his first year in high school, he was responding to derogatory statements with replies such as "I'm Ainu, what's wrong with that?" and "So what if I'm a little hairier than you?"[140]

After Akibe graduated, he began working in his father's shop making Ainu crafts. The Ainu tourist *kotan* at Lake Akan remains one of the most popular tourist spots to experience the Ainu in Hokkaido. Akibe realized how most Wajin were clueless about the indigenous people within their very own country. Tourists asked Akibe if he was Iranian, Italian, or Israeli. Such remarks, and the remarks of Nakasone, made many Ainu feel as if they were not Japanese. In summer, Akibe began participating in the dance of the sword (*Emushi Rimse*), the dance was free and used to bring in tourists who often bought souvenirs, Akibe felt this was his chance to teach the Wajin about the real Ainu, and he became interested in attending and participating in Ainu festivals around the country, and Ainu who witnessed the events were encouraged. Despite Nakasone's statement, there was a cultural revival occurring at the same time and this movement had been gathering pace long before 1986.

In 1982, the Hokkaido Utari Association began campaigning for new Ainu legislation to repeal the Former Aboriginal Act, marking a significant break away from accepting the assimilation policy. In 1984, legislation drafted to recognize the historical context of the Ainu included this sentence:

> "As the modern Japanese nation state formed and took its first steps, the Japanese government integrated *Ainu Mosir* in its entirety without consulting the Ainu who are the indigenous people."[141]

Ainu culture was also gaining prominence during this same period. In 1987, Sapporo Television Broadcasting began a program called *Irankarupte* (Hello in Ainu), teaching the Ainu language, and in 1989 weekly 15-minute radio sessions to learn the Ainu language started to be broadcast. Further steps towards political empowerment of the Ainu came in 1994 when Kayano Shigeru became the first-ever Ainu member of the Diet.

Yet even after this success problems remained, such as when the politician Suzuki Muneo in July 3, 2001 made the claim that the "Ainu have become completely assimilated", Suzuki's comments were met with a wave of criticism, and some commentators argued that such comments were in violation of Article 14 of the Japanese constitution, which states that: "All of the people are equal under the law and there shall be no discrimination in political, economic or social relations because of race, creed, sex, social status or family origin."

While progress was being made, there was still a way to go. In

2014, an elementary school attempted to use designated foreign language class time to teach the Ainu and Okinawan languages, but a Liberal Democratic Party member of the Diet took the issue to the Board of Education and the lessons were shut down.

Perhaps a time will eventually come when these languages are taught in school and a revival movement such as with the Welsh language in the United Kingdom will breathe new life into the Ainu language.[142]

There also continues to be a lack of general knowledge about the Ainu in many parts of Japanese society. Takeuchi Hayato (born 1992), who worked in the Shiraoi Ainu Museum (the predecessor to *Upopoy*), was surprised when tourists commented that his Japanese was very good, or asked him questions about whether Ainu still hunt. Despite such questions, Takeuchi is determined to increase people's knowledge of the Ainu. Responding to Suzuki's comments in an *Asahi Shimbun* article in the early 2000s the author Natsuki Ikezawa (born 1943) summed up the reality of Japanese attitudes:

"There is a way of thinking that the Ainu, Zainichi-Koreans, Chosen people (North Korea), and the Okinawans have been 'assimilated,' that is to say that they have been absorbed into a sea of Japanese (Wajin). However, ethnicity is a self-awareness. While the state may determine citizens' nationality, ethnicity is determined by oneself. If you say you are Ainu, or so-and-so ethnicity, as long as there is at least one such Japanese citizen alive, it cannot be said that Japan is a homogenous ethnic state. Multiculturalism is not an ideology, it is reality."[143]

15

THE AINU IN JAPAN AND THE WORLD

THE MOST SIGNIFIGANT legislation for the Ainu came as recently as the past three decades and is in part thanks to the Hokkaido Utari Association which became increasingly involved internationally from the 1980s. The association compiled a list of laws that affected the Ainu and had sent these to the United Nations to try to campaign for a fairer lot for the Ainu. The association also strengthened its network with other indigenous groups throughout the world, in countries including China, Australia and the United States. In 1990, the United Nations declared that 1993 would be the year of indigenous people; this marked a watershed moment and put pressure on the Japanese government to acknowledge that indigenous people existed within the country's borders. On December 10, 1992, the Giichi Nomura (director of the Hokkaido Utari Association), gave the following speech at the United Nations (abridged):

"For the Ainu who since ancient times have maintained a unique culture and history throughout Hokkaido, the Kuril Islands and south Sakhalin, this day of the tenth of December has to be especially commemorated. That is to say, only a mere six years ago in 1986, the Japanese government denied our very existence. Japan was

a special case in the world boasting that it was an
unparalleled example of a 'homogeneous ethnic state'.
Through the United Nations our existence has been
recognized. If such a ceremony were to be held a mere
few years ago, surely it would have been impossible
for me to give such a speech here as a representative
of the Ainu. In the eyes of the Japanese government
we, the Ainu, are an ethnic group that does not exist.
You need not worry, we never became ghosts [...] The
Ainu people with the year of indigenous people seek
to form a new partnership between the government
of Japan and member states with indigenous peoples.
We want to talk together about our current unlawful
status, the important values of our traditional societies
and together wish to seek solutions to the issues we
face. From now Japan can be a formidable ally and I
would like to invite the Japanese government to discuss
things together with us. The attitudes of the Japanese
government towards the rights of indigenous people
is never a problem limited to Japan itself. Overseas,
the activity of Japanese companies and aid from the
Japanese government has serious effects on indigenous
people throughout the world. Their indifference to the
indigenous people of their own country cannot be
separated from these matters. Through the experience
of a new partnership, the Japanese government can
develop an understanding of not just responsibility to
the Ainu, but all indigenous people. This is something
which we have great confidence in. What we are
requesting is a high level of autonomy, the rights to
carry out our traditional ways of life 'coexistence with
nature and peace through discussion', these are our

fundamental principles. This is not something that is a confrontation to already established states. Through our own values, we can maintain and develop a society full of ethnic dignity and achieve the co-existence of all ethnicities. In the Ainu language we call the earth *'ureshipamosir'*. This means an earth that raises all things together. In this era with the end of the Cold War, in a period in which a new international order is being searched for, we seek a partnership between indigenous people and non-indigenous people, and a period in which through this contribution we can all contribute to international society. I would like to end this speech by saying that it is our wish as indigenous peoples to bring forth a future full of hope for humanity."[144]

Giichi finished the speech by thanking the audience in Ainu, *Iyairaikere*.

Of utmost importance was the repeal of the Former Aboriginal Act, in place since 1899 and the legislation that made the assimilation ideology a political reality. Before the repeal of the act in 1997, Ainu campaigned for a number of things including the guarantee of human rights and readdressing historical and contemporary discrimination, political rights, such as parliamentary seats for indigenous people. New Zealand was a model for the Ainu of indigenous peoples succeeding to have their voices heard.

Education was also an issue that had long been campaigned for, as a lower proportion of Ainu students proceeded to high school and on to university after the compulsory education period, which in turn diminished job prospects for them. There was also fishing, farming and foresting, all legacy issues from the Meiji era, which prevented Ainu from pursuing traditional means of living. There were calls for a fund to be set up to provide support for the Ainu to achieve stronger economic standing and to readdress historical discrimination, and finally cultural promotion.

The act replacing the Former Aboriginal Act only addressed the last of these issues in the Ainu Cultural Promotion Act of 1997.[145] Though it did not go as far as many Ainu had campaigned for, it was significant for recognizing that the Ainu language and culture were in danger. National recognition of the Ainu as indigenous people, however, did not come until a decade later.

What is the position of the Ainu within Japanese society and the international community in the 21st Century? When the author was a student in Tokyo in 2018, posters for the popular *manga* and anime *Golden Kamuy*, lined the subway stations of Tokyo, while that same year the Ainu band *Oki Dub Ainu Band* headlined the Sumida Jazz Festival. In Hokkaido, it was announced that in Biratori, three buses would run routes in the Ainu language. Meanwhile, Sapporo station hosted displays of Ainu embroidery and placed a wooden statue of an Ainu at its center. Outside of the city's most popular tourist spots, the former Hokkaido Government building erected an electric sign, counting down the days until the opening of the National Ainu Museum in Shiraoi in 2020.

The renewed interest in things Ainu was not limited to Japan. A 2019 British Museum exhibition on manga featured one of the main Ainu characters from *Golden Kamuy* on its poster, and for a while, posters with an Ainu girl wearing traditional clothing featured throughout the London underground rail system and along the fences of the British Museum. In the late 2010s, the Ainu were becoming more recognizable, and more than this, they were becoming an object of pride for Japanese society. After all, the Ainu are part of Japan and one of the many things that makes Japan unique.

Though there remains a way to go to strengthen the rights of Ainu and the extent of their acknowledgement within Japan and the world, the author expects this positive trend to continue.

The legacy, today, then, is the fruit of past generations' labor. In the 1980s and 1990s, the Ainu made significant steps both nationally and internationally. In 1986, for the first time Ainu attended the United Nations at the working group on indigenous people held in Geneva. From this, they went on to attend UN events on many other occasions. By 1991, Japan had recognized the Ainu as a minority group within Japan but not yet as an indigenous people. In 1993, Kayano Shigeru was elected to the Japanese diet and in 1997 the Ainu were declared as the indigenous peoples of Hokkaido in a Sapporo court ruling. In April 2007, the Center for Ainu and Indigenous People was established in Japan, the first of its kind. It also carried a name in the Ainu language *Aynu Teetawanoankur Kapinuye Cise* and was founded by Sapporo University with the goal of raising awareness of Ainu culture among the general populace as well as to conduct research on the linguistics, archeology, history and anthropology of indigenous people. Another watershed moment came in September 2007 when the United Nations passed a resolution on the rights of indigenous people, and Japan, unlike Australia, Canada and New Zealand, did not abstain and passed the motion.

In the following year, on June 6, 2008 both the lower and upper house of the Diet unanimously adopted a resolution that recognized the Ainu as the indigenous people of Japan and, following this, the Council for Ainu Policy was formed as an agency chaired by the Chief Cabinet Secretary. What this ultimately culminated in was the establishment of *Upopoy* – the National Ainu Museum and Park, the only national museum in Hokkaido, which opened in 2020. This museum has its roots in the half-a-century-old Shiraoi Ainu Museum, and tourism in Shiraoi *kotan* dates back to the Meiji era.

Following the United Nations Declaration on the Rights of Indigenous Peoples, the Japanese government arranged a colloquium in August of 2008 and published a report the same year. The colloquium was composed of experts on international law, constitution law, anthropologists, the former minister of education, the governor of Hokkaido and representatives from the Ainu Association of Hokkaido. The report recognized that the Ainu had undergone discrimination during Japan's modernization and had been left in unnecessary poverty. The report also acknowledged that the Ainu possess a unique language and culture and were indigenous people. The report called for a "symbolic space" which could become the basis of ethnic harmony, a place that allowed both those in Japan and those from around the world to understand Ainu history and culture, as well as to build connections for the future.

The recommendation for the site was Lake Poroto for its natural surroundings, geography and the legacy of the institutions that had been established there. Further progress was made on April 26, 2019 when the Japanese government passed new legislation, the first law in Japanese history, to recognize the Ainu as indigenous people.[146] The law pledged financial support for the traditions and customs of the Ainu. The formal name of the new law can be translated as "Promotional Measures to Realize a Society in which the Ainu People are Respected". Article 1 of the law reads:

"This law takes into account the situation of Ainu

culture and tradition, which is a source of pride for the Ainu people, [this law also takes into account] the international state of affairs of indigenous people in recent years. [The Ainu people] are the indigenous people of the northern part of the Japanese archipelago, above all Hokkaido. This law establishes the responsibility of the government to enact measures related to the establishment and management of a symbolic space for ethnic coexistence, for cities, towns and villages to create plans for the promotion of the Ainu which will be approved by the Prime Minister and the certification of special measures for projects based on regional promotion policy for the Ainu. This act will also set up the Council for Ainu Policy Promotion. From these measures the Ainu people will be able to live with pride as an ethnic group, and [this law] works towards a society in which the Ainu people can live with pride and are respected. This law also aims to contribute to the realization of a society in which all people can coexist with each other respecting each person's character and individuality."[147]

Thus, in 2020 almost 200 years after the Former Aboriginal Act and following centuries of conflict between the Ainu and the Wajin, Japan has finally reached a state of maturity where it proudly celebrates both the culture of the Wajin and the Ainu.

EPILOGUE

THE AINU TODAY

HOKKAIDO IS AN example of the amount of diversity to be found in a single country. The island's ecology, indigenous people and history differ dramatically from Japan's other three main islands and there is certainly a feeling of excitement when one visits such a region for the first time. The author hopes that this book has allowed the reader to not just reassess their perceptions of Hokkaido, but that of Japan as a whole.

The focus of this book has been the peoples who have lived their lives in Hokkaido, making it the unique place that it is today. A history stretching back to the Jōmon ancestors of the Japanese and the Ainu who first inhabited the island, to Hokkaido's colonization and incorporation into the Japanese state and on into the 21st Century. Along this historical trajectory, there has been both times of tension and cooperation between the Wajin and Ainu, as well as Westerners and others from further afield.

In school, we are taught to visualize the world as a collection of nation-states, and many of us unconsciously accept that this is how the world is. From this narrative, it is easy to slip into the assumption that a fixed entity such as Japan, with Hokkaido in the north and Kyushu in the south, has been the same since time immemorial.[148] As this book has attempted to show, historically the boundaries of nation-states are, and have always been, far from fixed. In early modern history, Hokkaido was hardly thought of as part of Japan proper, and after colonization began in the 19th Century, for a few decades, Japan's borders extended further north beyond Hokkaido, into Sakhalin and the northern Kuril Islands. If history had played out slightly differently, we might think of Karafuto today in much the same way as we do Hokkaido. Then there is the matter of the Northern Territory dispute between Japan and Russia, which brings in the question of whether there will ever be a time again when Japan's territory extends further north than Hokkaido.

There are many things that will go into shaping Hokkaido's future, some gradual and practical such as the declining birthrate, others more hypothetical such as a proposal to build a tunnel under the sea to connect Hokkaido and Sakhalin. But a renaissance of the Ainu within Japanese culture has occurred, something that would have been unthinkable to generations who grew up during the peiod of the assimilation policy. The months before the opening of *Upopoy* show just how drastically society has changed.

The Japanese government invested 200 billion yen in the 10-hectare site that makes up *Upopoy*, and as the organization neared its opening in April 2020, promotional activities took place across Hokkaido. By January 2020, 150 organizations had signed up to support the opening of the first national museum for the Ainu. In Sapporo, the JR Tower Hotel began selling its teddy bear mascot, Ciel, with Ainu-inspired clothes whose design had been supervised by the Sapporo Ainu Association. The hotel also hosted an Ainu art exhibition.

This was not the only hotel to join in the promotions. From January 2020, the Sapporo View Ōdori Hotel off Ōdori Park began offering a lunch buffet that included Ainu dishes such as the stew Ohau. Japan's major airlines also sought to encourage interest in *Upopoy*. From September to November 2019, ANA aired an in-flight promotional video about *Upopoy* and JAL began offering a special "*Upopoy* fare" and included a piece about the museum in its in-flight magazine. Everyday brands such as the confectionary company Megmilk Snow Brand and the delivery company Sagawa Express began putting *Upopoy* logos onto their packages, and Hokkaido Bank made plans to provide its staff and their families with time off work to attend *Upopoy*'s opening day and paid for their attendance.

The Hokkaido Government also sought to increase international attention, arranging for Ainu-related events including live music and opportunities to try one's hand at Ainu embroidery in America, Vietnam, London, Harbin and Hong Kong. The demand for school trips within Japan to *Upopoy* was also significant, and from December 2019 to the end of January in 2020, 269 schools had already applied for school trips to the museum. The biggest event to promote the opening of *Upopoy* was the 71st Sapporo Snow Festival.

The Sapporo Snow festival is one of Hokkaido's largest tourist attractions of the year, with tourists coming from across the world to see the tall and intricately detailed snow sculptures. the 71st festival, from January 2020 to February 2020 significant for having a giant Ainu-themed snow sculpture at its center to capture the spirit of *Upopoy*. Numerous events also sought to attract the attention of attendees, at night projection mapping projected the culture of the Ainu onto the white sculpture. Promoting this centerpiece snow sculpture and *Upopoy* were the Japanese actor Ukaji Takashi whose mother is the Ainu poet and artist Shizue Ukaji, and Sakaguchi Nagisa who is a member of the J-pop girl band AKB 48 who hails from Asahikawa. Along with these high-profile names in Japan, traditional Ainu dances were also performed in the snow festival ensuring that *Upopoy* was well promoted before its planned opening in April, eventually delayed to July 2020.

Although the Covid-19 pandemic cut off not just Hokkaido but all of Japan from international travel. Even during a press briefing during this period there was an unexpected minor topic of note. Suga Yoshihide as the Chief Cabinet Secretary in May of 2020 was seen during a press conference wearing a face mask with an Ainu motif on it. When asked about the mask Suga commented

"I was given the mask from Ainu in Noboribetsu (*Noboribetsu Ashiri no Kai*), it's handmade. The embroidered pattern is said to be a talisman that keeps pathogens out of the body.[149] As a talisman it also serves as a means to transmit Ainu culture, and that is why I am wearing it."[150]

Suga went on to become the Prime Minister of Japan in September 2020.[151] This seemingly insignificant event shows how the recognition of the Ainu has changed within Japan, and seems a world apart from the days of Prime Minister Nakasone Yasuhiro.

Despite the limits on travel, when *Upopoy* did finally open over 10,000 people within Japan visited *Upopoy* in just the first ten days of its opening.[152] And by October 11, 2020 a total of 120,414 had visited the site.

To conclude this work, I would like to provide an overview of *Upopoy*: The National Ainu Museum and Park. With the opening of such an important institution in Hokkaido, it is perhaps difficult to imagine that only a few decades ago there were politicians in Japan who denied Ainu people still existed. Such false perspectives serve to underscore the significance of *Upopoy* to Japan.

Each building in *Upopoy* is named in the Ainu language beginning with the entrance plaza, (*ūerankarap mintar*), followed by the site's entrance building (*hoskian chise*), which also contains a restaurant serving Ainu food and a souvenir shop. The large building towering over the plaza is the National Ainu Museum (*anunkokor aynu ikor oma kenru*).

Upopoy provides visitors the opportunity to experience the culture and history of the Ainu. To the west of the entrance building, on the banks of Lake Poroto, there is a large multipurpose hall (*uekari chise*) where performances of Ainu dance and music, customs registered as UNESCO intangible heritage, are performed. There is also an experience center (*yaihanokkar chise*), where visitors can play Ainu musical instruments such as the *Mukkuri* and *Tonkori* and attempt Ainu cooking.

North of the National Ainu Museum is a traditional Ainu *kotan* (*teeta kane an kotan*) where visitors can view traditional *chise* and Ainu clothing. The site also provides a setting for traditional Ainu ceremonies. There is also a nearby workshop (*ikar ushi*) where visitors can observe experts creating Ainu carvings and embroidery. Visitors may also take a stroll around the lake and

The National Ainu Museum (photograph kindly provided by Upopoy)

view over forty species of trees and plants which have deep connections with Ainu culture.

The site is of course more than a tourist attraction, it is also a communal space to be used by the Ainu and other guests to ensure the legacy and future of Ainu culture thrives, as seen in the dances, music and productions of Ainu crafts on site. This also extends to the memorial building (*shinnurappa ushi*). Neighboring the memorial building is a tomb for the remains of Ainu forcibly removed by researchers during the Meiji Period and thereafter. In 2008, both houses of the Diet passed a resolution for universities across the country to return the remains of Ainu people that had been taken without permission. The tomb itself is a concrete building with the reliefs of Ainu graves embossed on the entrance walls. Traditional Ainu tombstones (*kuwa*) are around four-feet and are formed of long pieces of wood with a spear-like shape for men and a Y-shape for women. Next to the memorial building, a white totem-pole-like structure adorned with Ainu motifs looks out over the lake on one side and the Pacific Ocean on the other.

The largest building at the *Upopoy* site is the National Ainu Museum which houses a permanent exhibition, special exhibitions and a library (*kanpisos nukar tunpu*). At the time of the site's opening, the permanent exhibition in the museum revolved around six themes: '*Itak*' (language), about the Ainu language, a game that allows users to try and pronounce Ainu words, and the differences in the Ainu language across regions; '*Inomi*' (prayer), about Ainu ceremonies, such as Iomante and the soul (*Ramat*) which inhabits all living things; '*Urespa*' (To raise), on the general life, clothing, food, dance, music and children's games of the Ainu; '*Upaskuma*' (traditions), history left by the Ainu about themselves and a history by the surrounding people who encountered them; '*Nepuki*' (work), about traditional Ainu jobs such as fishing and hunting etc. and the tools used as well as crafts during the Meiji era, and the jobs of modern Ainu today; last of all, *'Ukoapukas'* (interactions), about the interactions between Ainu and surrounding peoples as well as the wider world, including other indigenous groups around the world who have a shared experience similar to the Ainu in Japan.

In the Ainu language the word *'Upopoy'* can be translated as 'singing together', *Upopoy* is significant as it is an attempt to address past wrongs, as seen in the tomb and memorial center. The establishment of *Upopoy* was supported by the Japanese government, who have committed to readdressing ignorance about the Ainu in Japan and to include the Ainu in the narrative of the history of Japan and its people. *Upopoy* also lays a foundation for the future of the Ainu, becoming a beacon of prosperity in Japan and the wider world.

The reader may have questions about the Ainu in Japan today, how many are there? How many people speak the language? What is their economic situation and their future?

Since the Japanese government does not collect any statistics of the number of people who identify as Ainu in Japan, it is difficult to arrive at a precise number. A 2013 survey by the Ainu Association of Hokkaido put the number of Ainu in Hokkaido at 16,786, with 38% of these in Hidaka Subprefecture and 32.1% in Iburi Subprefecture.[153] However, such a survey does not take into account those living outside of Hokkaido, and of course lacks the resources a national government survey would have. A 2017 survey by the Hokkaido Government found that the number of Ainu had fallen to 13,118. However, with the Ainu increasingly viewed in a positive light in Japanese society, there is a possibility that more people will begin to associate themselves as Ainu or partly-Ainu in the future.

The number of Ainu speakers is also tricky to define. The Japanese Agency for Cultural Affairs has recognized that Ainu is an endangered language under UNESCO and works to record Ainu speakers as well as to translate their recordings into Japanese. Unfortunately, as with population numbers, there is a lack of government statistics. It is difficult for researchers to survey speakers of the Ainu language, since all researchers can do is attempt to ask individuals, and some will not respond due to concerns over privacy and other personal reasons. While there are still individuals who have a high fluency in the Ainu language, they tend to be of advanced age, and the Ainu language is indeed endangered. But this does not mean that the language is destined to become extinct. There are Ainu language classrooms across Hokkaido and in Tokyo, and there is also an Ainu radio program which publishes its texts and shows online, making the language more accessible for those who are interested. There are also multiple Ainu language textbooks in Japanese written for those in Japan who wish to learn the Ainu language.

Traditional Ainu religious practices continue though at a low level. A 2008 survey found that less than 10% of the Ainu who responded took part in *Kamuy-Nomi* (communicating with the gods) and *Shinnurappa* (ancestor worship). Even fewer respondents still carried out the bear-sending ceremony — 1.1% (for both animals and substitutes).[154] Much debate surrounds the practice of bear sacrifice in *Iomante* even within the Ainu community. While live bears are rarely used, debate remains around whether they should be. This can be seen in the 2020 documentary *Ainu Mosir* directed by Takeshi Fukunaga, where members of the Akan community debate whether the sacrifice of a live bear should take place. Some members point out that they are not hunter-gatherers like their ancestors, they instead rely on tourism and that this would put people off, or simply they do not have the heart to do it. Another member stresses that the whole point of *Iomante* is that they treat the bear well and when they send it back to the *Kamuy Mosir*, it tells the other gods who return to Earth as other animals such as owls and bears how great it is in the land of the humans. If the Ainu people cannot carry out their religious practices, how Ainu are they really? As with many issues in communities such as the Ainu, there is not always a unanimous opinion on contentious issues.

As the Ainu have been assimilated into Japanese society, traditional Ainu religious customs have certainly weakened. In the 2008 survey, the most common religious practice amongst those surveyed was Buddhism at 46.2%, although this was not necessarily exclusive of only Buddhism and it is possible to practice Ainu religious customs alongside another faith.[155]

The economic position of the Ainu has improved in recent years, in a 2013 survey by the Ainu Association of Hokkaido, in the 41 years up to 2013, the number of Ainu working in the primary sector (mining, forestry, fishing etc.) fell by about half, while those in the tertiary sector more than doubled. In 2013, 36% of Ainu were working in primary industries, 19% in secondary industry (manufacturing etc.) and 40.4% in tertiary industries (mostly the tourism industry), while 4.6% were in undefined industries.[156] Nonetheless, many Ainu view this as still not enough, and will not be satisfied until they reach economic parity with their Wajin compatriots.

The Japanese government is now heavily involved in the promotion of Ainu culture, as can be seen from the financial commitment to the creation of *Upopoy*. The Office of Ainu Promotion within the Japanese government states that its mission is the creation of a society in which the Ainu people can be proud as an ethnic group, and the promotion of Ainu culture.

While there are no Ainu politicians in the national government at present, there is an organization of Diet members focused on Ainu policy, and also a similar organization within the government of Hokkaido.[157] Advocacy for the Ainu, then, mostly falls to the hands of Ainu organizations across the country, most notable the Ainu Association of Hokkaido which plays the largest role.

There is still much to be done to increase general Japanese awareness of the Ainu. A 2016 government survey asked 1,727 people the question, "Have you come into contact with Ainu people and Ainu culture?", and 74.1% responded "no", 24.7% "yes", and 1.3% as "unsure".[158]

Many Ainu are still concerned about racism. In the 2017 survey by the Hokkaido government, 23.2% of respondents replied "yes" to the question, "Have you been the target of racism?" while 13.1% responded "yes" to the statement, "While I have not been the target of racism, I have seen it with other (Ainu)" and only 35.2% responded "yes" to "I have not been the target of racism."[159] In terms of the response to such incidents of racism, 18.6% of respondents said "I did nothing" while only 10.9% said "I protested." Examples of other responses are not worrying about it (12.2%) bearing it (12.2%) being proud of ones Ainu heritage (1.9%), consulting with family (1.9%), consulting with a public organization or teacher (1.3%), while 26.9% of respondents did not answer this question.[160] In order to remove discrimination to the Ainu, most respondents (58.6%) agreed the priority was to "increase the understanding of the Ainu through school education"[161]

For Ainu culture to flourish in modern times it is necessary for people to feel proud of their culture and history. The survey in 2008 indicated an increase in pride amongst young people in their Ainu heritage, with 45.7% of respondents (1,167) citing Ainu culture as a source of pride, and 34.5% (881) cited Ainu

History.[162] In regards to the importance of Ainu *puri* (habits and customs of the Ainu) one respondent commented:

> "Ainu *puri* is a way of life. I believe *puri* reveals itself in everything – ways of thinking about things or people and Ainu culture as a whole, including mentality. It shows in our minds, such as in ways of communing with nature, having gratitude for things, and affection for my Ainu husband, I have come to love the concept of Ainu *puri*. I feel the utmost peace of mind and the gentleness of the world."[163]

The opening of *Upopoy*, which serves as an education facility as well as a celebration of the Ainu, will hopefully help serve these functions. In only its first year, it has drastically changed the situation for many young Ainu, who can work at the facilities and teach visitors about the Ainu, while learning about their own culture and language themselves, thereby increasing their pride as Ainu.

However, there is also a small backlash towards this movement from right-wing groups which seek to deny the existence of minorities in Japan, including the Ainu. The opening of *Upopoy* is a landmark event for the Ainu, but there is still much more to be done and continued efforts are required to push forward.

The opening of the National Ainu Museum in 2020 saw lower turnout than initially anticipated because of the coronavirus pandemic, but it will surely play a role in increasing interest and understanding in the indigenous people of Hokkaido both at home and around the world in the years to come. In December, 2020 the Hokkaido Government opened on its website a viritual tour of *Upopoy* for any of those who are interested but cannot make the journey to Hokkaido.

The significance of the site's opening was encapsulated by speeches from senior figures in both the Japanese Government and the Ainu Association of Hokkaido. At the Japanese government's commemorative ceremony to mark the opening of *Upopoy*, held in Tokyo, the then Chief Cabinet Secretary, now the 99th Prime Minister of Japan, Suga Yoshihide commented:

> "It is very important for the Ainu people to be able to maintain their honor and dignity while being able to pass this on to the next generation, and important [for us] to realize a society in which diverse values can coexist. We will do our utmost to improve the attractiveness of *Upopoy*, so that many people from both Japan and abroad will be able to empathize with the ideal of ethnic coexistence."[164]

During the opening ceremony in Hokkaido at the *Upopoy* site, Katō Tadashi, the Director of the Ainu Association of Hokkaido (from May 2004 to June 2020) said that, while tears fell from his eyes:

> "…the true value of being human is not the character of an ethnicity, but the mentality of the individual. I have confidence that the *Upopoy* will be an institution that contributes to the harmony and coexistence of humanity."[165]

As with any group, the Ainu will continue to change. One respondent to the 2008 survey captured this :

> "Even if we cannot do exactly as our ancestors did, I

believe we will find ourselves spiritually richer thanks to Ainu heritage, and will gradually come to cherish Ainu culture by being considerate to others, being appreciative of our food, learning about the history of the Ainu and studying how they have endured hardships."[166]

Indeed, not only those of Ainu heritage, but Japan and the wider world will also be richer for it. While the opening of *Upopoy* and the National Ainu Museum in 2020 is the end point for this book, the story of Hokkaido and the Ainu will surely continue.

ENDNOTES

1   The name for Wakkanai has its origins in the Ainu language as 'yam-wakka-nay' meaning the place of 'cold water'

2   The Northern Territory problem remains a point of contention between the Japanese and Russian governments. Japan continues to include the northern islands in maps of Hokkaido. The Russian government insists that Japan surrendered these territories at the end of World War II. Russia has made efforts to solidify its *de facto* control of the islands, such as the building of a fishery processing plant on the island of Shikotan. To further bolster this, on the 24th September 2020, Russia announced that it would be building the first paved road on Shikotan which will be more than 2.5 kilometers long as part of the 'Kuril Islands Socio-Economic Development Plan'

3   If theories about the Emishi people who fought with the Japanese throughout early Japanese history are correct, then people who can be seen as 'proto-Ainu' existed as far as south as modern day Tokyo and beyond. The role of the Shogun itself originates from driving back these so called 'barbarian' people and expanding the Emperor's control

4   Matsuura initially used the characters 北加伊道 ('Hokkaido'), showing how these are in part phonetic. Other names Matsuura proposed to the Meiji government included 'Hitakami', 'Hokkai' and even 'Chishima' the Japanese name for what is now the Kuril Islands. The 'dō' 道 in the name of Hokkaido is equivalent to the symbol

for prefecture 県, for example Okayama (岡山) Prefecture is written as 岡山県, with dō denoting a much larger administrative region. Hokkaido is the only region in the entirety of Japan that has this special definition as a dō / 道

5   *Upopoy* – The National Ainu Museum and Park was originally scheduled to open at the end of April in 2020, but the Covid-19 pandemic led to the date being moved on numerous occasions until it was opened July 12, 2020

6   The characters for Jō 縄 and mon 文 together literally mean 'rope patterns'

7   The Okhotsk culture formed around the Sea of Okhotsk and was active from the 3rd Century to the 13th Century. DNA analysis from remains at Okhotsk archeological sites shows common trends with those of Ainu descent, but not in Jōmon remains

8   Theories about Ainu places name stretch as far as the Kanto region, although these are hard if not impossible to prove. For example, the city of Kamakura on its official website gives one of the many and possible origin of the city name as from the Ainu 'Kamukuran' which means crossing over the mountains

9   Georg Schurhammer, *Francis Xavier: His Life, His Times, Indonesia and India 1545-1549* (Loyola Press, 1980), 336.

10 The characters for Iōzan 夷王山 can be literally translated as 'King of the Ezo' (Ainu). A museum to the historical remains of Katsuyama outpost can be visited today at the site. Katsuyama was built around the mid 15th Century by Takeda/Kakizaki Nobuhiro. At the summit of Iōzan is a shrine (夷王山神社) in which Takeda is enshrined

11 黒印状

12 津軽一統誌

13 Shinichirō Takakura, *Ainu Seisaku Shi* (Nihon Hyōronsha,

1943)

14   *Ibid*

15   Tatsujiro Kuzuno (1910-2002) has written the Ainu language name for Shakushain as Sakusain. There are also other Ainu language versions, such as Saksaynu and Samkusaynu. Shakushain is a Japanese transliteration, and since this is the most common version of his name used in Japan it is used here

16   蝦夷談筆記

17   松前蝦夷一揆聞書

18   蝦夷蜂起

19   Hiroto Hirayama, *Shakushain No Tatakai* (Sapporo: Jurosha, 2016), 120

20   *Chasi* are referred to as *Casi* in the Ainu language, and over 500 of these hill fortresses have been identified across Hokkaido

21   Hokkaido Shimbun. "新ひだかアイヌ協会は、シャクシャイン像を建て替える," *Hokkaido Shimbun*, February 15, 2015.

22   In 1989, a Nagasaki museum was founded to commemorate the life of Seibold. The Seibold Memorial Museum became the first museum in Japan dedicated to a European

23   Mamiya Yoshiaki (1939-2017) who was the chairman of the Ashikawa branch of the Foundation for Research and Promotion of Ainu Culture from 1990 to 2003, visited his ancestor Mamiya's hometown in Ibaraki Prefecture where he held the Ainu religious ceremony of *Kamuy-imi*. During the *Kamuy-imi* ceremony, the Ainu thank the *Kamuy* for providing them with food and warmth while also asking them to grant their prayers. Yoshiaki passed away in 2017, the Mamiya name is continued through his eldest son Mamiya Akihiko. By performing the *Kamuy-imi* in Ibaraki Prefecture, Mamiya Yoshiaki reminds us how the

exploration and cartography of Hokkaido, the Kuril Islands and Sakhalin was a joint Ainu and Japanese endeavor

24 This garment is in the *Rūnpe* style which involves adding pieces of thin white or colored cloth with Ainu embroidery onto a cotton garment. Other Ainu styles which use cotton are *Chikakarpe* (black and navy embroidery cloth with hardly any white), *Kaparamip* (Adding a large piece of cloth with Ainu embroidery to the garment), and *Chijiri* (stitching the design straight into the cotton garment)

25 松前蝦夷一揆聞書

26 蝦夷三官寺

27 The Tōshō-gū shrines are elaborate shrines of multi-colored reliefs of dragons, monkeys, and birds decorated in multicolored lacquer and gold. They are some of the most extravagant shrines in Japan, and they attract large numbers of tourists, particularly the world heritage Nikkō Tōshō-gū shrine in Tochigi Prefecture and the Ueno Tōshō-gū shrine in Tokyo's Ueno Park

28 尊王攘夷

29 The Japanese negotiations were led by Kawaji Toshiaki (1801-1868) who claimed that the Kuril island of Iturup was a Japanese territory since Japanese texts refer to the island. Putyatin countered Kawaji by pointing out that the majority of the people living on Iturup were not Japanese but Ainu. Kawaji followed the Shogunate's reasoning that the Ainu are Japanese subjects too, thereby showing that the Kuril Islands are Japanese, not Russian territory. After days of going back and forth, on February 17, 1855 the Treaty of Shimoda was signed at Chōraku-Ji temple. A sign commemorates the event at the temple today

30 Francis Hawks, *Narrative of the Expedition of an American Squadron to the China Seas and Japan* (D. Appleton and Co

Beverley, 1857), 436

31 *Ibid*, 441

32 洋夷名話

33 *Narrative of the Expedition of an American Squadron to the China Seas and Japan*, 438

34 The Meiji government dismantled the original Magistrate after the battle of Hakodate, and the Magistrate was reconstructed to its former glory in 2010, a feat taking over 20 years of archeological and historical research to complete

35 Further written entries can be seen within the Magistrate if one visits today

36 The Aizu clan were entrusted with the northeastern part of Hokkaido from around Betsukai to around Oumu. The Sendai clan were assigned the eastern region from Shiraoi to Nemuro as well as the Kuril Islands of Kunashir and Iturup. The Shōnai clan was given the western region from Niseko, and the Akita clan a small region around Mashige in the middle of territory assigned to the Shōnai clan, the area around Cape Sōya to Oumu and the islands of Rishiri and Rebun off Hokkaido's northeastern coast. The Tsugaru clan were entrusted the eastern half of the Oshima Peninsula with the Morioka clan were entrusted the right half

37 Today Goryōkaku is one of the major tourist attractions of Hakodate, and a viewing tower offers views of what is now Goryōkaku Park

38 The temple that Rice used as the American consular is unfortunately no longer standing in Hakodate. In 1858, the temple changed its name from Jōgen-Ji temple to Higashi Hongan-Ji temple (東本願寺) and was subsequently burnt down during the Great Fire of Hakodate in 1907. The Higashi Hongan-Ji that stands in Hakodate today was moved west from the original site and was rebuilt as the

first reinforced concrete building in Japan

39 *Hakodate Kaika To Beikoku Ryōji* (Sapporo: Hokkaidō Shinbunsha, 1994), 29

40 *Ibid*, 23

41 *Ibid*, 77

42 In Japan, Masuda received a house on the grounds of Zōjō-Ji Temple now in Tokyo's Shibakoen beneath Tokyo tower. Many things had changed during Masuda's absence, for one the new Meiji government had renamed the city of Edo as Tokyo in 1868 and instead of viewing Westerners with suspicion, students and politicians flocked to his Tokyo office to learn about the Western powers such as Russia

43 With the opening of the Hokkaido bullet train in 2016, the last stop was Hakodate and posters of the Orthodox Church lined the walls of Tokyo station

44 On Nikolai's parting from his family, his father handed him a figure of Christ that went on to adorn Nikolai's private room in Hakodate, and later in Tokyo, for the rest of his life

45 Hokkoku Ryōsei, *Bakumatsu Ishin Ezochi Ibun: Gōshō, Mononofu, Ikokujintachi No Yūhi* (Sapporo: Hokkaidō Shuppan Kikaku Senta⁻, 2009), 183

46 *Ibid,* 187

47 The seeds of the Shogunate's downfall were sown during the regime's birth. It was after the battle of Sekigahara in 1600 that the samurai domains were split into two categories: *Fudai* who had fought on the side of the Tokugawa and *Tozama* who had opposed them. *Fudai Daimyō* were given strategic lands and allowed to rise to positions of power within the Shogunate, with the *Tozama* lacking political influence and being under heavy surveillance

48 *Hakodate Kaika To Beikoku Ryōji* (Sapporo: Hokkaidō Shinbunsha, 1994), 117

49 Hijikata has become a historical celebrity of sorts in Japan today, and versions of him have featured in television, anime and manga stories. He has also become a mascot for the Goryōkaku castle

50 *Bakumatsu Ishin Ezochi Ibun*, 253

51 Both monuments are in Hakodate today and every year in mid-May at the start of the 'Hakodate Goryokaku Festival' Hakodate citizens dressed as the Meiji and Enomoto army parade through the city. One of their stops is the Hekketsu-Hi and on June of every year, a memorial service is held for the fallen

52 Sapporo is derived form the Ainu name 'Sat Poro Pet' (Great Dry River) (Sat = dry), (Poro = large) (Pet = river). 'Pet' in particular is a very common sound that can be found in many of Hokkaido's place names and can be spotted across Hokkaido

53 Another key difference between Qing China and Meiji Japan is in who was blamed for the problems caused by the arrival of the foreign powers. In Qing China the majority of ethnically Han Chinese were ruled by a Manchu minority and resentment towards this state of affairs was often directed at them alongside the foreigners. In Japan this rage was often directed towards the Shogunate and the foreigners themselves. The Meiji government was able to stabilize the country and turn this anger towards foreign things into a means for Japan to become more modern and Western

54 The flag of the Development Commission later became the basis for the Hokkaido flag that can be seen throughout the island today

55 Sapporo Gakuin University, ed., *Daigakuteki Hokkaido Gaido: Kodawari No Arukikata* (Sapporo: Showado, 2012), 79

56 帰農御免願

57 Morie Enomoto, *Samuraitachi No Hokkaidō Kaitaku* (Dōshin, 1993)

58 From Tohoku samurai from the Hirosaki (Aomori Prefecture) Yonezawa and Tsuruoka (Yamagata Prefecture) and Aizu (Fukushima Prefecture) domains. From Kantō came samurai from the Mito domain (Ibaraki Prefecture), and from Chūbu came the Kanazawa (Ishikawa and Toyama Prefectures) and Nagoya (Aichi Prefecture) and Shizuoka (Shizuoka and Yamanashi Prefectures) domains. From Kansai came the Wakayama and Hikone (Shiga Prefecture) domains. From Chugoku came the Yamaguchi, Hiroshima and Totori domains. From the island of Shikoku came samurai from the Tosa (Kōchi Prefecture) and Tokushima domains. From the island of Kyushu came samurai from the Kumamoto, Saga (Saga and Nagasaki Prefectures), Satsuma (Kagoshima Prefecture) and Fukuoka domains

59 移民扶助規則

60 The Escape King continues to be a main attraction of the Abashiri Prison Museum built inside the former Prison, and a mannequin depicts Shiratori during his infamous escape. Shiratori's reputation has also enjoyed a recent revival due to the manga and anime *Golden Kamuy* (beginning in 2014), in which the character Shiraishi Yoshitake is based on the real life Shiratori Yoshie, as well as a 2017 live action film

61 The Jōmon tunnel is still in use today and the JR Hokkaido Sekihoku Line between Engaru Town and Kitami City passes through it. In 1980, a monument was built to the dead whose remains were found in the tunnel in the 1970s and 1980s

62 北海道土地払下規則

63 北海道移民答問

64   The Sapporo Agricultural College was also notable for its uniform, the *'Gakuran'* clothes with a black jacket, stand-up collar and metal buttons. The Western-style uniform coincided with the introduction of Western technology and thought, and was introduced into Sapporo Agricultural College and the Imperial College of Engineering in the early 1870s. Today the *Gakuran* has become a symbol of Japanese middle school and high school boys and has also been popularized internationally through popular manga characters such as Kūjō Jōtarō in the series *JoJo's Bizarre Adventure*

65   Hideshi Seki, *Hokkaidō No Rekishi* (Sapporo: Hokkaidōshinbunsha, 2006), 52

66   The phrase 'boys be ambitious' became well known throughout the country. In Sapporo, a statue of Clarke at Hitsujigaoka has the phrase inscribed with his left hand behind his back, and his arm stretched out forth. It remains on souvenirs from Hokkaido and is echoed in the motto of Kitahiroshima: *'the ambitious city'*

67   Today a statue in front of Kagoshima station commemorates the students and a 150-year memorial of the Satsuma study abroad mission is commemorated on limited cans of Sapporo beer: 'The gold' which included a picture of the statue with the phrase 'Sapporo Beer, the beer that Kagoshimans created'

68   The highway now forms part of the national highway thirty-six and five

69   Kenji Nozoe, *Saharin Ga Takara No Shima to Yobareteita Koro*: Umi o Watatta Dekasegi Nihonjin (Tōkyō: Shakai Hyōronsha, 2015), 168

70   *Ibid*, 63

71   *Ibid*, 46

72 *Ibid*, 72

73 Not all came by force, some arrived via north Hokkaido or travelled south through Russia (after Japan lost control of Russia's maritime provinces)

74 *Ibid*, 207

75 Kosaka Yōsuke, *Ryūbō: Nichi-Ro Ni Owareta Kita Chishima Ainu* (Sapporo: Hokkaidō Shinbunsha, 1992), 208

76 北海道巡回記

77 *Ryūbō*, 226

78 北千島調査報文

79 Masato Kuwabara and Jun Kawakami, *Hokkaidō No Rekishi Ga Wakaru Hon: Sekki Jidai Kara Kingendai Made Ikkiyomi* (Arisusha, 2018), 290

80 Isabella Bird, *Unbeaten Tracks in Japan: An Account of Travels in the Interior Including Visits to the Aborigines of Yezo and the Shrine of Nikko.* (Edinburgh: R. & R. Clark, 1888), 177

81 *Ibid*

82 北海道地貸規則 & 北海道地券発行条令

83 北海道土地払下規則

84 Denmei Ueda, *Ainu Minzoku o Kangaeru.* (Kyōto: Hōritsu Bunkasha, 2007), 27

85 *Unbeaten Tracks in Japan*, 189

86 *Ibid*

87 アイヌの碑

88 Shigeru Kayano, *Ainu No Ishibumi* (Tōkyō: Asahi Shinbunsha, 1994), 73-75

89 *Ibid*

90 北海道旧土人保護法

91 "教育ニ關スル勅語（明治二十三年十月三十日），" 文部科学省, https://www.mext.go.jp/b_menu/hakusho/html/others/detail/1317936.htm

92 Fred C. C. Peng and Peter Geiser, *The Ainu: The Past in the*

Present (Hiroshima: Bunka Hyoron, 1977), 201

93 Junichi Tomimura, *Kōhei To Ainuhei* (JCA Shuppan, 1981), 21-22

94 *Ibid*

95 *Ibid*, 56-57

96 白老土人協会

97 Kimio, Miyatake, *Umi o Watatta Ainu: Senjūmin Tenji To Futatsu No Hakurankai*. (Tōkyō: Iwanami Shoten, 2010), 141

98 *Unbeaten Tracks in Japan*, 189

99 Iwao Nitami, *Ikyō No Shito: Eijin Jon Bachirā Den* (Sapporo: Hokkaidō Shinbunsha, 1991), 34

100 *Ibid*, 136

101 The site of Batchelor's Sapporo residence is now located inside the Hokkaido University Botanical Gardens

102 若きウタリに

103 The monument to John Batchelor can be found in Uckfield Cemetary in the UK today. The monument includes a silhouette of Hokkaido, and two separate stone panels, one with the Kanji for "love", the other "HOKKAIDO JAPAN". The main text of the monument reads "The Venerable John Batchelor O.B.E D.D. 1854-1944, Missionary to the AINUS 1877-1941"

104 *Ainu No Ishibumi*, 108

105 *Kōhei To Ainuhei*, 118

106 国家総動員法

107 *Kōhei To Ainuhei*, 131

108 It would be Kawakami who recorded the final days of Tsukamoto's life and told this testament to Tomimura Junichi

109 *Kōhei To Ainuhei*, 177

110 While Kawakami was in the camp, he read Tsukamoto's wartime journal and learnt more about Tsukamoto's

experience as an Ainu in Japan. At that time, Kawakami
wanted to return the journal to Tsukamoto's family, but
25 years passed before he was able to do so. The chance
occurred when his daughter was planning to go to Okinawa
for her honeymoon, and Kawakami told her the story of
Tsukamoto and his experience of the Battle of Okinawa. She
encouraged him to go to the Ministry of Health and Welfare
in Tokyo, and Kawakami was able to find Tsukamoto's
family. With his daughter he went to Hokkaido and
confirmed that Tsukamoto's wife had remarried, and that
his baby, a son, had grown up to have a family of his own.
It was during this visit that he found Tsukamoto's older
journals and letters which were published in the book 『皇
軍とアイヌ兵－沖縄戦に消えたアイヌ兵の生涯』

111 *Ainu No Ishibumi*, 109

112 *Ibid*, 112

113 *Ibid*

114 *Saharin Ga Takara No Shima to Yobareteita Koro*, 238

115 Kudō Toshiyuki, *Karafuto Eien Naru Daichi* (Bokkasha, 2017),
335

116 *Saharin Ga Takara No Shima to Yobareteita Koro*, 37

117 Kudō Toshiyuki, *Karafuto Eien Naru Daichi* (Bokkasha, 2017),
349

118 *Saharin Ga Takara No Shima to Yobareteita Koro*, 245

119 *Ibid*, 237

120 *Ibid*, 183

121 Today some of the tanks from the battle of Shumshu are
preserved in the Sakhalin State Museum

122 The Japan Times, September 22, 2007. https://www.
japantimes.co.jp/news/2007/09/22/reference/
specialpresentations/nemuro-raid-survivor-longs-for-
homeland/.

123 アイヌ神謡集

124 Yukie Chiri, *Ainu Shinyōshū* (Tōkyō: Iwanamishoten, 2009), 3-5

125 十勝アイヌ旭日社

126 北海道アイヌ協会

127 旭川市旧土人保護法地処分法

128 By this point, the Ainu had been naturalized as Japanese citizens, and most of those who held Ainu heritage had Wajin ancestors also, and this is the case today

129 Hiromi Nishiyauchi, *Shiraoi Ni Okeru Ainu Minzoku No Henyō*, 65

130 *Ibid*, 24

131 *Ainu No Ishibumi*, 127

132 *Ibid*, 139

133 *Ibid*, 129

134 平取町二風谷アイヌ語教室

135 Akibe Hideo and Ōtani Yōichi, *Ainu Bunka No Genzai* (Sapporo: Sapporo Gakuin University, 1997), 164

136 *Ibid*, 167

137 Hiromi Nishiyauchi, *Shiraoi Ni Okeru Ainu Minzoku No Henyō: Iomante Ni Miru Shinkan Kinō No Keifu* (Tōkyō: Tōshindō, 2018), 83

138 *Ibid*

139 *Ibid*, 84

140 *Ainu Bunka No Genzai*, 10

141 Hiroto Hirayama, *Ainu No Rekishi: Nihon No Senjū Minzoku o Rikaisuru Tame No 160-Wa* (Tōkyō: Akashi Shoten, 2014), 306

142 Revival efforts of indigenous languages in both Hokkaido and Okinawa are ongoing, and this has gained particular traction in Okinawa with numerous language schools. Similar efforts are making progress in Hokkaido, although

they have yet to gain the same traction as in Okinawa Prefecture

143 *Shiraoi Ni Okeru Ainu Minzoku No Henyō*, 98

144 "1992年12月10日国連総会「世界の先住民の国際年」記念演説," 公益社団法人北海道アイヌ協会

145 アイヌ文化の振興並びにアイヌの伝統等に関する知識の普及及び啓発に関する法律 (1997) also known as the Ainu Cultural Promotion Act

146 The law's full name is アイヌの人々の誇りが尊重される社会を実現するための施策の推進に関する法律 (2019) The Realization and Creation a Society in which the Ainu People can be Proud Act. But this is often shortened to アイヌ新法 The New Ainu Law

147 "アイヌの人々の誇りが尊重される社会を実現するための施策の推進に関する法律," e-gov 法令検索, https://elaws.e-gov.go.jp/document?lawid=431AC0000000016.

148 Japan's southern border extends down to Yonaguni Island neighboring Taiwan, but this is left out of many maps, and is difficult to see on most world maps

149 Protection talismans or '*Omamori*' are very popular in Japan and are often sold at shrines and temples

150 "官房長官着用で話題 アイヌ民族の魔よけ文様マスク が人気." NHKニュース, May 17, 2020. https://www3.nhk.or.jp/news/html/20200518/k10012434091000.html.

151 Suga is the 99th Prime Minister of Japan, beginning with Itō Hirobumi in the Meiji era

152 This was on a reservation system to maintain social distancing measures. On the average working day, 1,000 people visited the site between July 12 and July 21, this number climbed to 1,800 on weekends

153 Ainu Association of Hokkaido. "アイヌの生活実態." 公益社団法人北海道アイヌ協会. Accessed December 26, 2020.

https://www.ainu-assn.or.jp/ainupeople/life.html

154 Toru Onai, ed., Report on the 2008 Hokkaido Ainu Living Conditions Survey - Living Conditions and Consciousness of Present-Day Ainu (Center for Ainu and Indigenous Studies, Hokkaido University, 2011), 110

155 *Ibid*, 108

156 Ainu Association of Hokkaido. "アイヌの生活実態." 公益社団法人北海道アイヌ協会. Accessed December 26, 2020. https://www.ainu-assn.or.jp/ainupeople/life.html

157 アイヌ政策を推進する議員の会 (national) & アイヌ政策推進北海道議会議員連盟 (Hokkaido)

158 "「国民のアイヌに対する理解度に関する世論調査」の概要." Cabinet Office, February 2016. https://survey.gov-online.go.jp/tokubetu/h27/h27-ainu.pdf

159 北海道環境生活部. "北海道アイヌ生活実態調査報告書平成29." Government of Hokkaido, 2017. http://www.pref.hokkaido.lg.jp/ks/ass/H29_ainu_living_conditions_survey_.pdf

160 *Ibid*

161 *Ibid*

162 Onai, Report on the 2008 Hokkaido Ainu Living Conditions Survey - Living Conditions and Consciousness of Present-Day Ainu, 28

163 *Ibid*, 28

164 NHK Hokkaido, "ウポポイ開業前日に政府が式典 #アイヌ: NHK北海道," NHK札幌放送局, July 11, 2020, https://www.nhk.or.jp/hokkaido/articles/slug-n19825cc197ba

165 *Ibid*

166 Onai, Report on the 2008 Hokkaido Ainu Living Conditions Survey - Living Conditions and Consciousness of Present-Day Ainu, 111

BIBLIOGRAPHY

Yamashita Tsuneo, Daikokuya Kōdayū: Teisei Roshia Hyōryū No Monogatari. Tōkyō: Iwanami Shoten, 2004.

Wakayama Akihiko, "アイヌ新法成立、交付金の活用に工夫を（風紋）." 日本経済新聞 電子版. 日本経済新聞社, April 28, 2019. https://www.nikkei.com/article/DGXMZO44276730W9A420C1SHB000/.

Utagawa Hiroshi, Ainu Bunka Seiritsushi. Sapporo: Hokkaidō Shuppan Kikaku Sentā, 1988.

Ueda Denmei, Ainu Minzoku o Kangaeru. Kyōto: Hōritsu Bunkasha, 2007.

Tomimura Junichi, Kōhei To Ainuhei. JCA Shuppan, 1981.

Tanimoto Akihisa ed, An Introduction to Ainu Studies. Sapporo: Center for Ainu and Indigenous Studies, Hokkaido University, 2018.

Tanaka Akira, Hokkaido To Meiji Ishin: Henkyo Karano Shiza. Sapporo: Hokkaido University Press, 2000.

Takakura Shinichirō, Ainu Seisaku Shi. Nihon Hyōronsha, 1943.

Takahara Kanako. "Nemuro Raid Survivor Longs for Homeland." The Japan Times, September 22, 2007. https://www.japantimes.co.jp/news/2007/09/22/reference/special-presentations/nemuro-raid-survivor-longs-for-homeland/.

Shinoda Kenichi, DNA De Kataru Nihonjin Kigenron. Iwanami Shoten, 2015.

Shimizu Kensaku, "幕末の函館に「幻の出島」 突き止めた着工の史実 開港経緯や外国人居留地 古地図で調査." 日本経済新聞 電子版. 日本経済新聞社, January 17, 2020. https://www.

nikkei.com/article/DGXKZO54463600W0A110C2BC8000/.

Seki Hideshi et al, Hokkaidō No Rekishi (Shita). Sapporo: Hokkaidōshinbunsha, 2006.

Schurhammer Georg, Francis Xavier: His Life, His Times, Indonesia and India 1545-1549. Loyola Press, 1980.

Satō Kōji, Nihon Kokkahō to Senjūminzoku Dearu Ainu No Hitobito. Sapporo: Center for Ainu and Indigenous Studies, 2013.

Sato Tomomi, "アイヌ語の現状と復興." 言語研究, no. 142 (2012): 29–44.

Sapporo Gakuin University, ed. Daigakuteki Hokkaido Gaido: Kodawari No Arukikata. Sapporo: Showado, 2012.

Plutschow Herbert, Gaikokujin Ga Mita jūkyūseiki No Hakodate. Tōkyō: Musashino Shoin, 2002.

Perry Matthew Calbraith, and Francis Hawkes, Narrative of the Expedition of an American Squadron to the China Seas and Japan, Performed in the Years 1852, 1853, and 1854: under the Command of Commodore M.C. Perry. New York: D. Appleton and Co.; 1857.

Peng Fred and Geiser Peter, The Ainu: the Past in the Present. Hiroshima: Bunka Hyoron, 1977.

Onai Toru, ed. Report on the 2008 Hokkaido Ainu Living Conditions Survey - Living Conditions and Consciousness of Present-Day Ainu. Center for Ainu and Indigenous Studies, Hokkaido University, 2011.

Nozoe Kenji, Saharin Ga Takara No Shima to Yobareteita Koro: Umi o Watatta Dekasegi Nihonjin. Tōkyō: Shakai Hyōronsha, 2015.

Nitami Iwao, Ikyō No Shito: Eijin Jon Bachirā Den. Sapporo: Hokkaidō Shinbunsha, 1991.

Nishiyauchi Hiromi, Shiraoi Ni Okeru Ainu Minzoku No Henyō: Iomante Ni Miru Shinkan Kinō No Keifu. Tōkyō: Tōshindō,

2018.

Nishino Tatsukichi, Ishikarigawa Kikō: Hokkaidō Bunmeishi o Saguru. Tōkyō: Nihon Hōsō Shuppankyōkai, 1975.

Nishiguchi Tadashi, Tanabe Yōko, and Billingsley Phil, Eikoku Seikōkai Senkyō Kyōkai No Nihon dendō to Hakodate Ainu Gakkō: Eikokujin Josei Edisu Bearingu=Gūrudo Ga Mita Meiji Nihon. Yokohama: Shunpūsha, 2018.

Nikkei Shimbun. "北海道の「ウポポイ」開業まで3カ月、官民で盛り上げ." 日本経済新聞. 日本経済新聞社, January 22, 2020. https://r.nikkei.com/article/DGXMZO54694710S0A120C2L41000?s=5.

Nikkei Shimbun. "「ウポポイ」開業3カ月で12万人来場." 日本経済新聞 電子版. 日本経済新聞社, October 12, 2020. https://www.nikkei.com/article/DGXMZO64894610S0A011C2L41000/.

NHK. "官房長官着用で話題　アイヌ民族の魔よけ文様マスクが人気." NHKニュース, May 17, 2020. https://www3.nhk.or.jp/news/html/20200518/k10012434091000.html.

NHK Sapporo. "ウポポイ入場者１０日で1万人超　#アイヌ：NHK北海道." NHK札幌放送局. NHK札幌放送局. July 22, 2020. https://www.nhk.or.jp/hokkaido/articles/slug-n74935f75f49c.

NHK Hokkaido. "ウポポイ開業前日に政府が式典　#アイヌ：NHK北海道." NHK札幌放送局. https://www.nhk.or.jp/hokkaido/articles/slug-n19825cc197ba.

Miyatake, Kimio. Umi o Watatta Ainu: Senjūmin Tenji To Futatsu No Hakurankai. Tōkyō: Iwanami Shoten, 2010.

Ministry of Education, Culture, Sports, Science and Technology. "大学が保管するアイヌ遺骨の返還について." 文部科学省, September 2016. https://www.mext.go.jp/a_menu/kagaku/ainu/index.htm.

Mieczkowski Bogdan, and Mieczkowski Seiko, "Horace Capron

and the Development of Hokkaido a Reappraisal." Illinois State Historical Society 67, no. 5 (November 1974): 487-504.

Maesawa Taka, Ainu Minzoku Inochi To Hokori: Maesawa Takashashinshū. Sapporo: Kurūzu, 2014.

MEXT. "教育ニ關スル勅語（明治二十三年十月三十日）." 文部科学省. https://www.mext.go.jp/b_menu/hakusho/html/others/detail/1317936.htm.

Kuzuno Tatsujirō, Kimusupo. Sapporo: The Foundation for Ainu Culture, 1999.

Kuwabara Masato, and Kawakami Jun, Hokkaidō No Rekishi Ga Wakaru Hon: Sekki Jidai Kara Kingendai Made Ikkiyomi. Arisusha, 2018.

Kuroda Tadao, "伊達の画家 小野潭の絵画資料について." Date-Shi.

Kudō Toshiyuki, Karafuto Eien Naru Daichi. Bokkasha, 2017.

Kosaka Yōsuke, Ryūbō: Nichi-Ro Ni Owareta Kita Chishima Ainu. Sapporo: Hokkaidō Shinbunsha, 1992.

Kayano Shigeru, Ainu No Ishibumi. Tōkyō: Asahi Shinbunsha, 1980.

JIJI PRESS. "色丹島で初の道路舗装　ロシア、実効支配強化：時事ドットコム." 時事ドットコム, September 25, 2020. https://www.jiji.com/sp/article?k=2020092500766.

Hokkoku Ryōsei. Bakumatsu Ishin Ezochi Ibun: Gōshō, Mononofu, Ikokujintachi No Yūhi. Sapporo: Hokkaidō Shuppan Kikaku Sentā, 2009. Hokkaido Shimbun. "新ひだかアイヌ協会は、シャクシャイン像を建て替える." Hokkaido Shimbun, February 15, 2015.

Ainu Association of Hokkaido. "アイヌの生活実態." 公益社団法人北海道アイヌ協会. Accessed December 26, 2020. https://www.ainu-assn.or.jp/ainupeople/life.html.

Hirayama Hiroto, Shakushain No Tatakai. Sapporo: Jurosha, 2016.

Hirayama Hiroto, Ainu No Rekishi: Nihon No Senjū Minzoku o Rikaisuru Tame No 160-Wa. Tōkyō: Akashi Shoten, 2014.

Hayasaka Hideo, and Yoshitaka Inoue, Kita No Bunmei Kaika: Hakodate Kotohajime Hyakuwa. Sapporo: Hokkaidō Shinbunsha, 1991.

Hara Teruyuki, and Amano Naoki, Karafuto Yonjūnen No Rekishi: Yonjūmannin No Kokyō. Tōkyō: All Japan Federation of Karafuto, 2017.

Hakodate Japan-American Association. Hakodate Kaika to Beikoku ryōji. Sapporo: Hokkaidō Shinbunsha, 1994.

Government of Hokkaido. 北海道環境生活部. "北海道アイヌ生活実態調査報告書平成29." 2017. http://www.pref.hokkaido. lg.jp/ks/ass/H29_ainu_living_conditions_survey_.pdf.

Gotō Haruki, Saharin o Wasurenai: Nihonjin Zanryūshatachi No Mihatenu Furusato Nagai Kioku. Tōkyō: DU BOOKS, 2018.

Gen. Horace Capron's Collection of Specimens of Antique Japanese Works of Art. Washington, D.C.: Smithsonian Institution, 1883.

Enomoto Morie, Samuraitachi No Hokkaidō Kaitaku. Dōshin, 1993.

Emori Susumu, Ainu No Rekishi To Bunka (1). Sendai: Sōdōsha, 2003.

Chiri Yukie, Ainu Shinyōshū. Tōkyō: Iwanami shoten, 2009.

Cabinet Office. "「国民のアイヌに対する理解度に関する世論調査」の概要." February 2016. https://survey.gov-online. go.jp/tokubetu/h27/h27-ainu.pdf.

Bird Isabella, 1888. Unbeaten Tracks in Japan: An Account of Travels in the Interior Including Visits to the Aborigines of Yezo and the Shrine of Nikko. Edinburgh: R. & R. Clark.

Akibe Hideo and Ōtani Yōichi, Ainu Bunka No Genzai. Sapporo: Sapporo Gakuin University, 1997.

Ainu Puri – Ainu No Kokoro Wo Tsunagu. The Foundation for

Ainu Culture, 2010.

Ainu No Hitotachi Totomo Ni – Sono Rekishi To Bunka. Sapporo: The Foundation for Ainu Culture, 2017.

Ainu Association of Hokkaido. "1992年12月10日国連総会「世界の先住民の国際年」記念演説." 公益社団法人北海道アイヌ協会, https://www.ainu-assn.or.jp/united/speech.html.

Aihara Hideki, 1945 Shumushuto No Shinjitsu: Shonen Senshahei Ga Mita Saigo No Senjo. PHP kenkyujo., 2017.

Agency for Cultural Affairs. "アイヌ語の保存 継承に必要なアーカイブ化事業: 文化庁." 文化庁 . https://www.bunka.go.jp/seisaku/kokugo_nihongo/kokugo_shisaku/kikigengo/archivejigyo/index.html.

Abashiri Prison Museum. "監獄秘話." 監獄秘話 囚人が開いた土地 | 博物館 網走監獄. https://www.kangoku.jp/kangoku_hiwa3.html.

CHRONOLOGY

Pre 14,000 BCE: Beginning of the Paleolithic Era in the Japanese Archipelago – The first people enter Japan

14,000 BCE – 300/1000 BCE: Jōmon Period throughout the Japanese Archipelago

1000BCE/300 BCE – 300 CE: Yayoi Period in Japan (excluding Hokkaido and northern Tohoku) – immigrants from the Chinese mainland and Korean Peninsula cross over to Japan, bringing with them rice cultivation.

340 BCE-700 CE: Jōmon culture continues in Hokkaido and northern Tohoku

250/300 CE – 538 CE: Kofun Period in Japan (excluding Hokkaido and norther Tohoku) – in which numerous Yamato clans vie for power and built large often key shaped tombs for their leaders

400s-900s CE: Okhotsk Culture enters Hokkaido from the north (although it appeared in the 3rd century around the sea of Okhotsk and would continue until the 13th century)

538-710: Japan enters the Asuka Period – Power is consolidated under an Emperor, Buddhism and Kanji arrives from China

700s-1200s CE: Satsumon Culture forms in Hokkaido and northern Tohoku

710-794: Japan enters the Nara Period – Capital city is formed in Nara modeled on Xi'an

794-1185: Japan enters the Heian Period – In which the golden age of court culture begins

1185-1333: Japan enters the Kamakura Period – In which power is taken from the imperial family and transferred to the

Kamakura Shogunate

1200s-1400s: Formation of Ainu Culture

1400s: Increase in the number of Wajin settling on Hokkaido's Oshima Peninsula.

1456: Murder of 'Okkai' at Shinori outpost

1457: Koshamain leads an attack on Wajin throughout the Oshima Peninsula

1458: Koshamain killed by Takeda Nobuhiro who would go on to form the Matsumae clan

1467-1603: Japan enters the Sengoku Period (Warring States Period)

1549: Francis Xavier the first missionary in Japan arrives at Kagoshima

1587: Shogun Toyotomi Hideyoshi orders all missionaries to be expelled from Japan

1600: Tokugawa Ieyasu wins the Battle of Sekigahara marking the beginning of the Tokugawa Shogunate

1603-1868: Japan enters the Edo Period in which there are centuries of stability under the Tokugawa Shogunate

1604: Tokugawa Ieyasu bestows the Black Seal to the Matsumae samurai, giving them monopoly over trade with the Ainu

1606: The Matsumae finish construction of Fukuyama Castle

1612: Tokugawa Shogunate orders a destruction of churches and forbids the preaching of Christianity

1618: Missionary Jerome De Angelis enters Hokkaido

1635: Alternate Attendance system begins in 1634 for Tozama Daimyō (in 1642 for Fudai Daimyō)

1639: Beginning of Sakoku with the banning of Portuguese ships

1639: Russians reach the Sea of Okhotsk

1669: Shakushain's Rebellion:

1697: First recorded encounter of Russians with the Ainu: party led by Vladimir Atlasov

1711: Russian expedition party enters northern Kuril Island of Shumshu and Paramushir

1713: Same Russian party clashes with Ainu and Kamchadals forcing a fur tax on the peoples of Shumshuand Paramushir

1778: Russians reach the southern Kuril Islands, and cross over into the area around Nemuro in Hokkaido

1782: Shinsho-Maru leaves Japan to be shipwrecked on the Aleutian Islands

1785: Mogami Tokunai undertakes the first of numerous surveys of Ezo (Hokkaido, the southern Kuril Islands, and later Sakahlin) under the Shogunate

1789: Kunashir-Menashi Rebellion

1792: Survivors of the Shinsho-Maru arrive in Hokkaido with the help of a Russian mission. They are taken to Tokyo and interrogated by the Shogunate

1799: The Shogunate designates eastern Hokkaido as under its direct control

1802: The Shogunate establishes the Hakodate Magistrate

1804: The Shogunate orders the creation of three Buddhist temples to convert the Ainu

1806: Tsugaru Samurai stationed on Sakhalin attacked by Russians led by Lieutenant Chwostoff

1807: The Shogunate designates western Hokkaido as under its direct control (including Matsumae)

1811: Glovnin Incident

1812: Napoleon's invasion of Russia puts a temporary stop in Russian expansion into Asia

1821: Shogunate returns supervision of Hokkaido to the Matsumae

1826: Franz von Seibold receives maps meets with Mogami, receives maps of Sakhalin

1853: Commodore Matthew Perry of the US Navy arrives at

Uraga

1854: Convention of Kanagawa signed between the US and Tokugawa Japan – Hakodate designated as one of the ports open to America

1855: Entirety of Hokkaido once again designated as under the control of the Shogunate, with the exception of Matsumae

1855: Treaty of Shimoda opens Hakodate, Nagasaki and Shimoda to Russian ships, Perry conducts a survey of Hakodate

1857: Elisha E. Rice arrives in Hakodate as the American Commercial Agent

1858: Russian Diplomat Iosif Antonovich Goshkevich arrives in Hakodate

1859: Construction of the Russian Orthodox Church in Hakodate

1860: Tohoku samurai ordered to guard parts of Hokkaido, southern Sakhalin and the southern Kuril Islands

1861: Nikolai arrives in Hakodate

1864: Hakodate Magistrate moved from the hills of Motomatchi to inside the Gryōkaku fortress

1865: British consular Francis Howard Vyse in Hakodate engulfed in controversy when Ainu bones grave robbed

1866: Sakamoto Ryōma brokers an alliance between Choshū and Satsuma samurai laying the foundations for the Meiji Restoration

1868: Meiji Restoration, 'Edo' renamed 'Tokyo'

1869: End of the battle of Hakodate, establishment of the Development Commission (開拓使), and change of name from 'Ezo' to 'Hokkaido'

1870: Date Kunishige leaves Tohoku for Hokkaido to become the first samurai colonizer

1871: Abolition of Feudal domains and the establishment of Prefectures

1871: Creation of the short-lived Tate Prefecture in July, by August

Tate Prefecture has been absorbed into Aomori (Hirosaki) Prefecture. In 1872 what was Tate Prefecture is returned to the jurisdiction of the Development Commission

1871: Horace Capron, who encourages dairy farming etc. in Hokkaido, arrives in Japan as advisor to the Meiji government

1871: Tattoos and Ninkari earrings banned, burning of houses banned

1871: The Development Commission begins a program of giving tools to Ainu who wish to take up farming

1872: (additional legislation in 1877 and 1886) land in Hokkaido is classified as ownerless and under the direct control of the state

1872: Abolishment of feudal class system

1872: Family register reforms lead to Ainu reclassified as commoners, in theory making them equal to the majority of the Japanese population

1872: Iomate banned by the Development Commission

1873: Ainu harpoon for catching Salmon, Marek begin to be outlawed across Hokkaido, in 1875 Ainu fishing nets also banned

1874: Kuroda Kiyotaka introduces the Tondenhei system

1874: Murder of acting consul of Germany Ludwig Haber in Hakodate

1875: Hekketsu-Hi monument for the war dead of Hakodate erected by Yanagawa Kumakichi

1875: Treaty of Saint Petersburg's gives Russia jurisdiction over the entirety of Sakhalin, with Japan having jurisdiction over the entirety of the Kuril Islands

1876: Deer hunting only permitted with a license, Ainu amappo trap and poison arrows banned.

1876: Predecessor to Sapporo Breweries constructs first distillery

1876: Reverend Walter Dening of the Church Mission Society

goes to Biratori to preach to the Ainu

1876: William S. Clarke arrives in Hokkaido

1876: over 800 Sakhalin Ainu are moved to Hokkaido

1878: Ban on salmon fishing and trout fishing around Sapporo, similar legislation across Hokkaido follows

1880: Code of Education makes school compulsory for three years (extended to four in 1886)

1880: Completion of the Hōheikan built in Sapporo for the Meiji Emperors' visit to Hokkaido

1881: The Meiji Emperor visits Shiraoi and watches a faux-Iomante ceremony

1882: Abolishment of the Development Commission and creation of Hakodate, Sapporo and Nemuro Prefectures

1882: First railway in Hokkaido created running from Mikasa to Otaru (Horonai Railway) to transport coal

1882: Hokkaido divided into three prefectures of Hakodate, Sapporo and Nemuro

1884: Northern Kuril Ainu relocated to Shikotan in the Southern Kurils

1886: Abolishment of the Three Prefectures system and establishment of the Hokkaido Government

1886: End of the three-prefecture system in Hokkaido, establishment of the Hokkaido Government

1887-1896: The Hokkaido Government instigates polices to encourage the mass colonization of Hokkaido

1890: First prisoners arrive in Abashiri

1890: Tondenhei system widened to not just include those of samurai households

1893: Hakodate Ainu Training School opens under Charles Nettleship

1894: First Anglican Ainu Church opens under John Batchelor in Biratori

1897: Prison labor ended in Hokkaido

1898: Nikolai visits the northern Kuril Ainu on Shikotan

1899: Passing of the Hokkaido Former Aboriginal Protection Act

1901: First government Ainu school built in Biratori

1904: Louisiana Purchase Exposition in St Louis – attended by Ainu

1904: Outbreak of the Russo-Japanese war

1905: Treaty of Portsmouth – concludes the Russo-Japanese war with Karafuto (southern Sakhalin) becoming formally part of Japan

1907: Great Fire of Hakodate

1908: Karafuto Government begins changing places names from Russian to Japanese

1910: Annexation of Korea – Korea becomes a Japanese protectorate

1910: Japan-British exhibition in London – attended by Ainu

1913: First paper mills open in Karafuto at Ōtomari (Korsakov)

1915: Tomamae-Sankebetsu Bear incident

1916: reconstruction of the Hakodate Orthodox Church

1920: Japan takes complete control of Sakhalin, returning the northern half in 1925

1923: Publication of 'A collection of Ainu mythology'

1930: Ainu Association of Hokkaido formed

1931: Mukden incident – provides pretext for Japanese invasion of Manchuria

1936: Sapporo becomes the most populous city in Hokkaido, overtaking Hakodate

1937: Marco Polo Bridge Incident – start of the second Sino-Japanese War (1937-1945)

1938: National Mobilization Law – gives the Japanese government control over civilian organizations

1939: Forced movement of Koreans to Karafuto began

1941: Soviet-Japanese Neutrality Pact

1941: The US and UK declare war on Japan

1942: Japan captures southern Aleutian island of Kiska (Attu captured in 1943), lost in 1943 – US now close enough to launch air raids on Japan's northern territories

1942: Japanese capture of Malaysia, Singapore, Burma, Indonesia

1944 March: thousands of workers from China bought to Hokkaido to bolster wartime economy

1944: Americans recapture Guam and Saipan – allowing air raids on much of mainland Japan

1945 February: Yalta Conference – Roosevelt and Churchill agree USSR can take Sakhalin and the Kurils if it launches an attack on Japan

1945 March: 88th Army Division formed in Karafuto

1945 April: Battle of Okinawa begins

1945 July: Allied naval bombardment of Muroran and Nemuro

1945 August: Atomic bombing of Hiroshima and Nagasaki, the USSR begins an offensive on Sakhalin, and the Kuril Islands. Emperor Hirohito announces Japan's surrender, but fighting continues in Japan's northern territories

1945 December: Ministry of Health and Welfare sets up an office in Hakodate to handle repatriates from Russian Sakhalin to Japan

1946 December: First round of repatriation from Soviet Sakhalin to Hokkaido begins

1947 August: Japanese citizens on Iturup relocated to Hokkaido

1972: 11th Winter Olympics opens in Sapporo

1972: Nibutani Ainu Culture Museum opens (name changes to Kayano Shigeru Ainu Museum after the opening of a municipal museum in 1992)

1973: Tokyo Utari Organization founded by Ukaji Shizue

1983: Kayano Shigeru's Ainu language school opens in Nibutani

1986: Prime Minister Nakasone Yasuhiro criticized over remarks that Japan is a homogenous society

1987: Biratori-Nibutani Ainu Language Institute opens

1991: Organization for the Ainu language formed

1994: Kayano Shigeru becomes first Ainu member of the Japanese Diet

1997: Repeal of the Former Aboriginal Act and introduction of the Ainu Cultural Promotion Act and replacement with the New Ainu Law 1997 (アイヌ文化の振興並びにアイヌの伝統等に関する知識の普及及び啓発に関する法律) (The Ainu Cultural Promotion Act)

1997: Sapporo District Court rules that the Ainu are the indigenous people of Hokkaido

2007: Center for Ainu and Indigenous People established at Sapporo University

2008: Ainu recognized as indigenous people by the Japanese Diet, and establishment of the Council for Ainu Policy Promotion

2010: Reconstruction of the Hakodate Magistrate complete

2016: Opening of the Hokkaido Bullet Train – for the first time Hokkaido is accessible from Tokyo via train

2018: New statue of Shakushain erected in Mauta Park

2019: New Ainu Law 2019 – the name of the law is (アイヌの人々の誇りが尊重される社会を実現するための施策の推進に関する法律) This replaced the 1997 law (The Realization and Creation a Society in which the Ainu People can be Proud Act)

2020 July: Opening of Upopoi – The National Ainu Museum and Park

Acknowledgments

I WOULD LIKE to thank my partner Eri for her support, and Drew Gwilliams for reading an initial draft of this work. Finally, I thank the reader for taking the time to read this book, and I hope it gives you a greater appreciation and understanding of Hokkaido and the people who continue to inhabit this fascinating island.

Index

About The Author

Ibrahim Jalal completed his postgraduate studies at Waseda University's Graduate School of Asia and Pacific Studies. He has lived throughout Japan, in Kurashiki, Yokohama and Tokyo, and currently resides in Cambridge in the United Kingdom.